the CALifornia Academy of Science.

a S. Francisco, nel tuo
mezzo del Golden Gate Park.

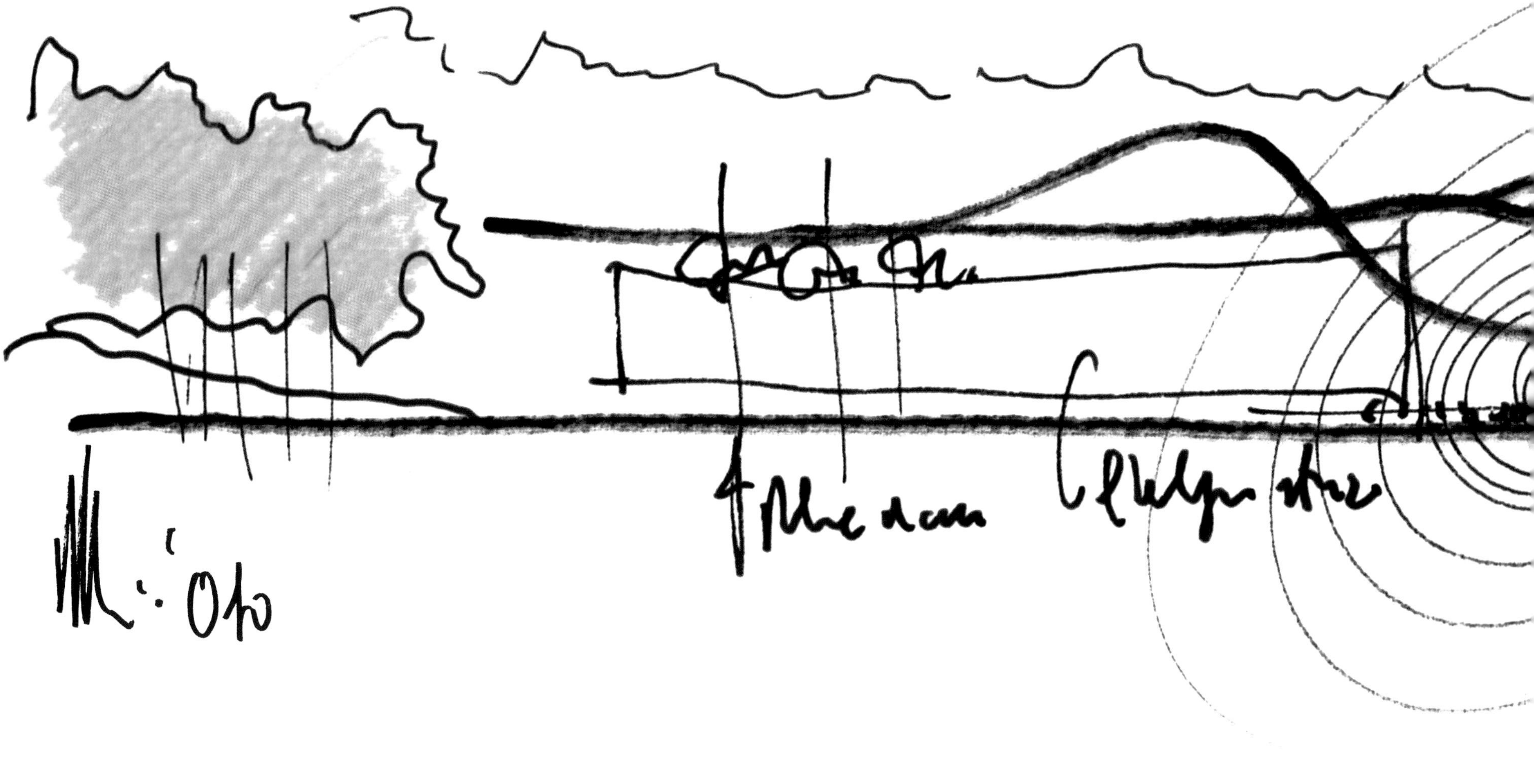

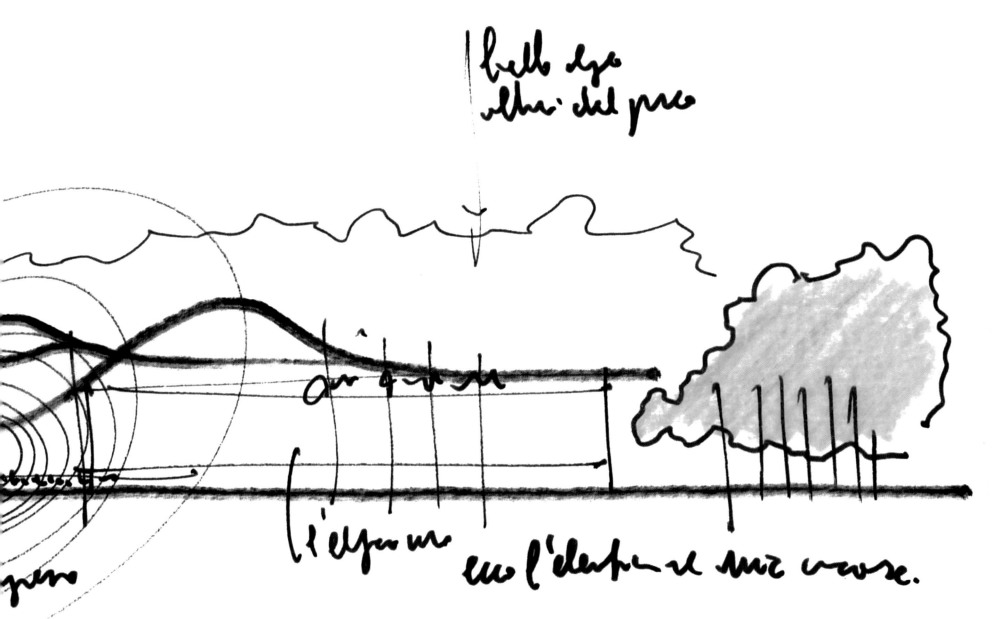

I bello dopo
ultimi del parco

(l'ellipse

ecco l'element...

Forse posso spiegare il tetto con un'immagine:
è un prato sospeso nel cuore del Golden Gate Park.
Come se un lembo del parco fosse stato tagliato
e sollevato a dieci metri di altezza,
per farci scivolare sotto il museo.

Perhaps I can explain the roof with an image:
like a meadow suspended over the heart
of the Golden Gate Park. It looks as if a piece of
the park has been cut away and lifted ten metres
above the ground to slide the museum underneath.

1853

1895

1906

1906

1916

1923

1900

1906

1915

U.S.G.S. Estimated Intensity Map
1989 Loma Prieta Earthquake on San Andreas Fault

Alla fine del 1800 fu costruita
la prima sede, all'angolo tra California
and Dupont Streets, quella che è oggi
Chinatown, e poco dopo si trasferirono
in Market Street. Nel 1906 il museo
venne distrutto da un terribile sisma,
e la collezione andò perduta.

1939

1960s

In the late 19th century, the first
museum premises were built
on the corner of California and
Dupont Streets, in what today
is Chinatown, moving to Market Street
soon afterwards. In 1906 the museum
was destroyed in a catastrophic tremor
and the exhibits were lost.

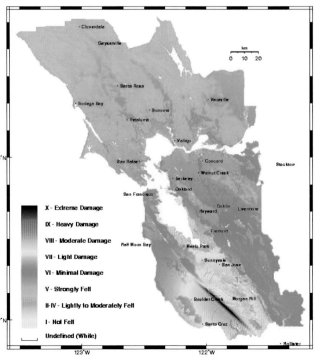

X - Extreme Damage
IX - Heavy Damage
VIII - Moderate Damage
VII - Light Damage
VI - Minimal Damage
V - Strongly Felt
II-IV - Lightly to Moderately Felt
I - Not Felt
Undefined (White)

1989

1989

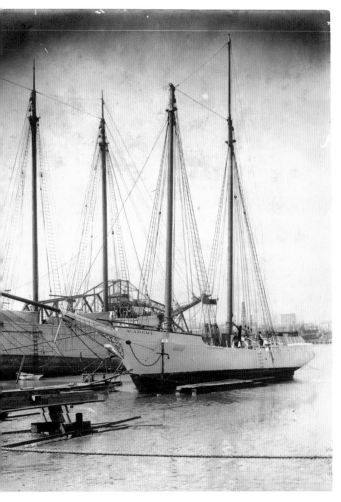

1905-1906

Il museo ricostruì la sua straordinaria raccolta di specie
grazie alla goletta Academy e alle spedizioni
alle Galapagos che si succedettero negli anni seguenti.

Thanks to the voyages of the schooner Academy to
the Galapagos Islands in subsequent years, the museum
was able to rebuild its marvellous collection.

1932

African Hall

Entrance to the Steinhart Aquarium

North American (California) Hall

1950

La California Academy of Sciences
era costituita da 12 edifici separati e 2 corti interne.

The California Academy of Sciences
was a complex of 12 separate buildings and 2 enclosed courtyards.

1916	Courtyard	8,364 sq. ft.	[777 m²]
1916	North American Hall Wild California Bird Hall	54,820 sq. ft.	[5.094 m²]
1923	Steinhart Aquarium	45,132 sq. ft.	[4.194 m²]
1931	African Hall	33,462 sq. ft.	[3.109 m²]
1951	Science Hall Morrison Planetarium Lowell-White Hall Auditorium African Annex	67,996 sq. ft.	[6.319 m²]
1959	Library Building	22,222 sq. ft.	[2.065 m²]
1969	Central Courtyard	20,787 sq. ft.	[1.931 m²]
1969	Cowell Hall and Porch/Deck	33,096 sq. ft.	[3.075 m²]
1976	Mc Bean/Peterson Gallery	13,395 sq. ft.	[1.244 m²]
1976	Wattis Hall	57,000 sq. ft.	[5.297 m²]
1977	Roundabout Building	12,044 sq. ft.	[1.120 m²]
1989	McBean/Peterson Addition	2,095 sq. ft.	[194 m²]
1989	Jewett/Linking Hall	5,510 sq. ft.	[512 m²]
1991	Herbst Portico	2,520 sq. ft.	[234 m²]
	Superficie totale Total surface	378,443 sq. ft.	[35.171 m²]

Morrison Planetarium
1951

Wattis Hall
1976

Steinhart Aquarium
1923

Cowell Hall
1969

Bird Hall
1916

Wild California
1916

African Hall
1931

Livello di rischio in seguito al terremoto di Loma Prieta (1989)
in base al "City Seismic Hazard Rating" (da 0 a 4)

Bird Hall: 4
African Hall: 3
Science Hall: 3
Roundabout Building: 3
Tutti gli altri edifici non raggiungevano gli standard di sicurezza
adottati a livello internazionale dopo il terremoto di Kobe (1995).

Seismic Hazard Rating after the Loma Prieta earthquake (1989)
from 0 to 4:

Bird Hall: 4
African hall: 3
Science Hall: 3
Roundabout Building: 4
All the others buildings didn't meet the new standards that
were adopted internationally after the earthquake in Kobe (1995).

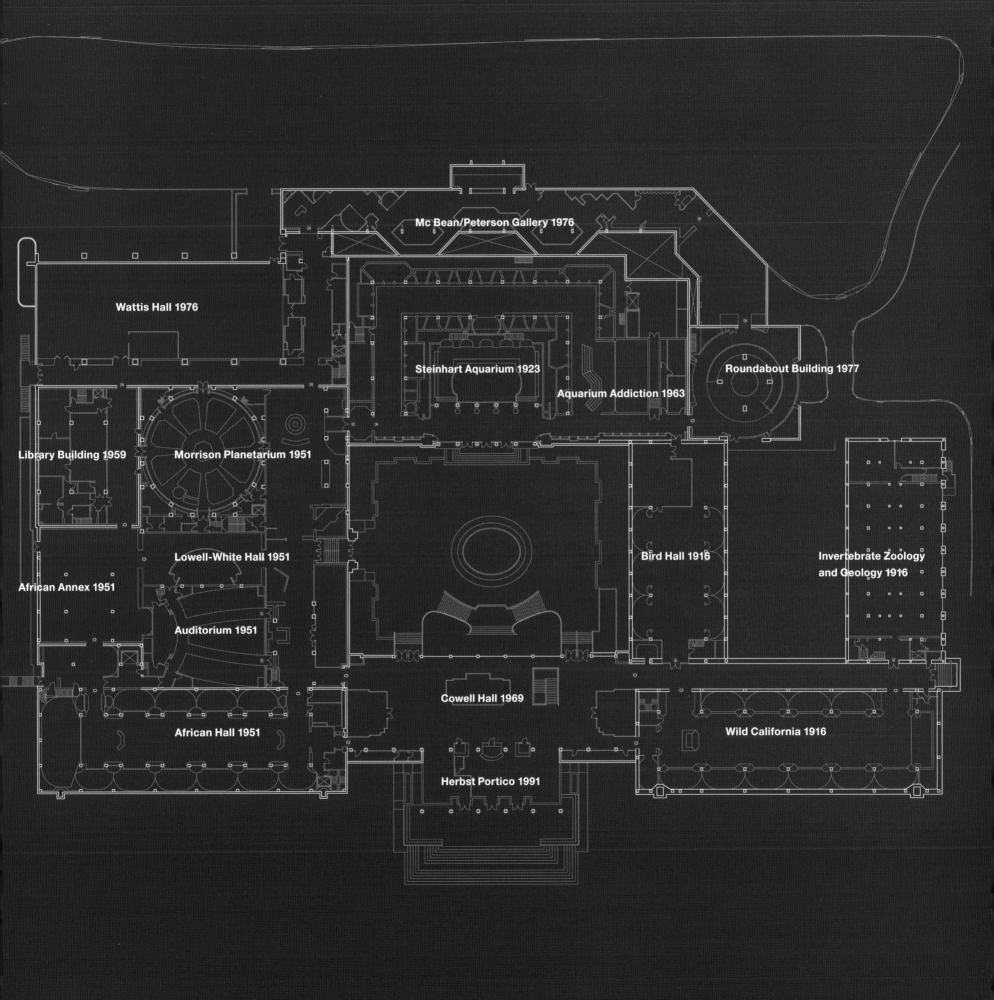

Mc Bean/Peterson Gallery 1976

Wattis Hall 1976

Steinhart Aquarium 1923

Aquarium Addiction 1963

Roundabout Building 1977

Library Building 1959

Morrison Planetarium 1951

Lowell-White Hall 1951

Bird Hall 1916

Invertebrate Zoology and Geology 1916

African Annex 1951

Auditorium 1951

African Hall 1951

Cowell Hall 1969

Wild California 1916

Herbst Portico 1991

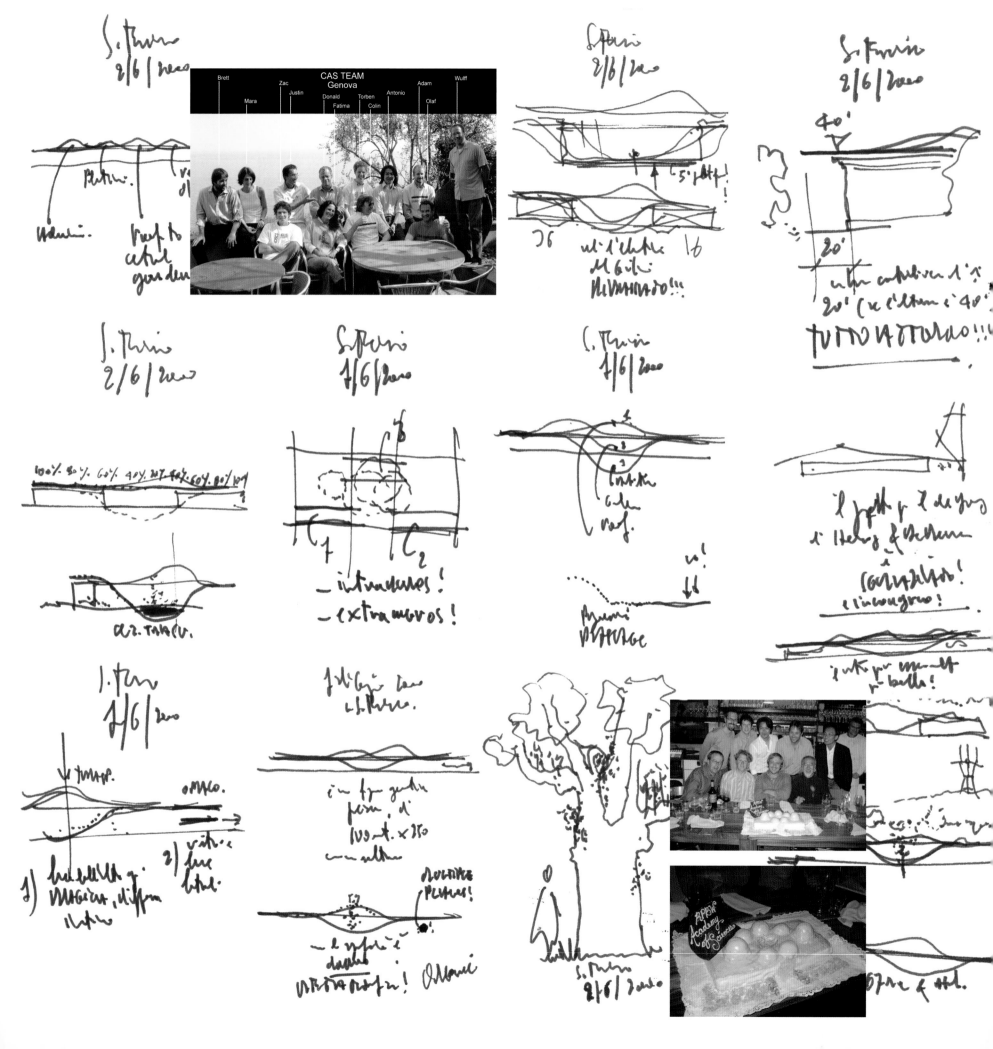

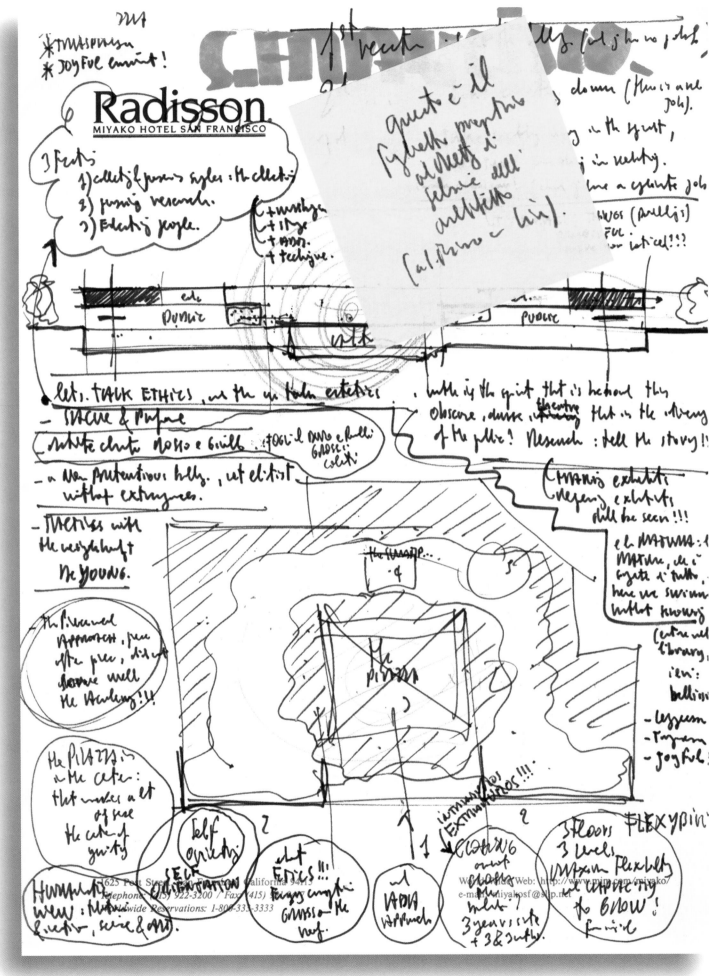

Gli appunti di Renzo Piano prima della riunione di selezione del progettista. Renzo Piano's notes before the meeting for the selection of the architect.

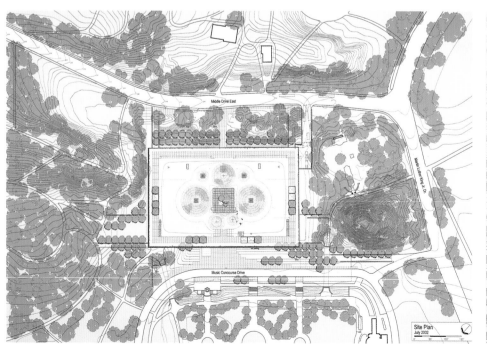

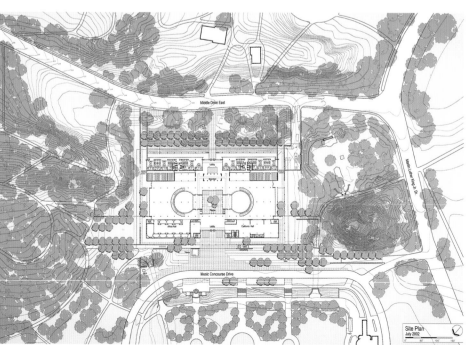

2005

2007

2008

Committee for the Defense of March about Delis Reum

C ⟶ D N AD

Delis's Nature About Reum

DNAD

from
Ciullo!

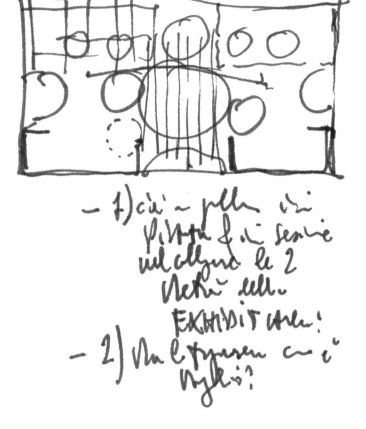

— 1) ciù in pulla in i
Pittupe f in sentire
incellguio le 2
Meter celle
EXHIBIT celle!

— 2) Vm e tipuren cm i
Nylon?

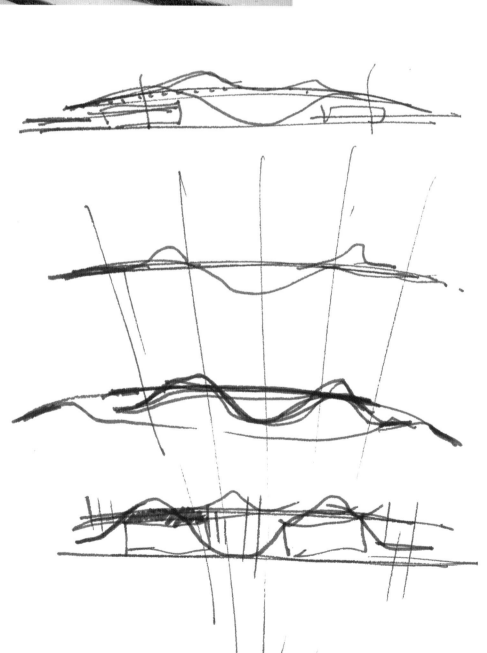

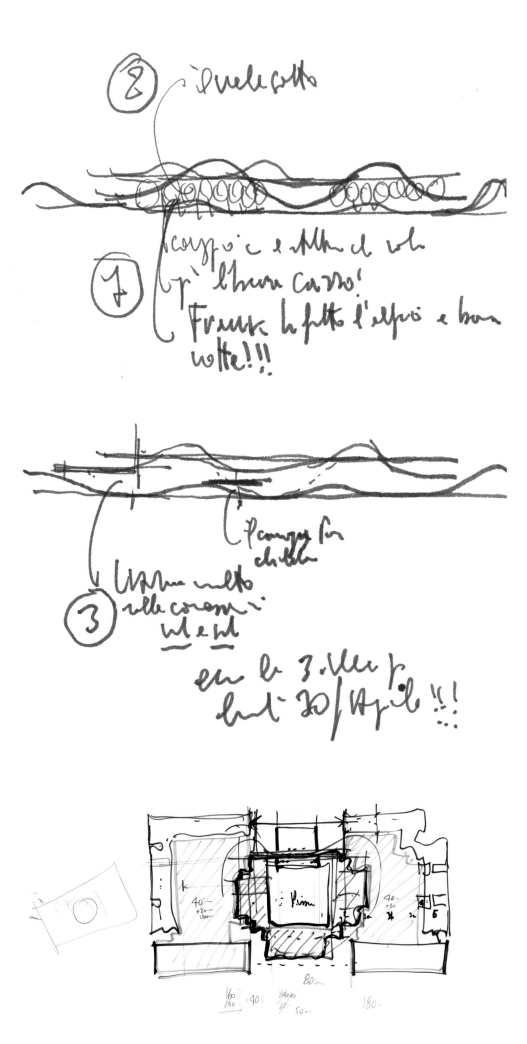

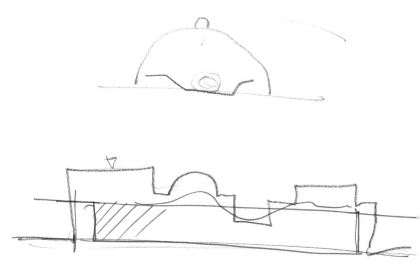

Camminando sul tetto capii come il nuovo museo, comunque lo si fosse fatto, avrebbe dovuto volare sul parco, mantenendo più o meno la stessa quota del tetto esistente.

As I walked across the roof, I realised that the new museum, no matter how it was designed, would have to soar over the park at more or less the same height as the existing roof.

La mattina del primo incontro si fece
una visita guidata del museo. Fui molto colpito
dai depositi in cui, lungo corridoi infiniti,
erano custodite le venti milioni di specie
che costituiscono la collezione.

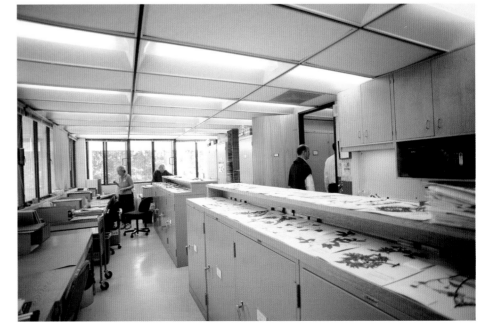

The morning of the first meeting there was
a guided tour of the museum.
I was very impressed by the storage areas,
the endless corridors lined with rooms where
the collection's twenty million species were kept.

"What we call the beginning is often an end.
And to make an end is to make a beginning.
The end is where we start from."
T.S. Eliot

This is a story about an architect, a building, a green pen and a pad of paper.

In the Loma Prieta Earthquake of 1989 the distinguished California Academy of Sciences in San Francisco suffered serious damage to its beautiful building but not its spirit. This disaster and subsequent planning of how to go forward, led the leaders of the institution to make bold plans for the future. After the decision is made to build, the most important step a building committee will take is the selection of an architect to whom they will entrust their plans and dreams for the future.

There are a number of methods by which architects are selected for commissions, public or private. Design competitions are one of the more popular. Competitions can be either open or invited, they can be conducted in one or more stages, they can be judged by a jury of peers, by the public, or in some cases by fiat. The combinations are many.

In the restrictive competition format, solutions are submitted without having had the benefit of the essential client-architect dialogue, which should play a central role in any successful design process.

In a design competition architects have no real client, only a program of requirements. The jury or public may believe they are selecting a design, not necessarily an architect. However, the design is inevitably changed, sometimes beyond recognition from the original, so instead an architect is selected, not a design, and no one has seen the body of work of the chosen architect. In the case of the California Academy of Sciences, the director and selection committee decided against a design competition because the committee did not want a fait accompli design from architects being considered.

The committee elected instead to engage in a selection process that was international in scope and by invitation. Materials and credentials were solicited from a select list of architects based on their experience and demonstrated design capability. In addition, the firm had to have a convincing history of successfully managing projects of a comparable size and complexity as that envisioned by the California Academy of Sciences.

Twenty-eight candidates were in the preliminary group of invited architects for consideration; that number was reduced to six finalists based on a review of submitted materials. Then there were personal visits by the committee to see representative buildings of this group, a tour of each candidate's office and a review of client references. The results of these activities enabled the committee to eventually narrow the list to three architects. The final and extremely important step was a personal interview by the committee of these three.

At the interviews the committee would hear the finalists' initial impressions and thoughts on the site, the program objectives, and other factors pertinent to the design, but actual speculative designs were not permitted.

For history, and the record, of which this book will soon become a part, it is useful to describe some of the circumstances of the interview that led to the engagement of Renzo Piano. Some of us present at the interviews can go back in time ten years ago when the decision was made. The committee came to the interviews armed with information gleaned from

visits to the architect's offices and were prepared to question the candidates based on the committee members' personal experience of having seen examples of each candidate's built work. References from previous clients were incorporated in the brief for the interviews and committee members were now in a position to engage each architect through a series of questions and responses. Lengthy discussions and debate among the committee in private would follow.

At the interview some architects chose to show the client a number of options, feeling this would not be as risky as presenting one proposal that the client might have reasons for rejecting out of hand.

Others passed out mini-publications of their preliminary conceptual designs. Some used simple models to illustrate their ideas in three-dimensional form, but a high level of detail was not permitted. There are, as in all interviews and auditions, attempts psychologically, oratorically, and dramatically to influence the committee. In the instance of the California Academy of Sciences one world-renowned architect displayed an abundance of conceptual drawings around the four sides of the meeting room in an effort to overwhelm the Committee with many alternatives and possibilities.

The day-long schedule of the interviews in a ground floor room called for two finalist interviews in the morning and one in the afternoon. The Committee took a luncheon break following the morning session leaving the room to Renzo Piano, the last architect of the three, who had come alone. When we returned from lunch, Mr. Piano was still alone. He had rearranged the tables into one large table and was seated on one side with a row of chairs for the committee on the other side, thereby changing the dynamics instantly to a more personal one. He had no boards or easels, no stacks of books, no projection equipment, only himself. He had a pad of paper spread out on the table. In his right hand he held a green felt-tip pen. He began to draw on the pad of paper speaking slowly, musing, and philosophizing about the project, and its many dimensions and challenges. At times it seemed like a soliloquy on a spot-lit stage. He seemed to be working things out in his mind as he proceeded, always accompanied by the Italian shrug and hand gestures. The time passed quickly, more like an interesting conversation than an interview.

Renzo Piano is one of the architects whose early sketches of a project are only fully understood when you play the record of the building's design backwards and see that the genius of the concept was there clearly at the beginning.

Even in this highly technological era the "mind-eye-hand-pencil" connection is still a potent force for architects who think and see and express their ideas in drawings and diagrams. Architects at a certain level have accumulated a storehouse of many experiences, which they can use to visually describe their ideas, concepts, and images.

To the casual observer, the scribbles Renzo makes on a drawing pad may seem like indecipherable marks on a piece of paper, but to him they are his personal hieroglyphics fraught with

architectural meaning. One should pay careful attention when Renzo sketches on a pad of paper. It may turn out to be a magnificent building.

At the end of his interview the committee knew they had been privy to seeing one of the master architects of our time at work, a scene that would be re-enacted many times during the years of design and building. Many people and machines would follow those conceptual lines – refine, define, calculate and create millions of other lines that would eventually become a building – one that will last for a long time and bring joy, education, and intellectual fulfillment to countless visitors, and will provide a haven for scientific investigation that can lead to any place where curiosity resides. When Renzo was finished he stood and spoke for a while; much of it praising his two fellow competitors.

"This is a very fine group of architects," he said, "Some of the best in the world." So it is up to you. You can hardly make a bad choice." He shrugged his shoulders and said, "It depends on whether you want Beethoven, Brahms, or Mozart."

That day we chose Mozart.

Bill Lacy, FAIA
Professional Advisor to the Selection Committee
22 September 2009

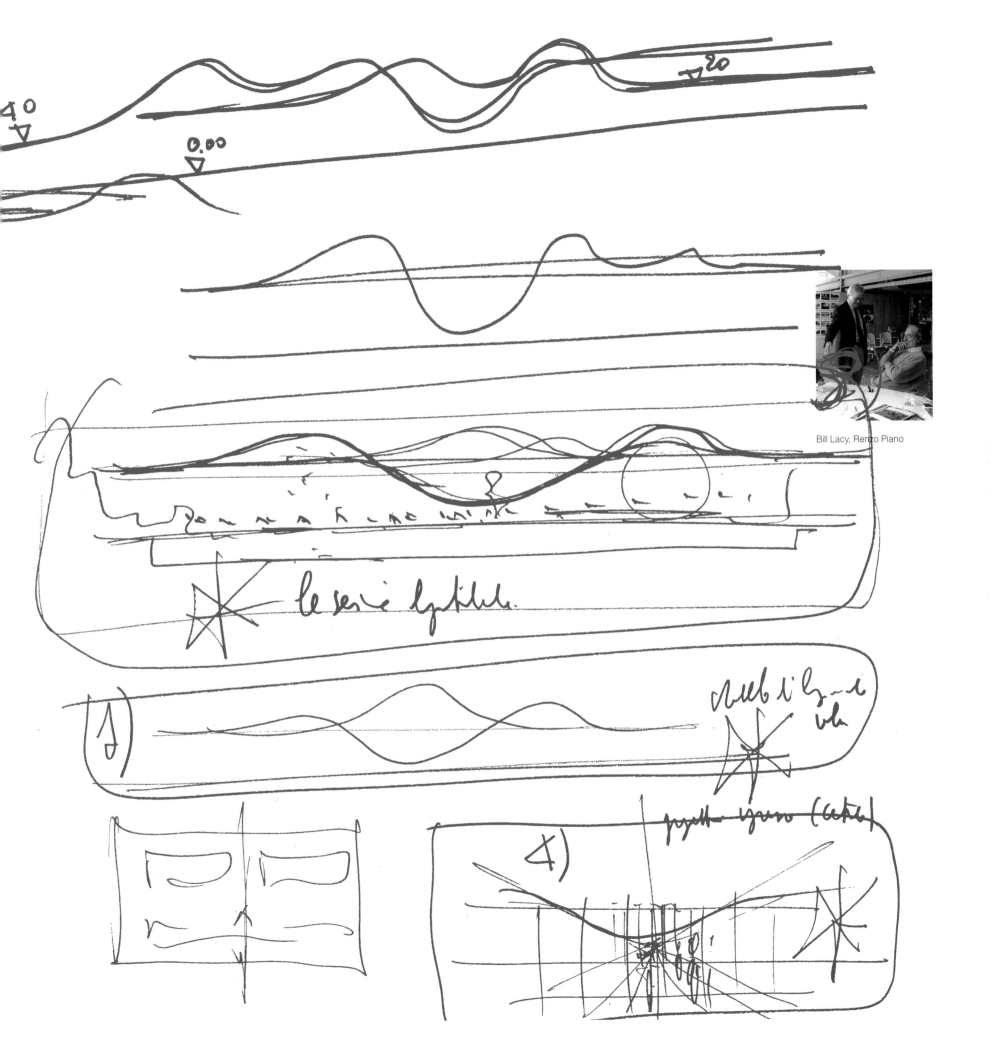

Bill Lacy, Renzo Piano

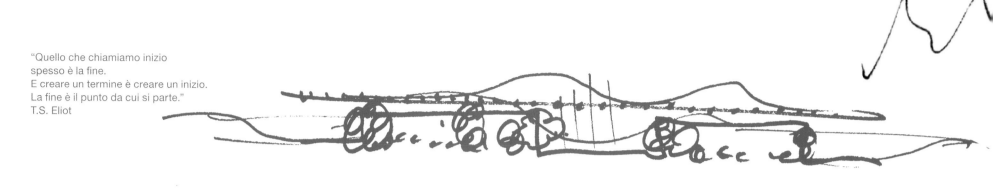

"Quello che chiamiamo inizio
spesso è la fine.
E creare un termine è creare un inizio.
La fine è il punto da cui si parte."
T.S. Eliot

Questa è la storia di un architetto, di un edificio, di un pennarello verde e di un blocco di fogli.

Durante il terremoto di Loma Prieta del 1989, il bellissimo edificio della rinomata California Academy of Sciences di San Francisco subì seri danni, ma il suo spirito restò intatto. Questo disastro e i piani che ne seguirono per decidere come intervenire spinsero la direzione dell'istituzione a fare dei programmi audaci per il futuro. Una volta presa la decisione di costruire, il passo più importante per la commissione edilizia è la selezione di un architetto al quale affidare progetti e sogni per il futuro.

Esistono diversi modi di selezionare gli architetti per le commissioni pubbliche o private. I concorsi di progettazione sono tra i più popolari. Possono essere dei concorsi aperti o su invito, possono svolgersi in una o più tappe, possono essere valutati da una giuria di colleghi, dal pubblico, o in alcuni casi per decreto. Le combinazioni sono innumerevoli. Nel caso di concorsi restrittivi, le proposte vengono presentate senza che si sia potuto beneficiare del dialogo essenziale cliente-architetto, che dovrebbe invece rivestire un ruolo centrale in un processo di progettazione di successo. In un concorso di progettazione, gli architetti non hanno un cliente reale, ma soltanto un programma di requisiti. La giuria o il pubblico possono pensare che stanno selezionando un progetto e non necessariamente un architetto.

Tuttavia, il progetto è inevitabilmente una trasformazione rispetto all'ipotesi iniziale, tale da renderla a volte irriconoscibile, quindi in realtà è l'architetto che l'ha ideata che si sceglie, senza però aver potuto seguire il logico sviluppo della sua elaborazione concettuale. Nel caso della California Academy of Sciences, il direttore e il comitato selettivo decisero di non scegliere la formula del concorso di progettazione, perché il comitato non voleva un progetto "chiavi in mano" dagli architetti valutati.
Il comitato optò invece per una procedura ad inviti di livello internazionale. Architetti selezionati in base all'esperienza e alla loro comprovata capacità di progettazione furono invitati a presentare materiali e credenziali. Inoltre, lo studio di architettura doveva avere nel curriculum la gestione di progetti affermati, di complessità e dimensione analoghe a quello immaginato dalla California Academy of Sciences.

Il gruppo degli architetti per la selezione preliminare era composto da trentotto candidati. Dopo l'esame del materiale prodotto, il gruppo di finalisti si ridusse a sei. Il comitato fece quindi un sopralluogo agli edifici più rappresentativi realizzati, una serie di incontri negli uffici di ogni candidato ed esaminò le referenze fornite dai loro clienti. Così facendo, ridusse a tre il numero degli architetti. L'ultima tappa, fondamentale, fu un'intervista personale. In tale occasione, il comitato ascoltò le prime impressioni dei finalisti, i loro pareri sul sito, gli obiettivi del programma e altri fattori pertinenti al progetto, senza che fosse permessa però la presentazione di progetti speculativi reali.
Per la cronaca, e per gli archivi di cui questo libro farà presto parte, è utile descrivere alcune circostanze dell'incontro che portò alla scelta di Renzo Piano.

Alcuni di noi, presenti durante le interviste, potranno fare un salto indietro nel tempo a dieci anni fa, quando la decisione fu presa. Il comitato si preparò alle interviste con le informazioni ricavate durante le visite agli studi degli architetti. Era pronto a fare domande ai candidati sulla base dell'esperienza personale ricavata dai membri del comitato nell'esame diretto di esempi costruttivi di ciascun architetto. Le referenze dei clienti precedenti erano contenute nel dossier preparatorio delle interviste, per cui i membri del comitato erano in grado di stimolare una serie di domande e risposte a ciascun architetto. A questa fase ne sarebbe poi seguita una di dibattito interno molto circostanziata tra i membri del comitato.
Alcuni architetti scelsero di mostrare nell'intervista un panorama di opzioni differenti per il cliente, convinti che proporre soluzioni alternative sarebbe stato meno rischioso che presentare un'unica proposta che, per qualche motivo, sarebbe potuto essere irrimediabilmente bocciata. Altri fecero girare delle mini-pubblicazioni dei loro progetti concettuali preliminari.
Alcuni usarono semplici modelli per illustrare le loro idee in una forma tridimensionale, perché non era permesso un alto livello di dettaglio. Come abitualmente avviene nelle interviste ed audizioni, furono messe in atto strategie di pressione psicologica, oratoria e di drammatizzazione per influenzare il comitato. Nel caso della California Academy of Sciences, un architetto di fama mondiale espose lungo i quattro lati della sala conferenza un gran numero di schizzi concettuali nella speranza di conquistare il comitato con la quantità di alternative e possibilità. Il giorno fatidico, le interviste dovevano svolgersi in una stanza al pianoterra, due al mattino e una al pomeriggio. Al termine della mattinata, il comitato fece una pausa per pranzo, lasciando la sala libera a Renzo Piano, l'ultimo dei tre architetti, che si era presentato da solo.
Al nostro ritorno dopo pranzo, Renzo Piano era ancora da solo. Aveva risistemato i tavoli per ricreare un unico grande tavolo ed era seduto da un lato, di fronte alla fila di sedie che aveva previsto sul lato opposto per il comitato, rendendo così molto più personale la dinamica della situazione. Non aveva né lavagne né cavalletti, nessuna pila di libri, nessun materiale di proiezione. C'era lui, e basta. Aveva un blocco di fogli sparso sul tavolo. Nella mano destra, teneva un pennarello verde.
Incominciò a disegnare sul blocco di carta mentre parlava lentamente, meditando e filosofeggiando sul progetto, sulle sue innumerevoli dimensioni e sfide. In certi momenti, sembrava fosse il monologo di un artista illuminato sul palcoscenico, che elaborava le cose nella sua mente di pari passo col procedere del suo discorso, sempre accompagnato dalla gestualità tipica degli Italiani. Il tempo passò veloce, nel clima di una conversazione interessante più che di un'intervista.

Renzo Piano appartiene a quella categoria di architetti in cui la comprensione piena dei primissimi schizzi di un progetto avviene solo a lavoro ultimato quando, ripercorrendo l'intera storia della progettazione dell'edificio, si capisce che la genialità concettuale era chiara e presente sin dalle origini.
Anche in questa epoca ipertecnologica, la connessione "mente-occhio-mano-matita" è sempre di grande forza per gli architetti che pensano, vedono ed esprimono le loro idee su disegni e schemi. Gli architetti che hanno raggiunto un certo livello hanno accumulato una tale quantità di esperienze che possono utilizzarle per visualizzare idee, concetti e immagini.

A un osservatore distratto, gli scarabocchi di Renzo su un blocco da disegno possono sembrare segni indecifrabili su un pezzo di carta, ma sono per lui geroglifici personali pieni di significato architettonico. Bisogna stare molto attenti quando Renzo fa uno schizzo su un pezzo di carta, perché potrebbe rivelarsi uno splendido edificio. Alla fine di questa intervista, il comitato era cosciente di aver visto all'opera uno dei maestri architetti della nostra epoca, scena questa che si sarebbe riproposta spesso durante gli anni della progettazione e della costruzione. Molti uomini e macchine avrebbero poi seguito queste linee concettuali – affinato, definito, calcolato e creato milioni di altre linee che si sarebbero poi trasformate in un edificio – un edificio che durerà a lungo e porterà gioia, cultura e appagamento intellettuale a innumerevoli visitatori, e che fornirà un rifugio per la ricerca scientifica che approda in tutti i luoghi in cui è viva la curiosità. Alla fine, Renzo si alzò e parlò un instante; espresse principalmente ammirazione per i suoi due concorrenti.

"È un grande gruppo di architetti", disse. "Tra i migliori del mondo." Ora spetta a voi decidere. Potete difficilmente sbagliare." Scrollò le spalle e disse: "Dipende se volete Beethoven, Brahms, o Mozart."

Quel giorno, scegliemmo Mozart.

Bill Lacy, FAIA
Consulente professionale per il comitato selettivo
22 Settembre 2009

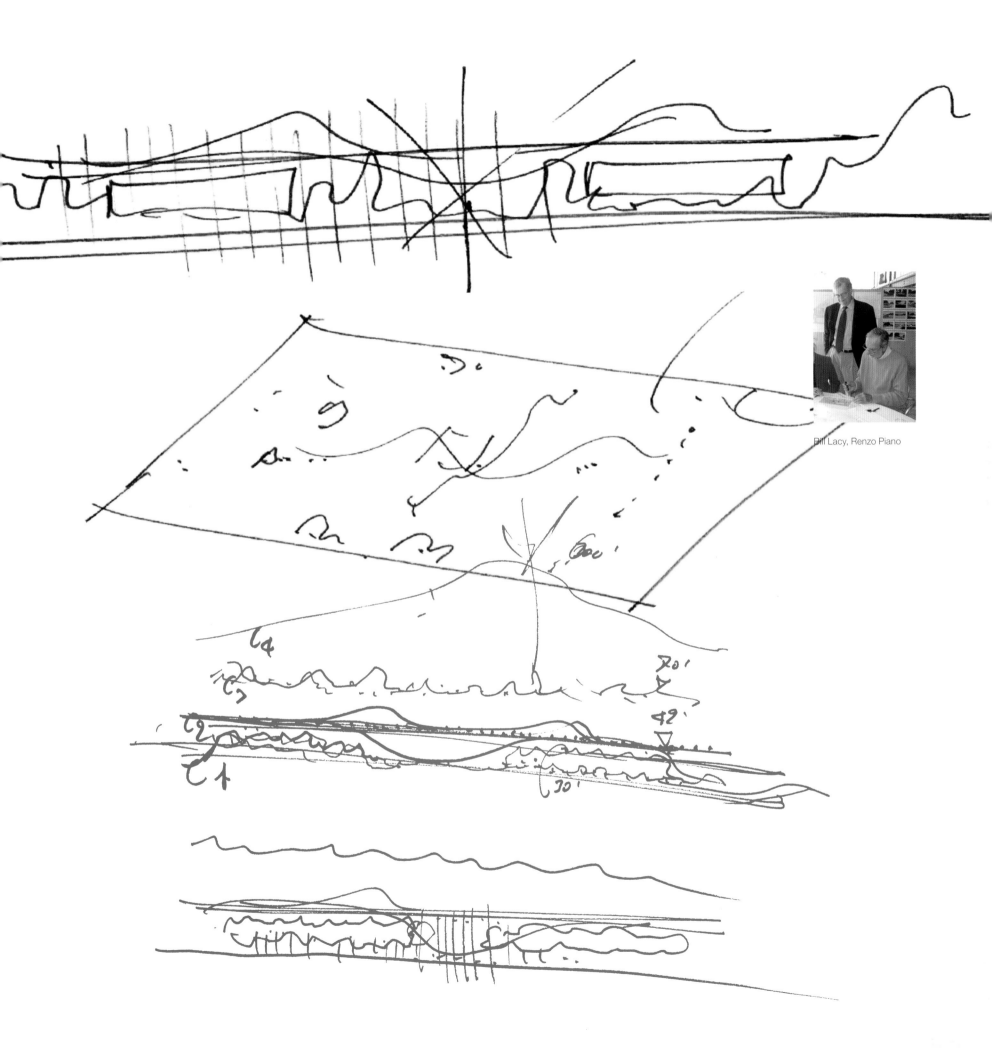

Bill Lacy, Renzo Piano

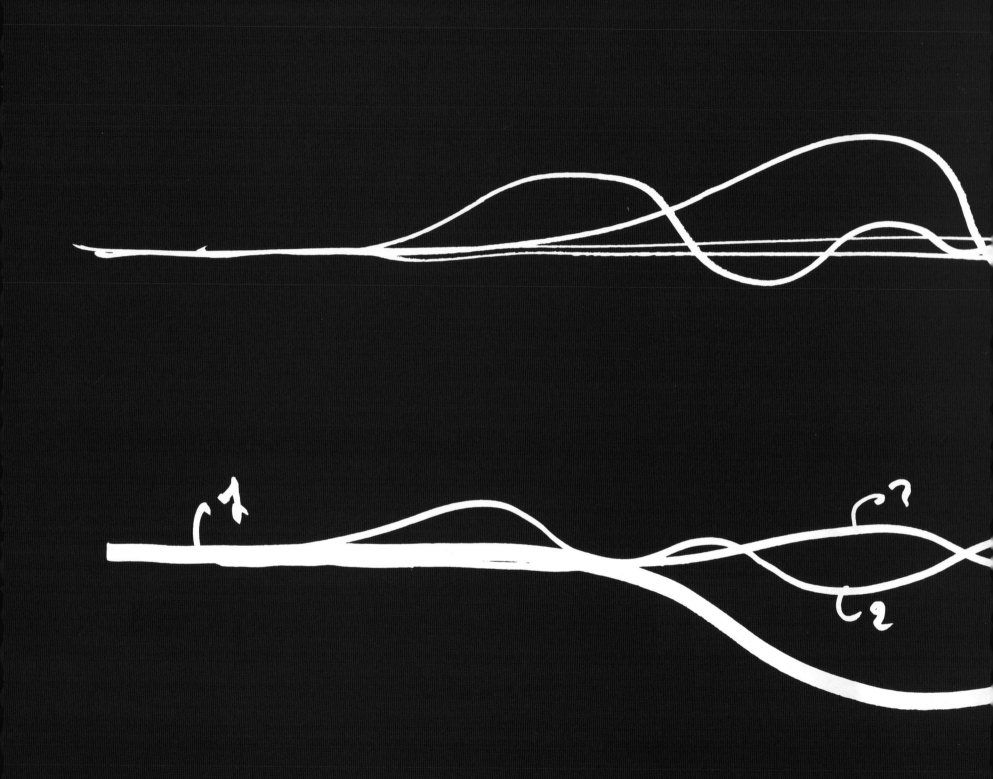

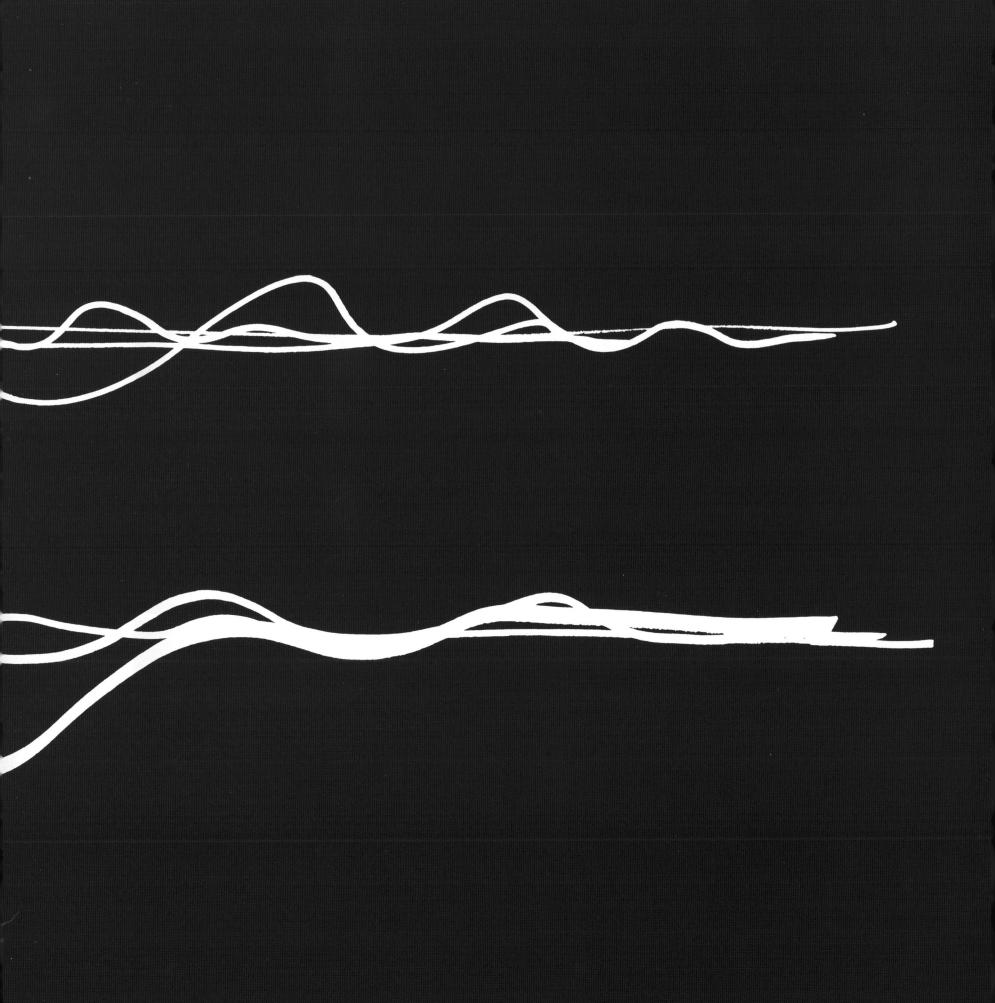

S.FRANCISCO

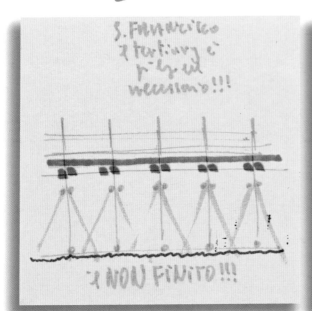

S. FRANCISCO
è tertiary è
pilgrim
necessario!!!

è NON FINITO!!!

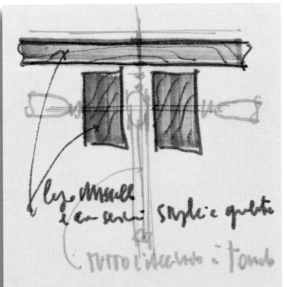

Styli e qualità
TUTTO l'acciaio è tondo

è una città, a little town fatta di 7 per
e streets & a Piazza!

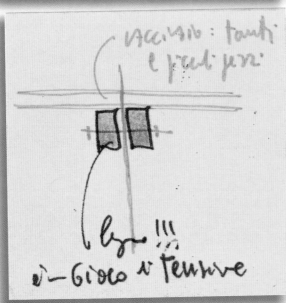

acciaio: tanti
e piccoli pezzi

è—Gioco e Tensive

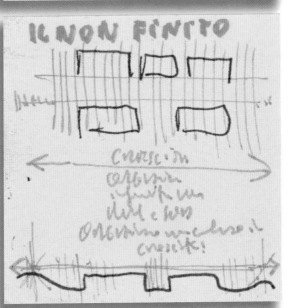

IL NON FINITO

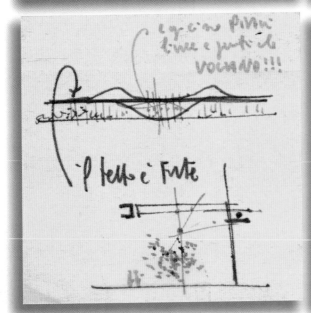

il tetto è fatto

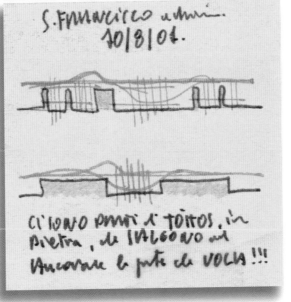

S.FRANCISCO urban.
10/8/04.

ci sono pinti i TETTOS in
Pietra, le IRIGONO in
ancorare le parti che VOLA!!!

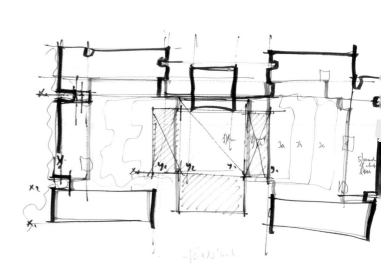

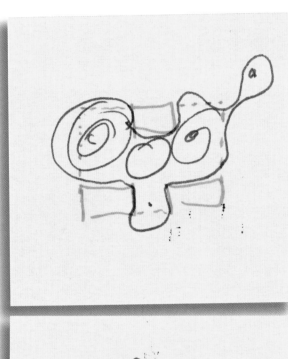

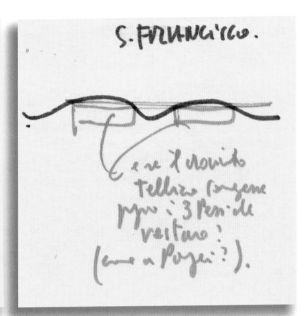

S. FRANCISCO.

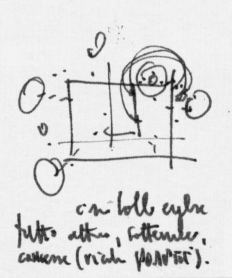

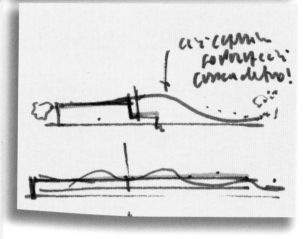

In qualche modo il museo era una piccola
città, costituita da 12 edifici separati.
C'era persino una piazza al centro.
Proprio così: tutti gli edifici erano cresciuti
lentamente attorno ad un quadrato,
che era una specie di piazza a cielo aperto.

In a sense the museum was a little town
of twelve separate buildings.
There was even a central plaza. That's right.
All the buildings had grown up around a
square, a sort of open-air Italian-style piazza.

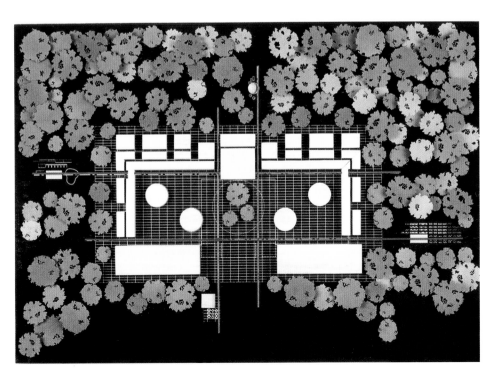

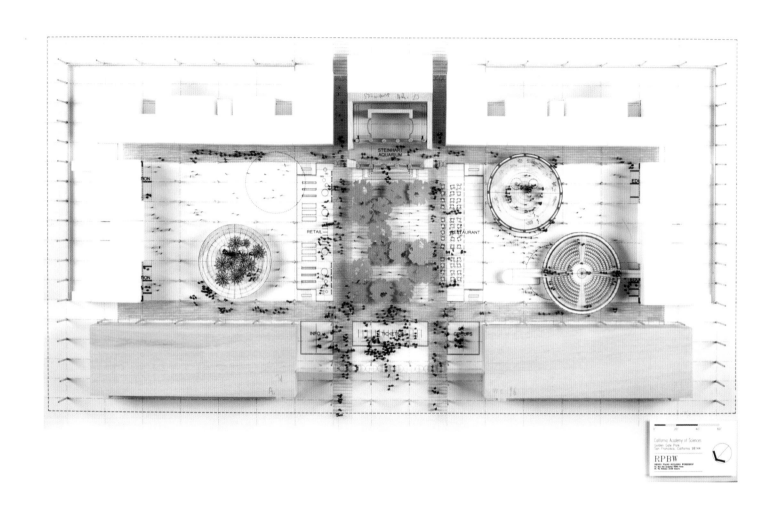

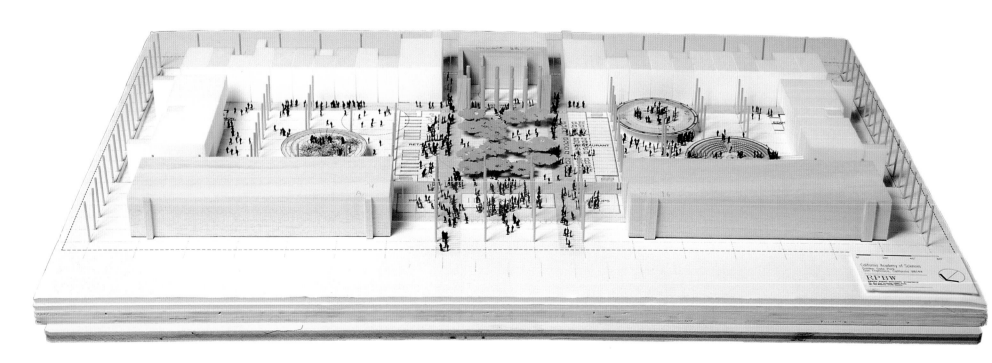

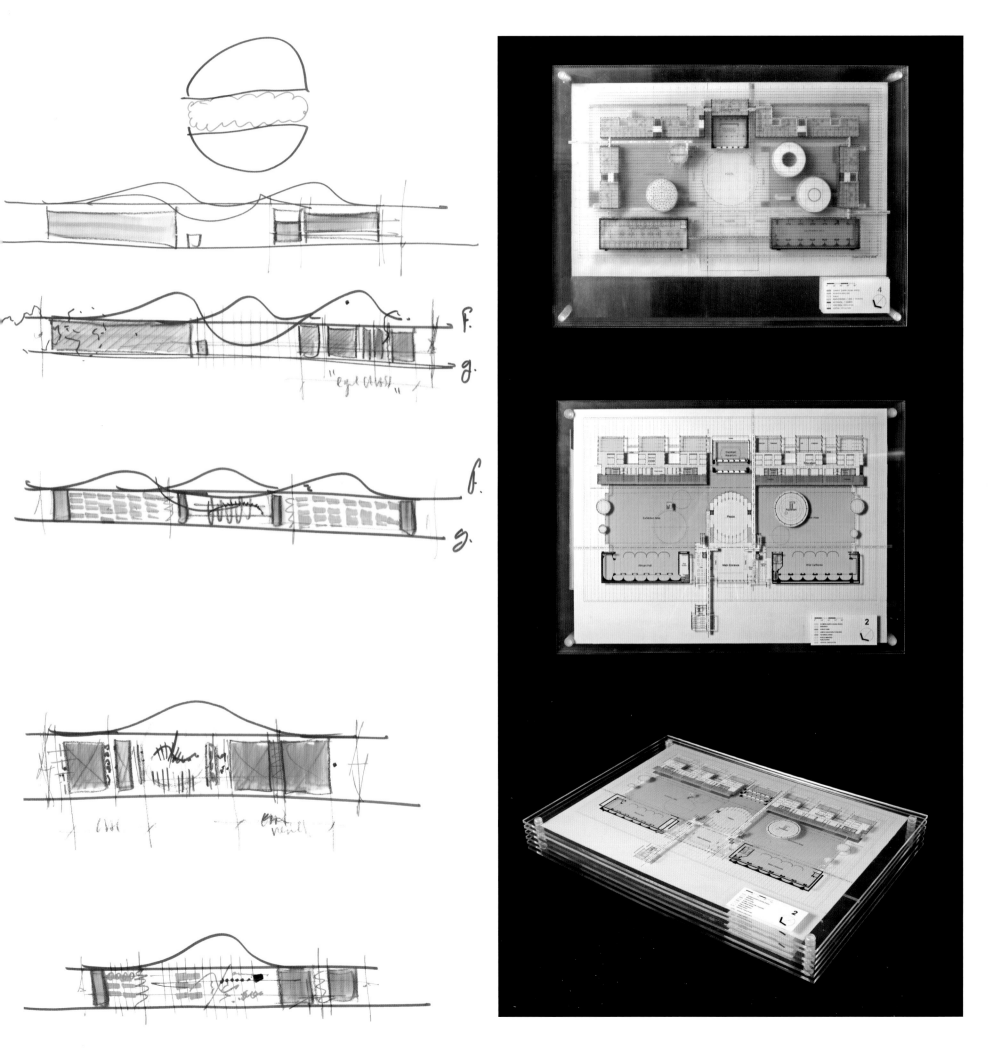

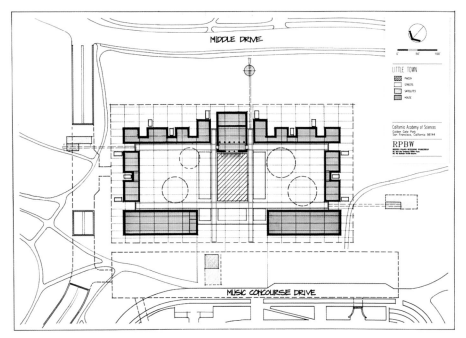
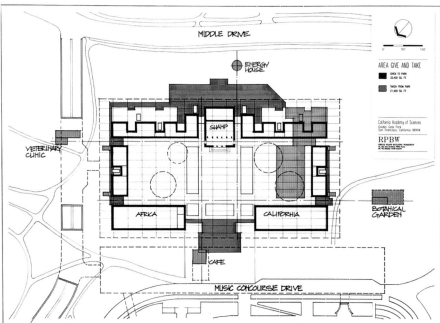
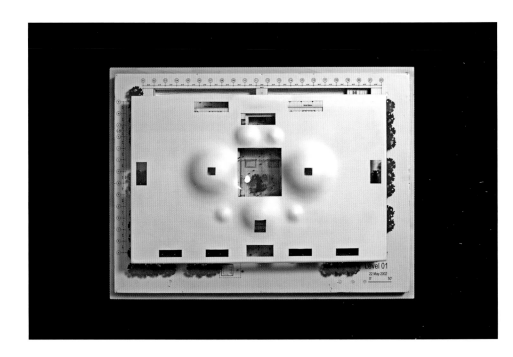
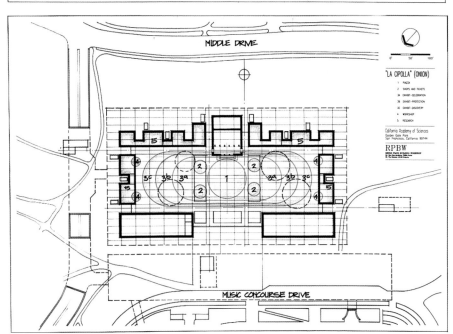

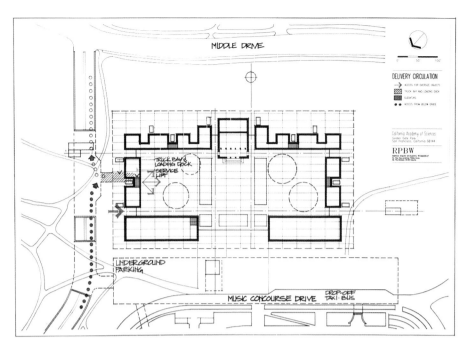

MIDDLE DRIVE

DELIVERY CIRCULATION

California Academy of Sciences
Golden Gate Park
San Francisco, California 98144

RPBW

TRUCK BAY &
LOADING DOCK

SERVICE
LIFT

UNDERGROUND
PARKING

MUSIC CONCOURSE DRIVE   DROP-OFF
TAXI · BUS

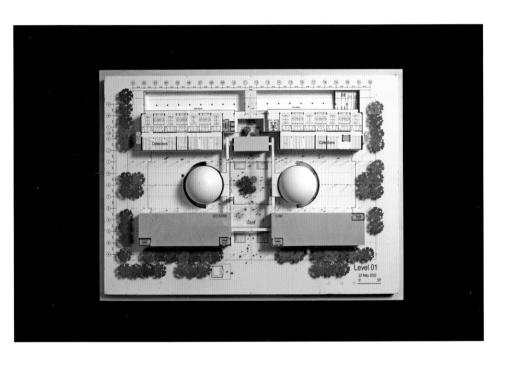

Collections   Collections

Closed

Level 01

22 May 2002
0'   50'

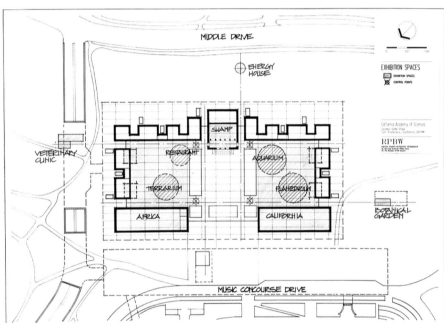

MIDDLE DRIVE

EXHIBITION SPACES

ENERGY
HOUSE

SWAMP

VETERINARY
CLINIC

RESTAURANT   AQUARIUM

TERRARIUM   PLANETARIUM

AFRICA   CALIFORNIA

BOTANICAL
GARDEN

California Academy of Sciences
Golden Gate Park
San Francisco, California 98144

RPBW

MUSIC CONCOURSE DRIVE

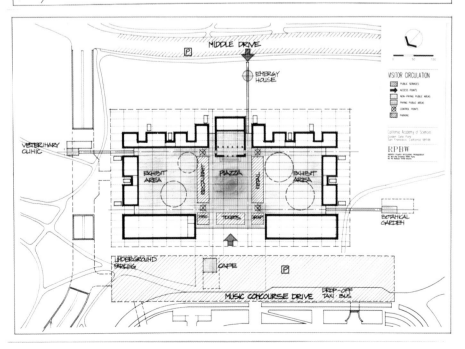

MIDDLE DRIVE

VISITOR CIRCULATION

ENERGY
HOUSE

VETERINARY
CLINIC

EXHIBIT
AREA   PIAZZA   EXHIBIT
AREA

RESTAURANT

TICKETS   SHOP

BOTANICAL
GARDEN

California Academy of Sciences
Golden Gate Park
San Francisco, California 98144

RPBW

UNDERGROUND
PARKING   CAFE

MUSIC CONCOURSE DRIVE   DROP-OFF
TAXI · BUS

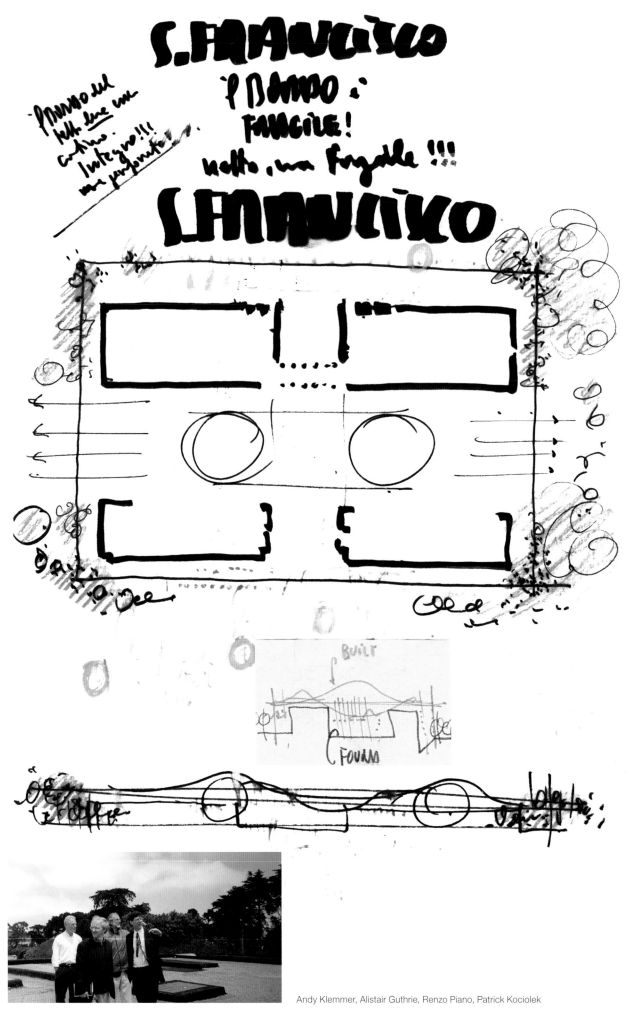

Andy Klemmer, Alistair Guthrie, Renzo Piano, Patrick Kociolek

To many visitors, museums can be places of richness and mystery. Diversity of collections, spaces that can be dark theaters, and content that helps to provide deeper understanding of concepts and events, help to open doors to new worlds. Yet, the complexity of the museum on the exhibitions side pales in comparison to the "back of house". Most museums have on display a small fraction of their collections, and the California Academy of Sciences is no exception. Away from the public eye include husbandry related to the Steinhart Aquarium, the technology associated with the Planetarium, educators, millions of artifacts and collections and research scientists. These additional levels of resources, like an onion, give the organization texture, richness and opportunities for unique stories - the field work carried out by the scientists, new observations of species and specimens, and insights into how people learn in informal settings are just a few sources of rich content. From microbes to man, San Francisco to Sao Tome, there are hundreds of stories unique to the Academy.

The scientists and the Academy's collections are a constant source of new ideas, resources to be celebrated, important to the "brand" of the Academy, locally, regionally, nationally and internationally. The collections are part of the history of the Academy and San Francisco. This complexity was one of the reasons the architect was intrigued by the commission.

The world of the public and the world of science are such different worlds, including the types and pace of the activities.

These different and diverse layers create a complexity not seen in many other museum types. In many other museums their juxtaposition (intellectually and physically) has been either ignored or been stark, such as offering picture windows in the research areas for the public to get a glimpse of this world. We rejected this approach, as the architect said, and we could affirm from personal experience, "To simply watch science is like watching grass grow." We ended up creating labs and places for the world of science and the public to come together, translated and interpreted by scientists themselves. And this was done while maintaining the environment for the world of science to exist and progress at its own pace.

But celebrating and maintaining this institutional richness almost did not happen. Although we had invested much time before, and into, the project to highlight and address this diversity, some member of the Academy community wanted to pull research and collections from the program, and out of the building. While, relatively speaking, the research and collection spaces were some of the least expensive that were created in the project, the idea was that cheaper space could be found away from Golden Gate Park. This debate was raised several times, as project costs were re-evaluated. The architect once suggested he would be less than interested in continuing the project if this unity of the organization was disrupted. In the end, the museum was kept whole. Some people see the new Academy as a beautiful building in and of itself. Some see it as a metaphor for San Francisco (and its seven hills), while others wonder at the interplay of nature and science (the organic form of the roof with California native plants and animals, married with high technology - solar panels, modern building techniques, etc.). For many people the new Academy building is a model of sustainability - the world's most sustainable museum. And the building is, of course, all of those, and depending upon my perspective I enjoy the building on all of those levels. But there are times that I see the building as a wonderful embrace, a blanket, fostering, encouraging and supporting the complete organization, celebrating the wonderful diversity of ideas, history and paces of the place.

The new Academy and the wonderful building in which it resides, is a wonderful, integrated institution, announcing and celebrating of the world and work of science and its place in our society.

Patrick Kociolek
Former Executive Director, California Academy of Sciences and
Director, Museum of Natural History, University of Colorado, Boulder

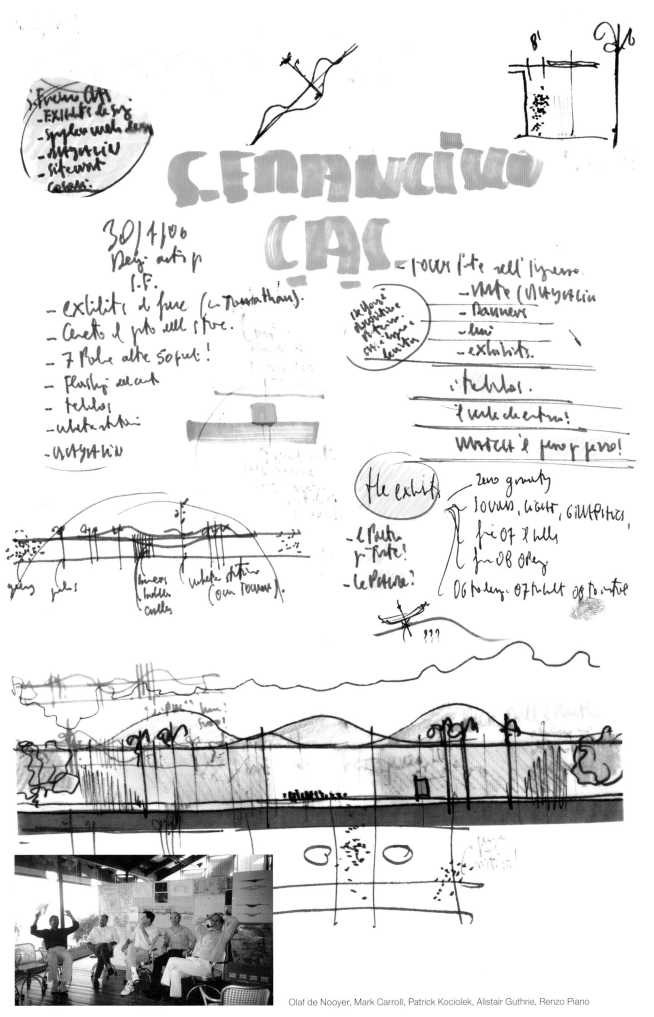

Olaf de Nooyer, Mark Carroll, Patrick Kociolek, Alistair Guthrie, Renzo Piano

Per molti visitatori, i musei sono luoghi di ricchezza e di mistero. Ci sono molti elementi che aiutano ad aprire la porta a nuovi universi: la varietà delle collezioni, gli spazi che possono essere dei "teatri oscuri", e il contenuto che permette una comprensione più profonda di concetti e di eventi. Eppure, la complessità della zona visibile del museo è poca cosa rispetto a ciò che non si vede. La maggior parte dei musei espone una parte minima delle collezioni, e la California Academy of Sciences non fa eccezione. Lontano dallo sguardo del pubblico, ci sono le coltivazioni legate all'acquario Steinhart, la tecnologia associata al Planetario, degli educatori, milioni di manufatti, collezioni e ricercatori.

Questi molteplici livelli di risorse, quasi fossero gli strati di una cipolla, conferiscono all'Academy consistenza, ricchezza e opportunità per delle storie uniche - il lavoro sul campo effettuato dagli scienziati, nuove osservazioni di specie ed esemplari, e visioni di come la gente impara in scenari informali. Queste sono solo alcune fonti ricche di contenuto. Ci sono centinaia di storie uniche all'Academy: dai microbi all'uomo, da San Francisco a Sao Tome. Gli scienziati e le collezioni sono una fonte costante di nuove idee, risorse da celebrare, importanti per il "brand" della stessa Academy, a livello locale, regionale, nazionale e internazionale. Le collezioni fanno parte della storia dell'Academy e di San Francisco. Questa complessità è stato uno dei motivi per cui l'architetto fu incuriosito dalla commessa. Il mondo pubblico e quello della scienza sono totalmente diversi, così come lo sono i tipi e i ritmi delle attività. Questa diversità di livelli crea una complessità non facilmente riscontrabile in altri tipi di musei.

In molti altri musei, la loro giustapposizione (intellettiva e fisica) è stata ignorata o interpretata in modo rigido, come ad esempio prevedendo delle finestre panoramiche nei settori riservati alla ricerca affinché il pubblico possa scorgere uno spaccato di questo mondo. Rifiutavamo questo tipo di approccio, come disse l'architetto, e potremmo affermare dalla nostra personale esperienza che "guardare semplicemente la scienza è come guardare crescere l'erba." Finimmo col creare laboratori e luoghi d'incontro tra il mondo della scienza e il pubblico, illustrato e interpretato dagli stessi scienziati. E fu possibile realizzare tutto questo mantenendo l'ambiente necessario perché il mondo della scienza potesse esistere e progredire al proprio ritmo.

Ma la celebrazione e la conservazione di questa ricchezza istituzionale sono stati sul punto di non realizzarsi. Benché avessimo investito molto tempo, prima e durante il progetto, per mettere in risalto questa diversità e concentrarci su di essa, alcuni membri della comunità dell'Academy volevano ritirare la ricerca e le collezioni dal programma e spostarli fuori dall'edificio. Nonostante, in termini relativi, gli spazi per la ricerca e la collezione fossero tra i meno costosi fra quelli realizzati all'interno del progetto, l'idea era che sarebbe stato possibile trovare uno spazio più a buon mercato fuori dal Golden Gate Park. Questo dibattito fu sollevato diverse volte, nel momento in cui si assisteva a una rivalutazione dei costi progettuali.

A un certo punto, l'architetto lasciò intendere che non sarebbe più stato interessato al proseguimento del progetto qualora venisse distrutta quest'unità organizzativa. Alla fine, il museo fu conservato nel suo insieme. Alcuni vedono la nuova Academy come un bellissimo edificio in sé. Alcuni la vedono come una metafora per San Francisco (e le sue sette colline), mentre altri si meravigliano davanti all'azione reciproca della natura e della scienza (la forma organica del tetto con piante e animali nativi della California unita all'alta tecnologia, ai pannelli solari, alle tecniche moderne di costruzione, ecc.). Per molti, il nuovo edificio dell'Academy è un modello di sostenibilità; il museo più sostenibile al mondo. E naturalmente, l'edificio è tutto ciò e, per quanto mi riguarda, mi piace per tutti questi aspetti. Ma a volte lo vedo come un bellissimo abbraccio, una coperta, che promuove, incoraggia e sostiene tutta l'organizzazione, che celebra la straordinaria diversità d'idee, di storia e di ritmi del luogo. La nuova Academy e il bellissimo edificio che la accoglie sono una magnifica istituzione integrata, che annuncia e celebra il mondo, il lavoro della scienza e il suo posto nella nostra società.

Patrick Kociolek
Ex direttore esecutivo della California Academy of Sciences e
Direttore del Museum of Natural History, University of Colorado, Boulder

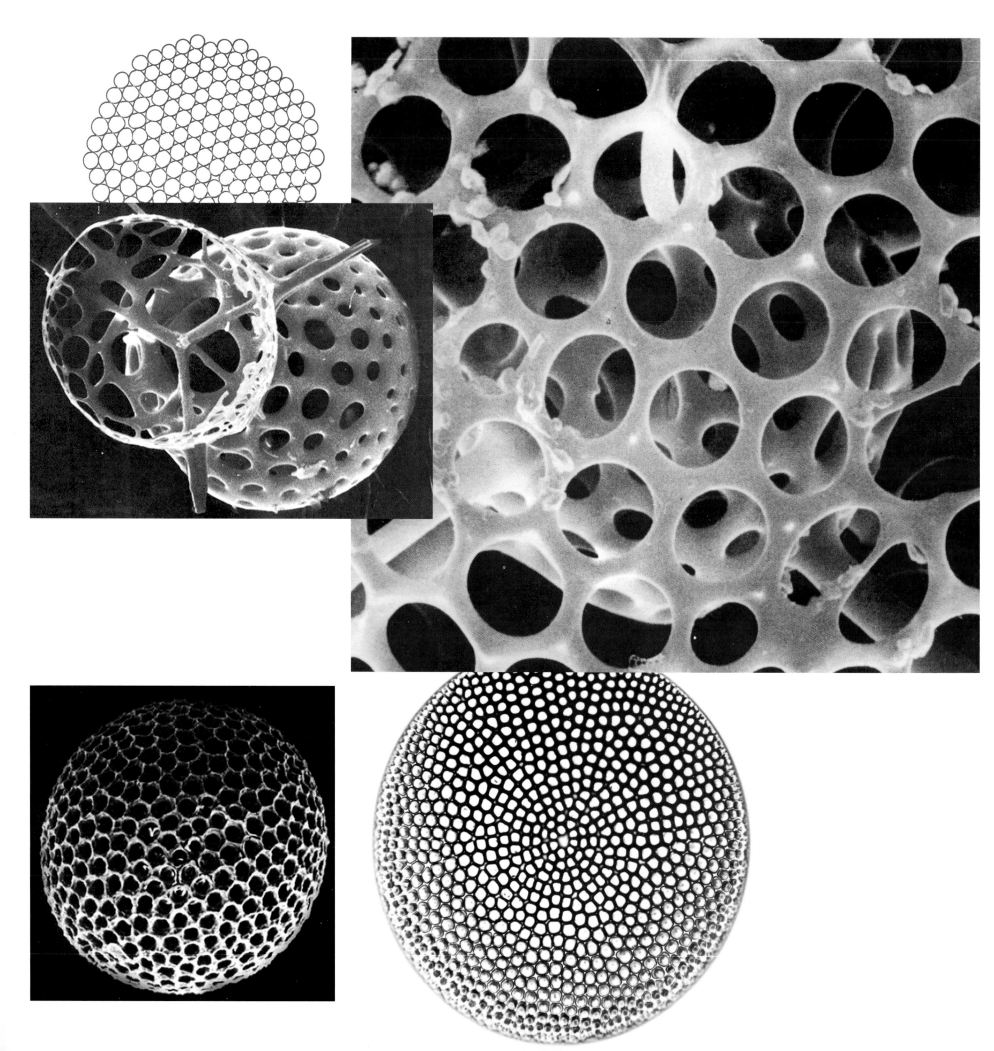

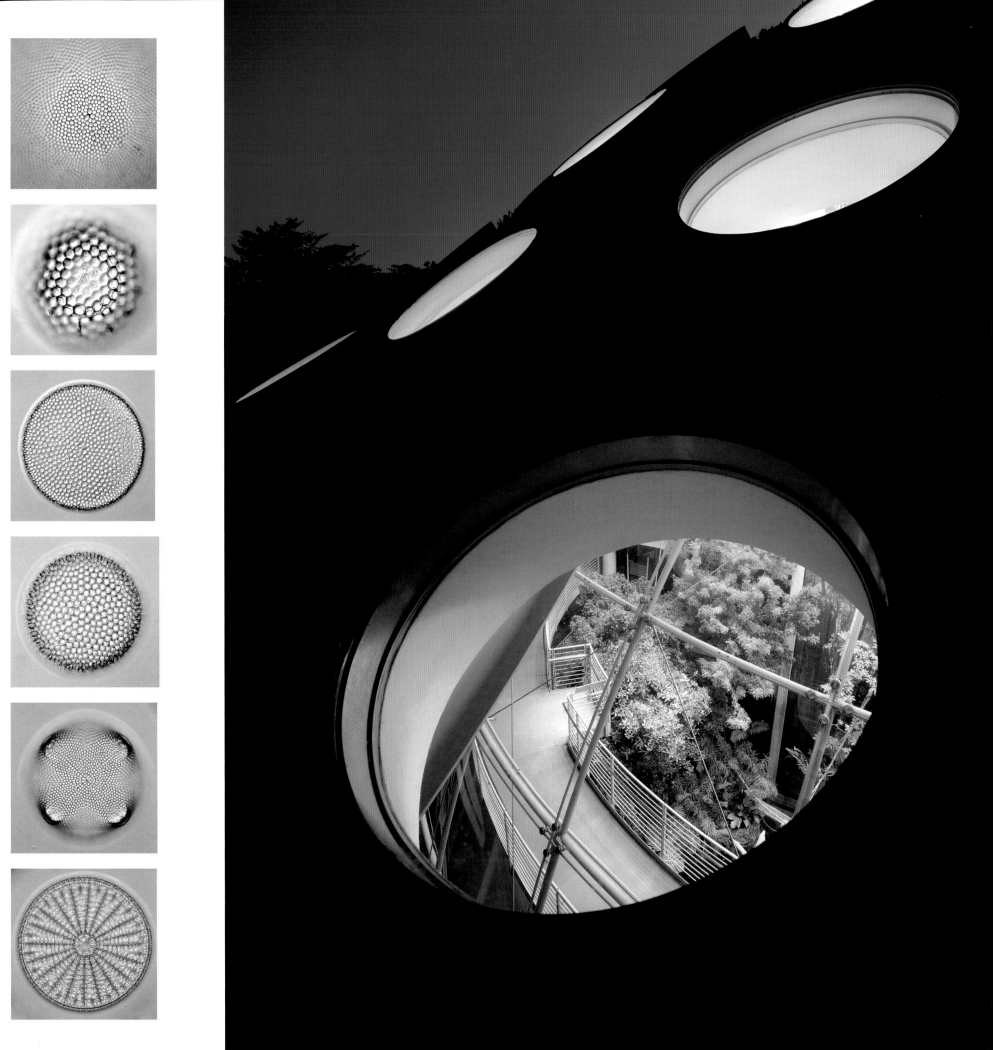

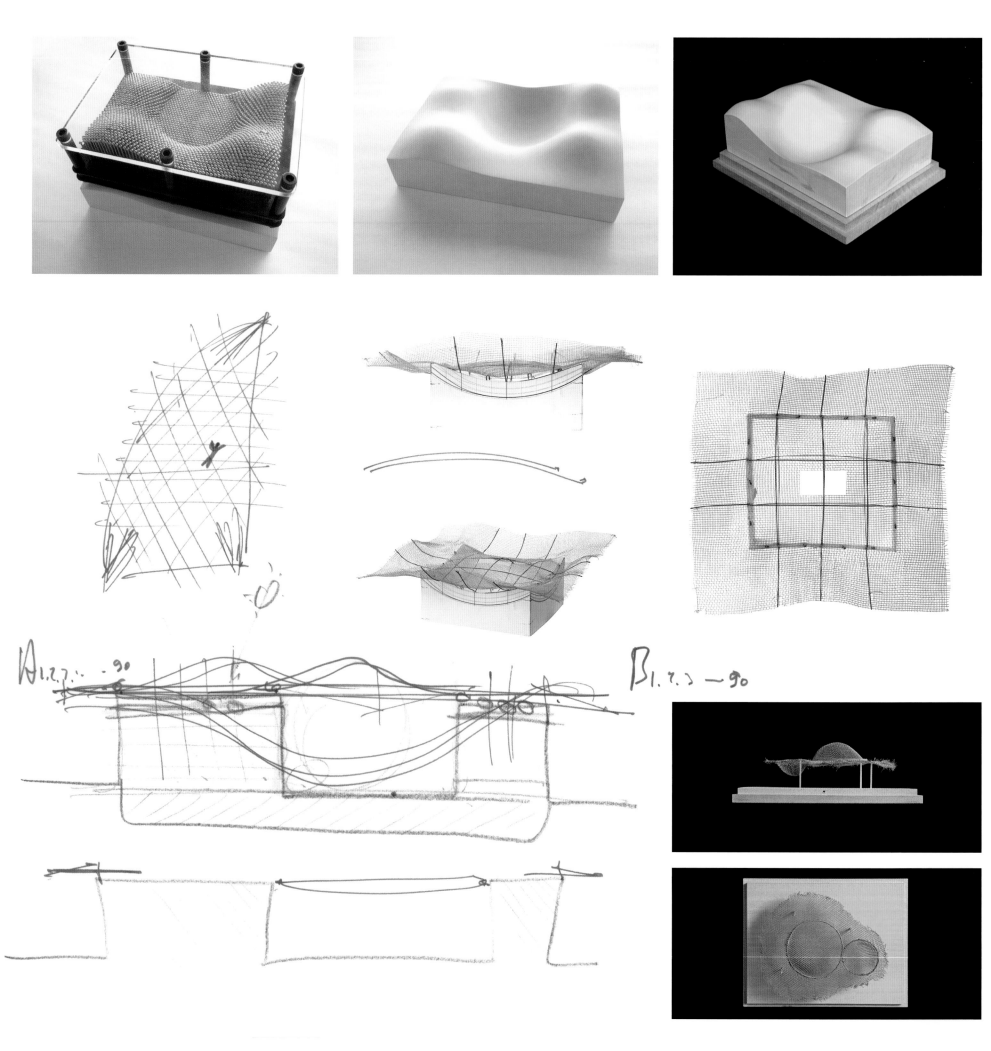

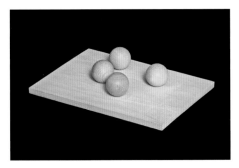

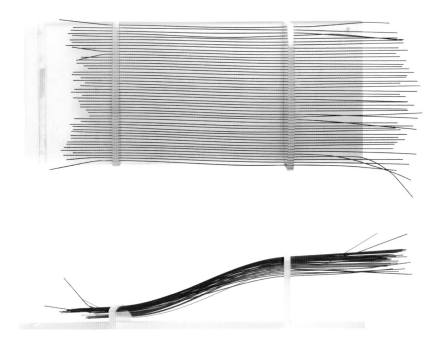
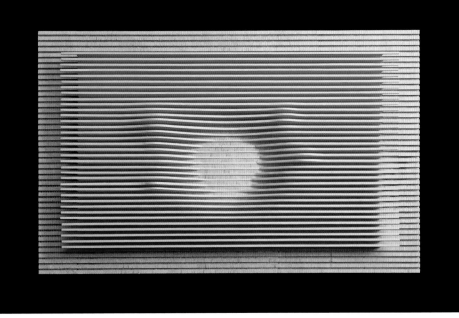
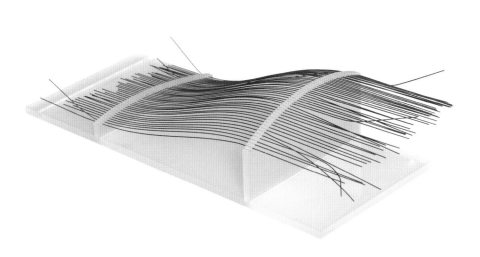
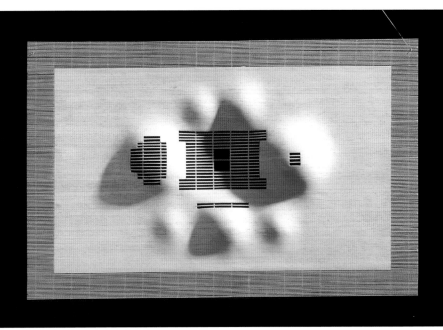

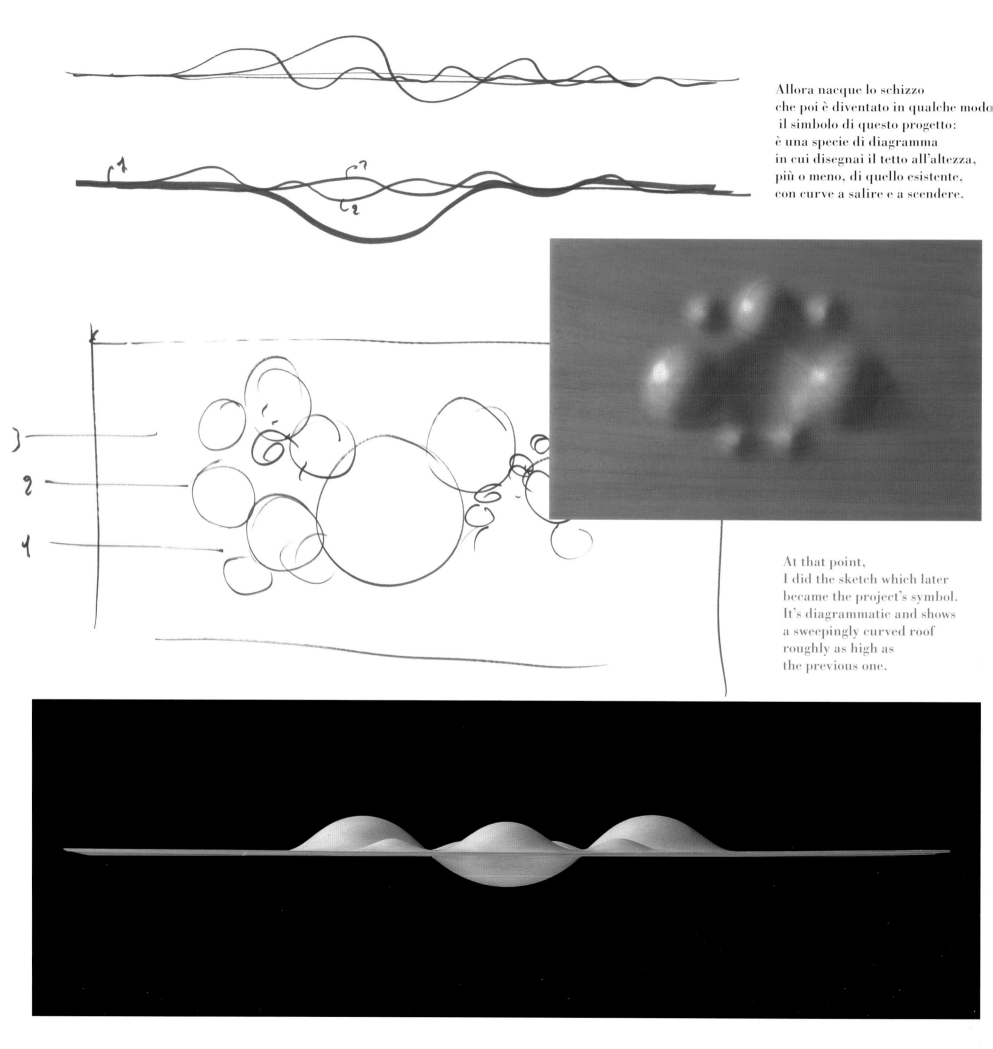

Allora nacque lo schizzo
che poi è diventato in qualche modo
il simbolo di questo progetto:
è una specie di diagramma
in cui disegnai il tetto all'altezza,
più o meno, di quello esistente,
con curve a salire e a scendere.

At that point,
I did the sketch which later
became the project's symbol.
It's diagrammatic and shows
a sweepingly curved roof
roughly as high as
the previous one.

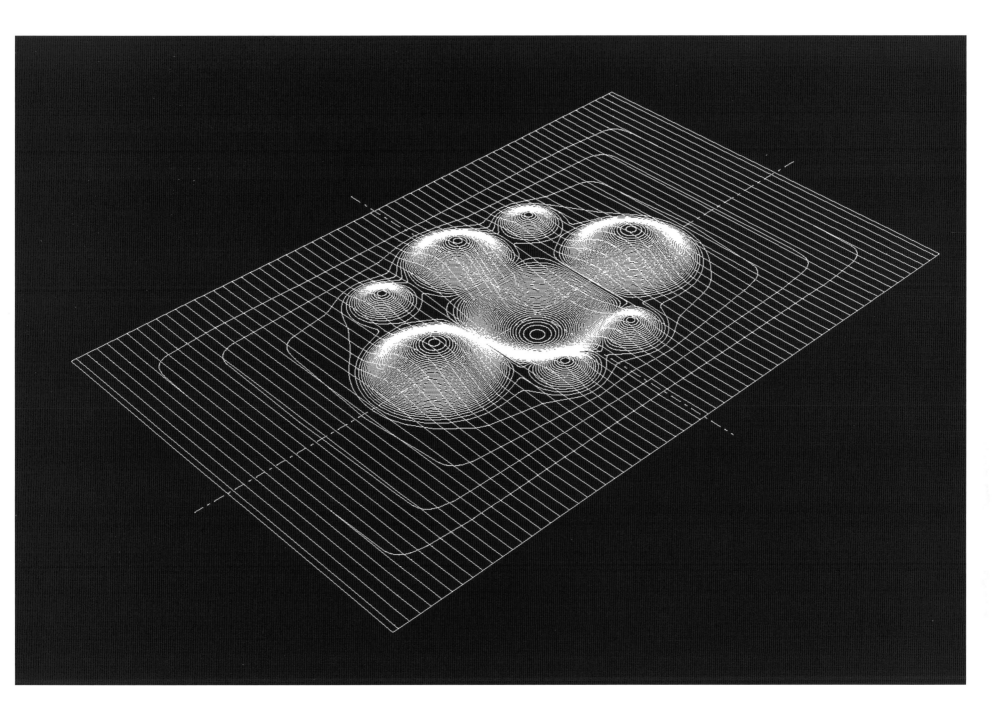

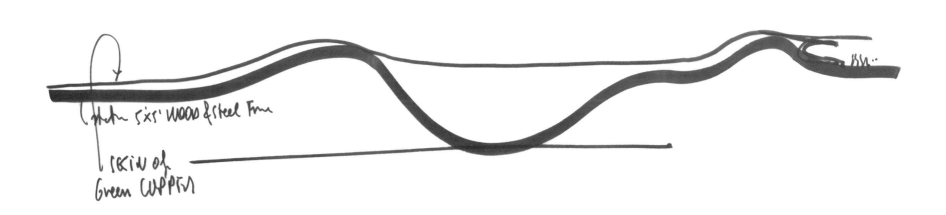

5x5' wood & steel frm

skin of
Green copper

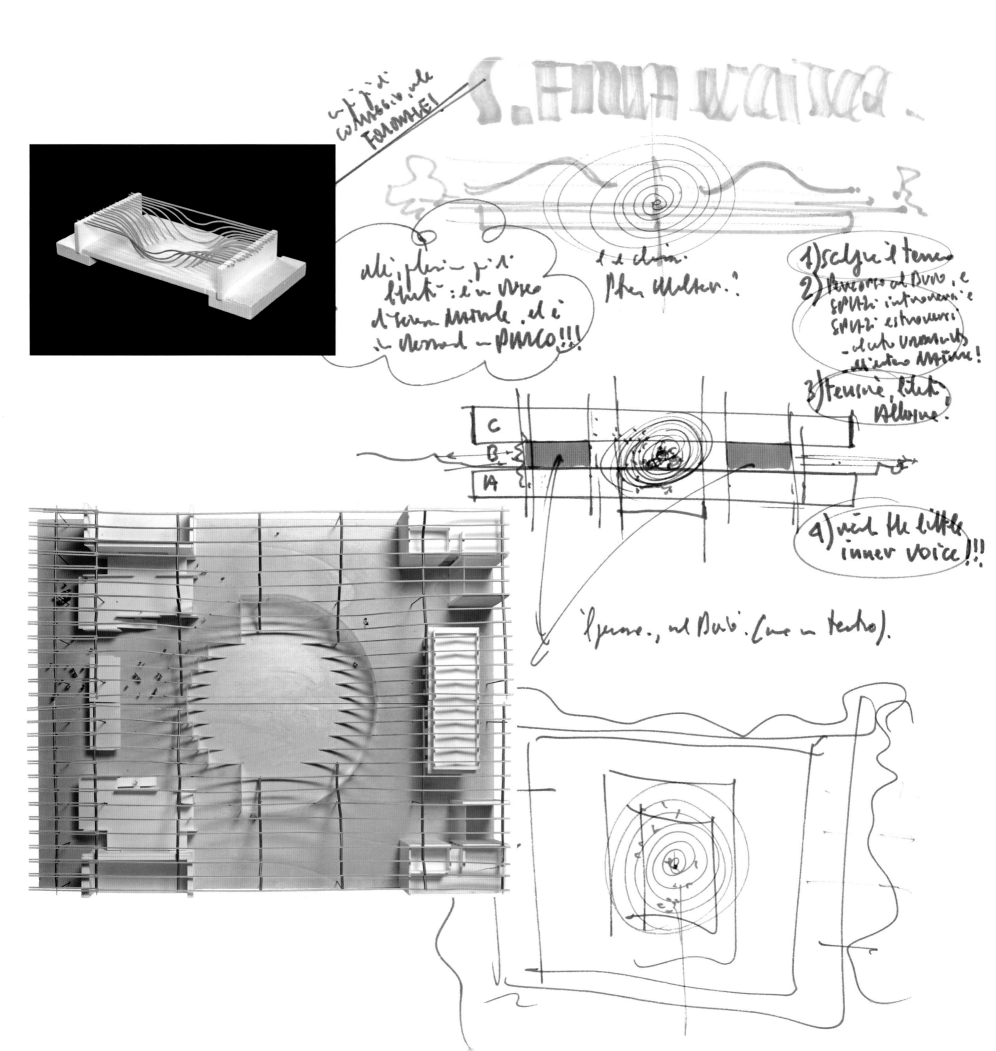

Una cosa che capii subito è che avrei tenuto la piazza.
"The Piazza", così poi battezzata in italiano,
è il punto intorno al quale si raccordano tutti i padiglioni
che compongono il museo. È l'elemento fondatore di tutto,
il vuoto che conta più dei pieni.

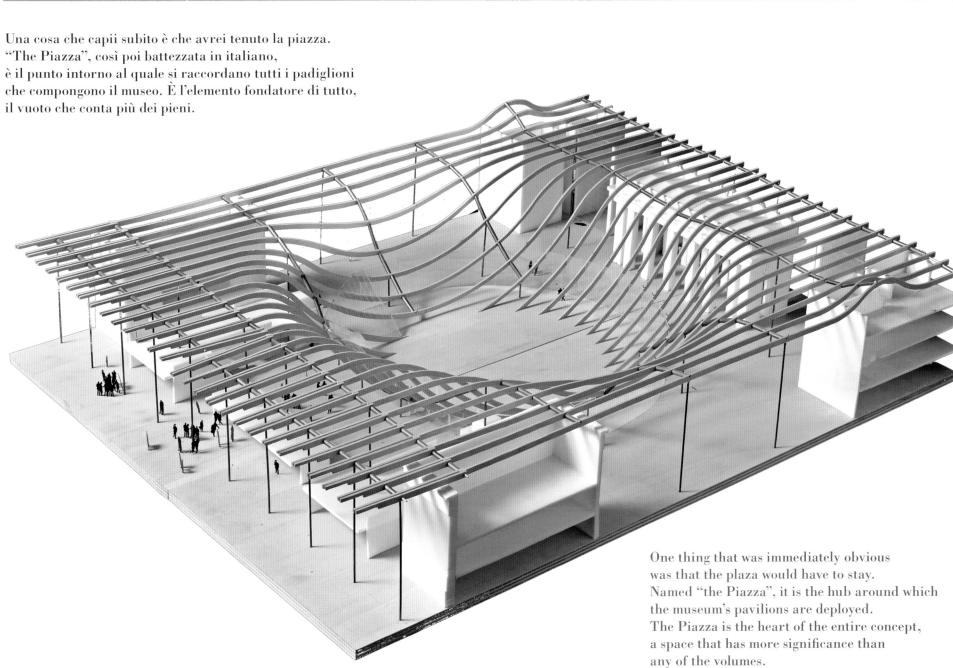

One thing that was immediately obvious
was that the plaza would have to stay.
Named "the Piazza", it is the hub around which
the museum's pavilions are deployed.
The Piazza is the heart of the entire concept,
a space that has more significance than
any of the volumes.

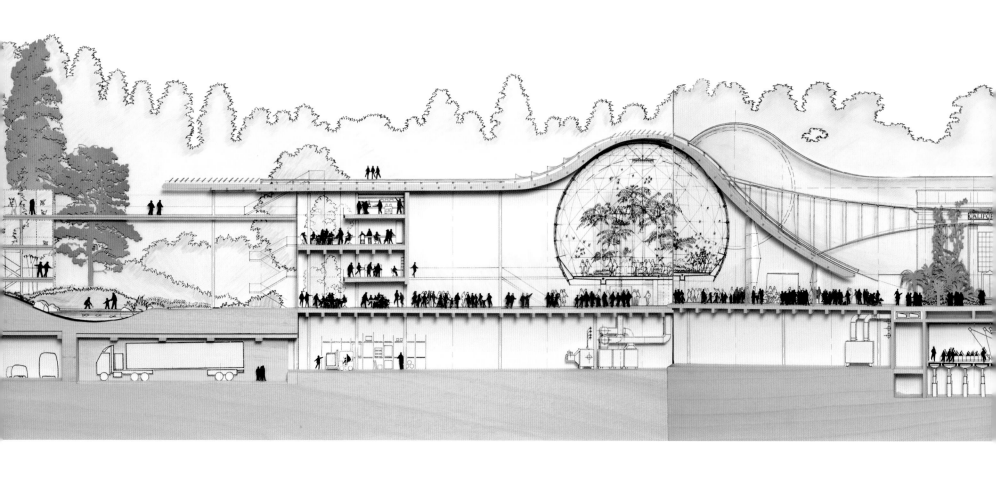

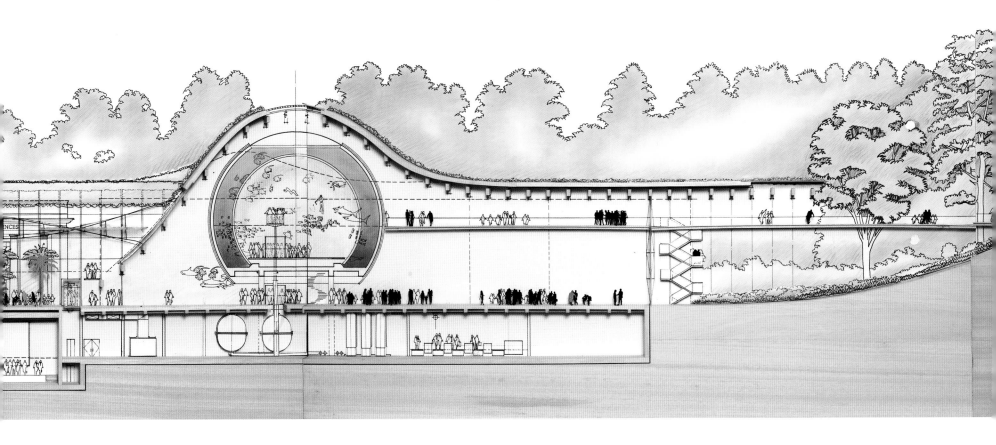

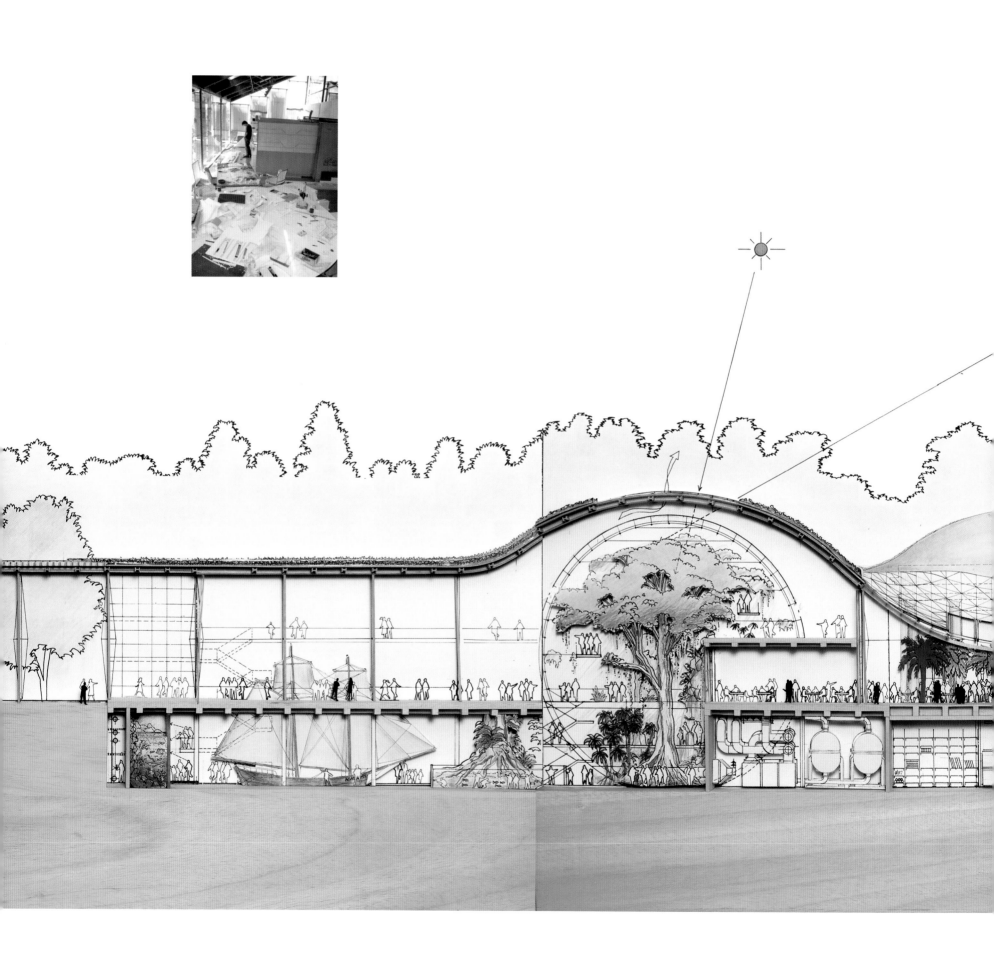

Alcune delle funzioni del museo sono troppo alte,
per cui sollevano il tetto. Altre devono essere più basse,
pensiamo alla piazza, ed ecco allora
che il tetto sprofonda e diventa una piazza.

Some of the museum's spaces
are too high, so the roof rises. Others, like the Piazza,
need to be lower so the roof descends
to become a square.

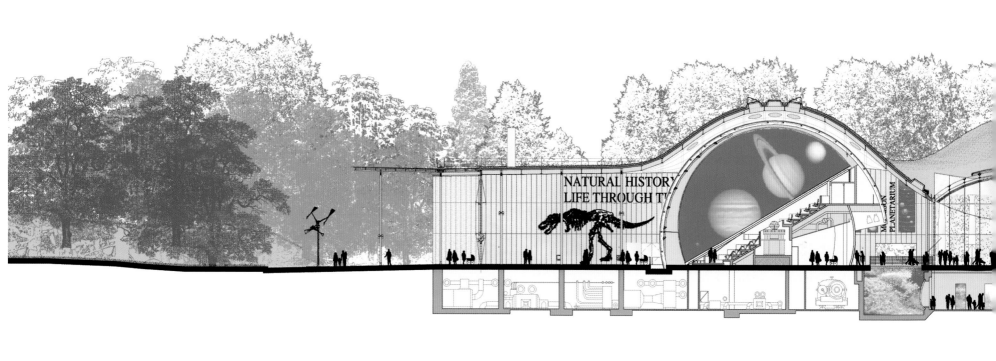

NATURAL HISTORY
LIFE THROUGH TI

PLANETARIUM

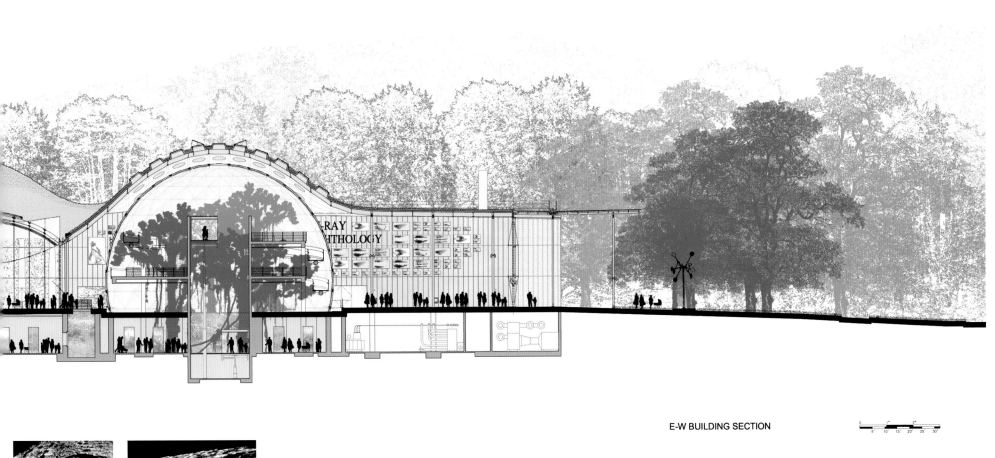

E-W BUILDING SECTION

N-S BUILDING SECTION

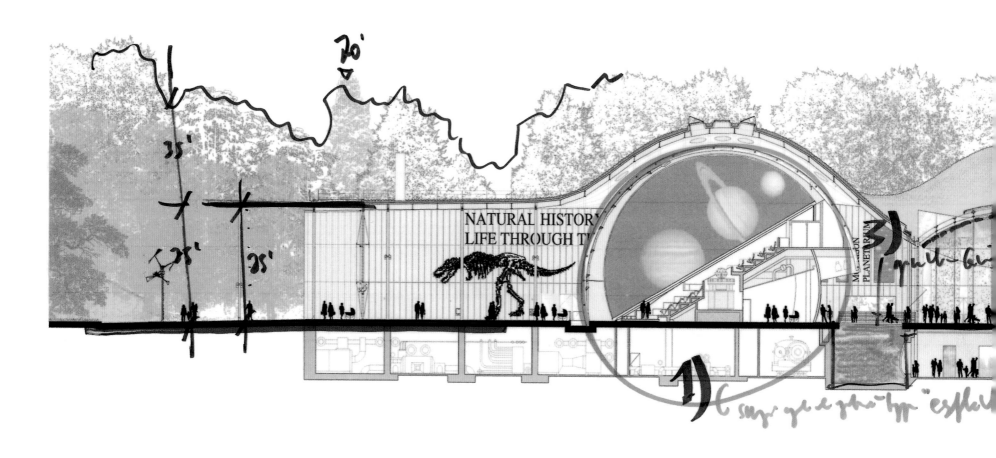

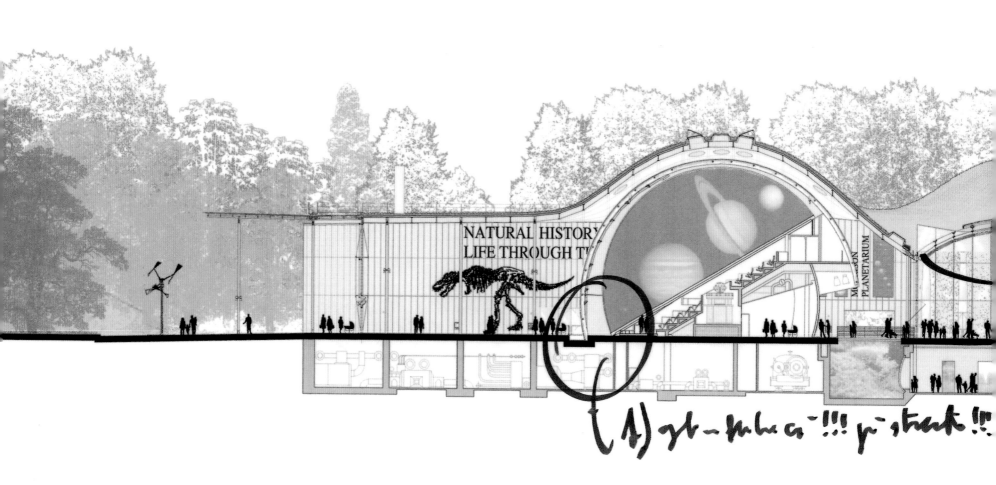

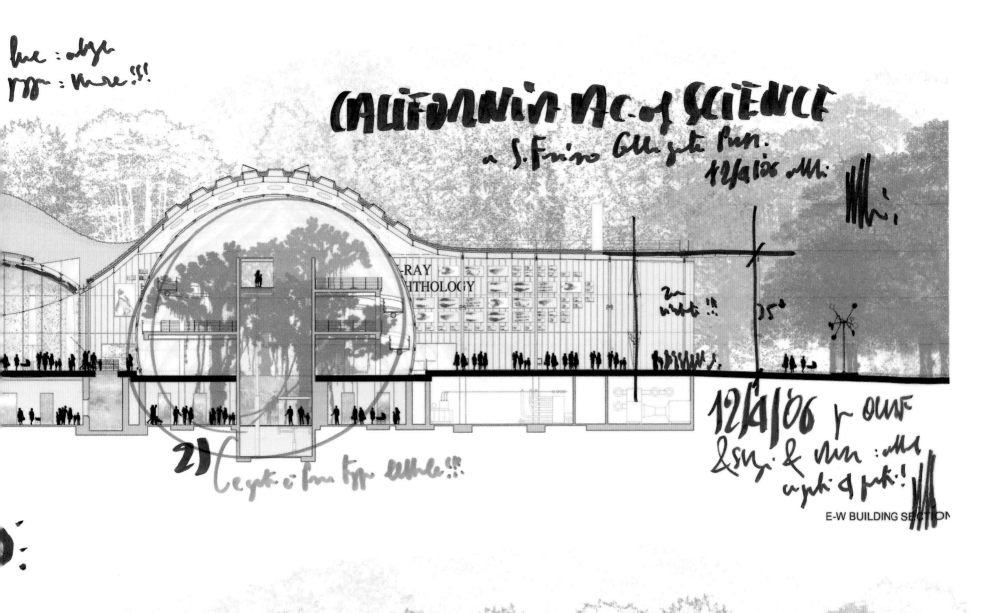

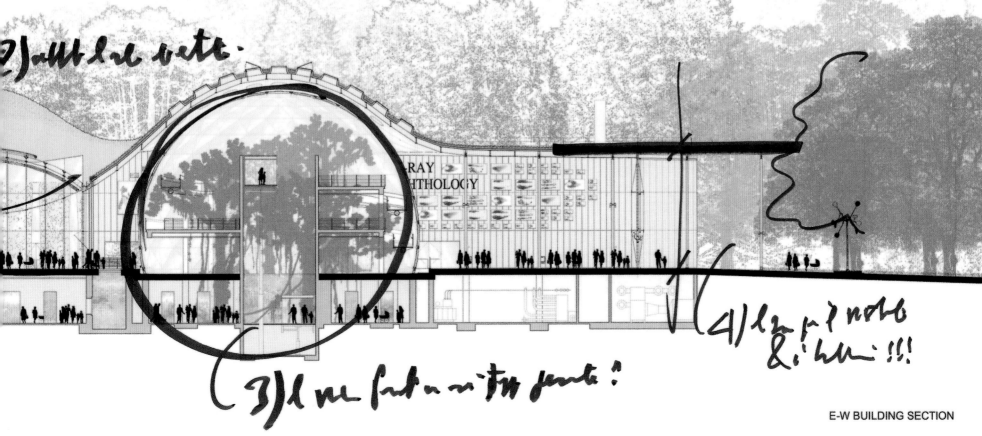

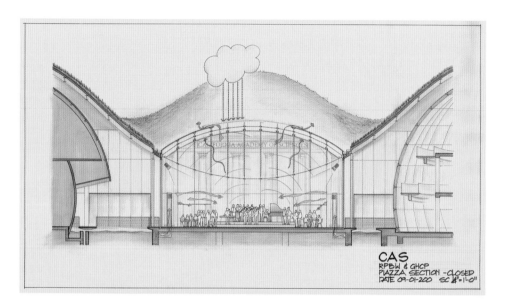

CAS
RPBW & GHCP
PIAZZA SECTION -CLOSED
DATE 09-01-200 SC 1/8"=1'-0"

CAS
RPBW & GHCP
PIAZZA SECTION -OPEN-
DATE 09-01-2004 SC 1/8"=1'-0"

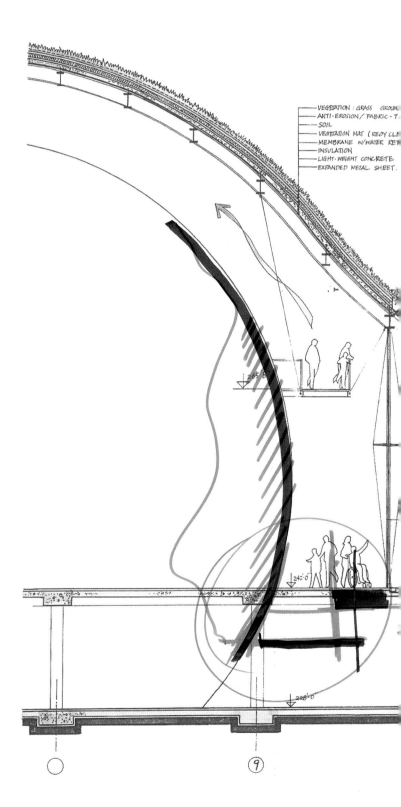

VEGETATION : GRASS GROUN
ANTI-EROSION / FABRIC - T
SOIL
VEGETATION MAT (RECYCLE
MEMBRANE W/WATER RE
INSULATION
LIGHT-WEIGHT CONCRETE
EXPANDED METAL SHEET

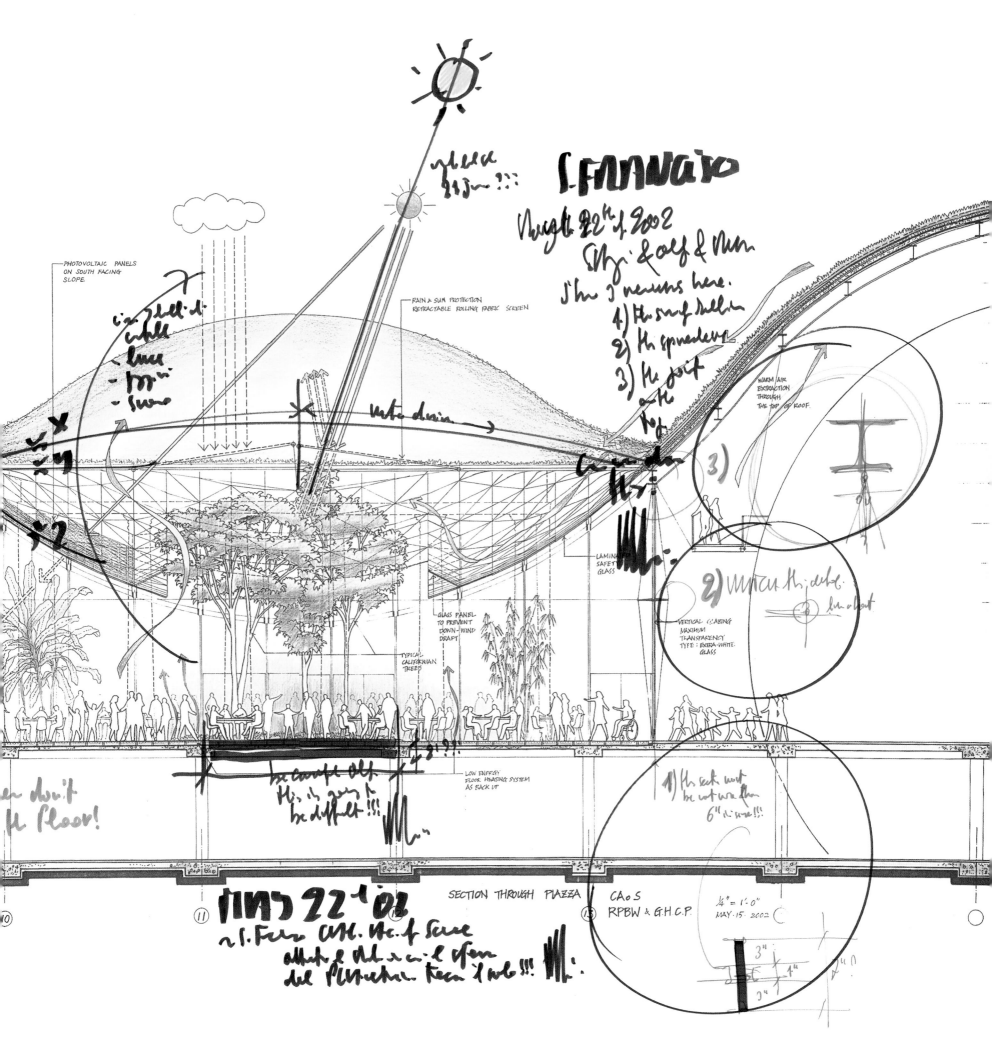

PHOTOVOLTAIC PANELS
ON SOUTH FACING
SLOPE.

RAIN & SUN PROTECTION
RETRACTABLE ROLLING FABRIC SCREEN

WARM AIR
EXTRACTION
THROUGH
THE TOP OF ROOF.

LAMINA.
SAFETY
GLASS

GLASS PANEL
TO PREVENT
DOWN-WIND
DRAFT

TYPICAL
CALIFORNIAN
TREES

VERTICAL GLAZING
MAXIMUM
TRANSPARENCY
TYPE : EXTRA-WHITE.
GLASS

LOW ENERGY
FLOOR HEATING SYSTEM
AS BACK UP

SECTION THROUGH PIAZZA

CA o S
RPBW & G.H.C.P.

¼" = 1'-0"
MAY. 15. 2002

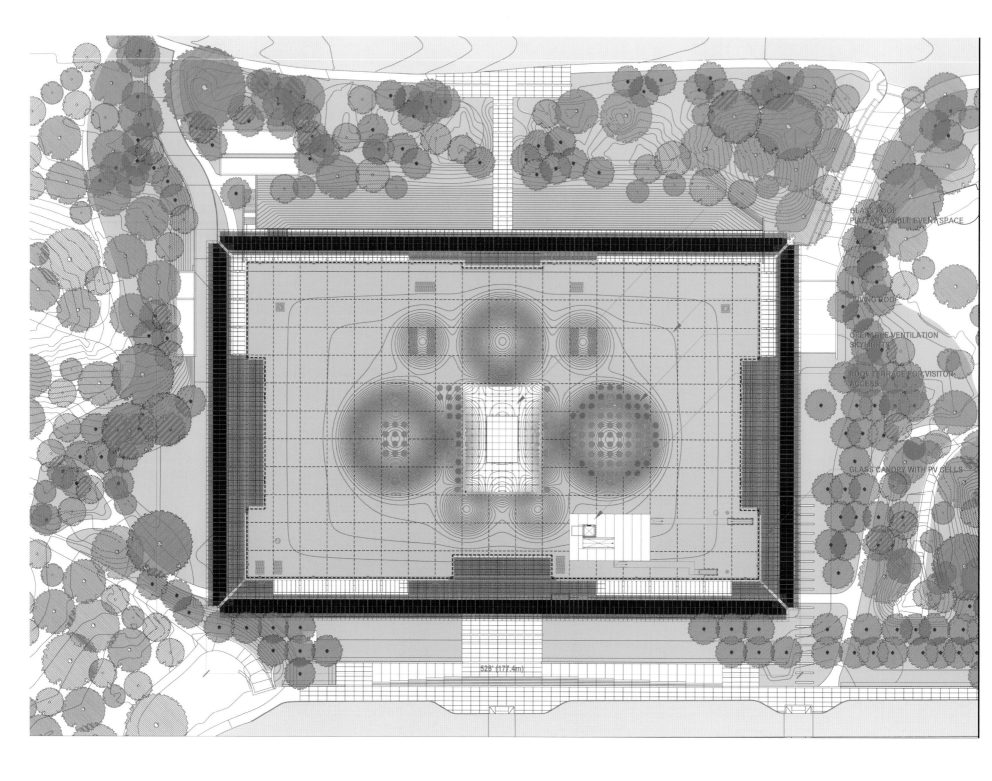

GLASS ROOF
PIAZZA FLEXIBLE EVENT SPACE

LIVING ROOF

OPERABLE VENTILATION
SKYLIGHTS

ROOF TERRACE FOR VISITOR
ACCESS

GLASS CANOPY WITH PV CELLS

528' (177.4m)

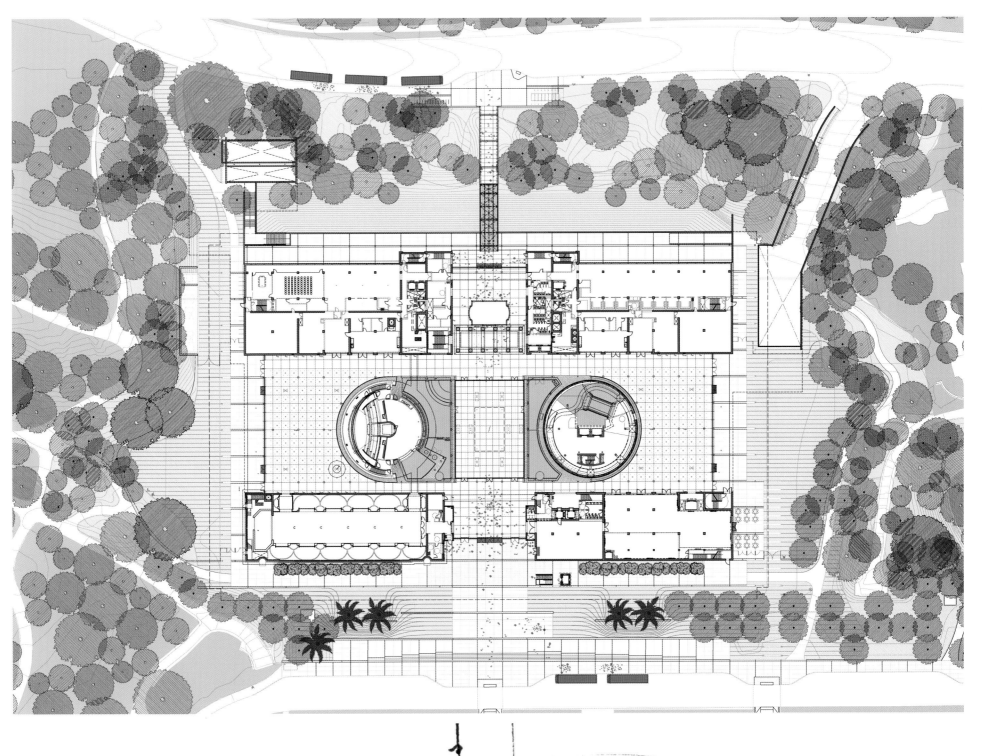

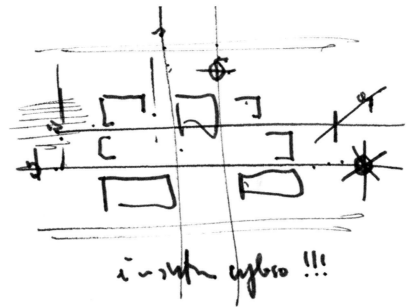

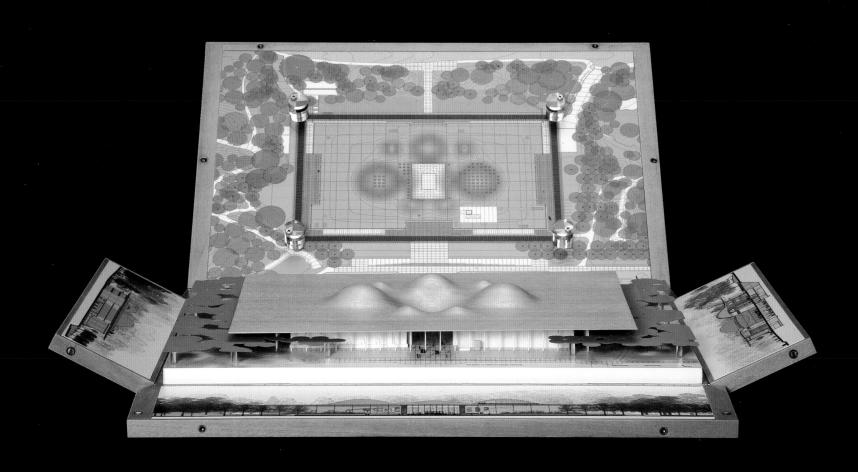

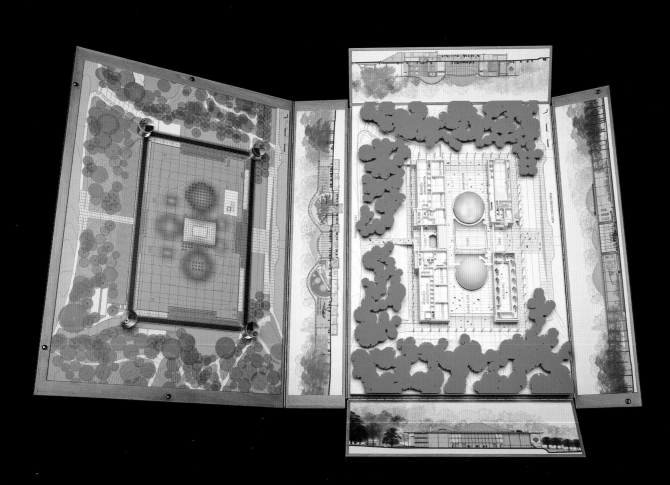

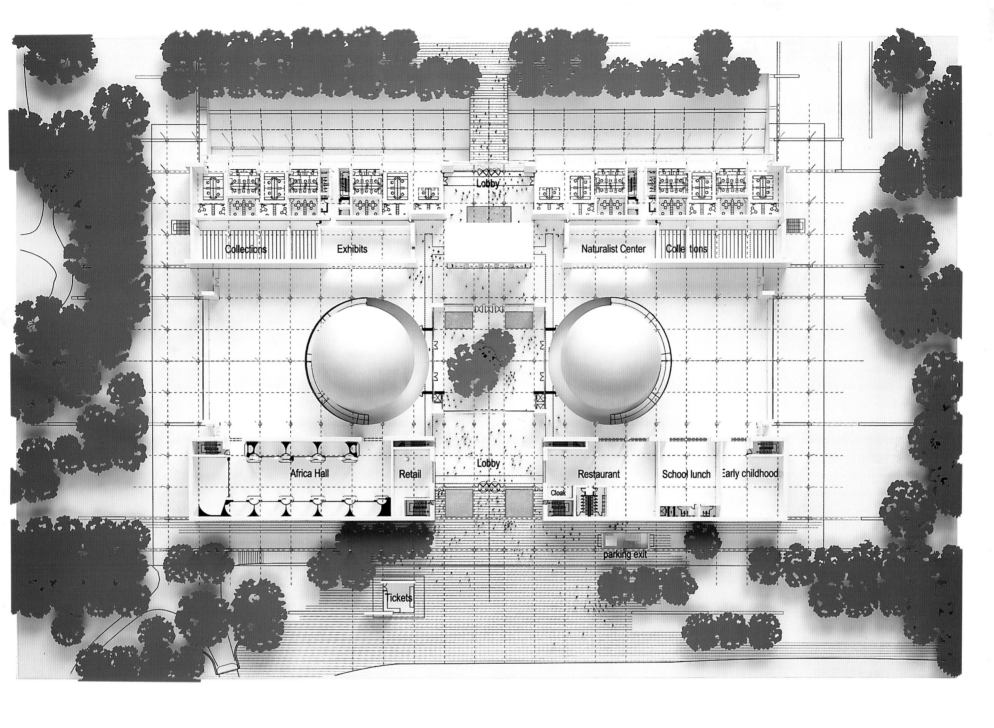

Collections   Exhibits   Lobby   Naturalist Center   Colle tions

Africa Hall   Retail   Lobby   Restaurant   School lunch   Early childhood

Cloak

parking exit

Tickets

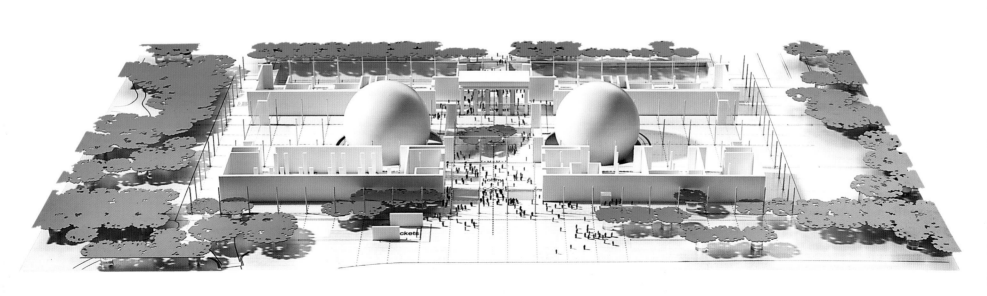

ckets

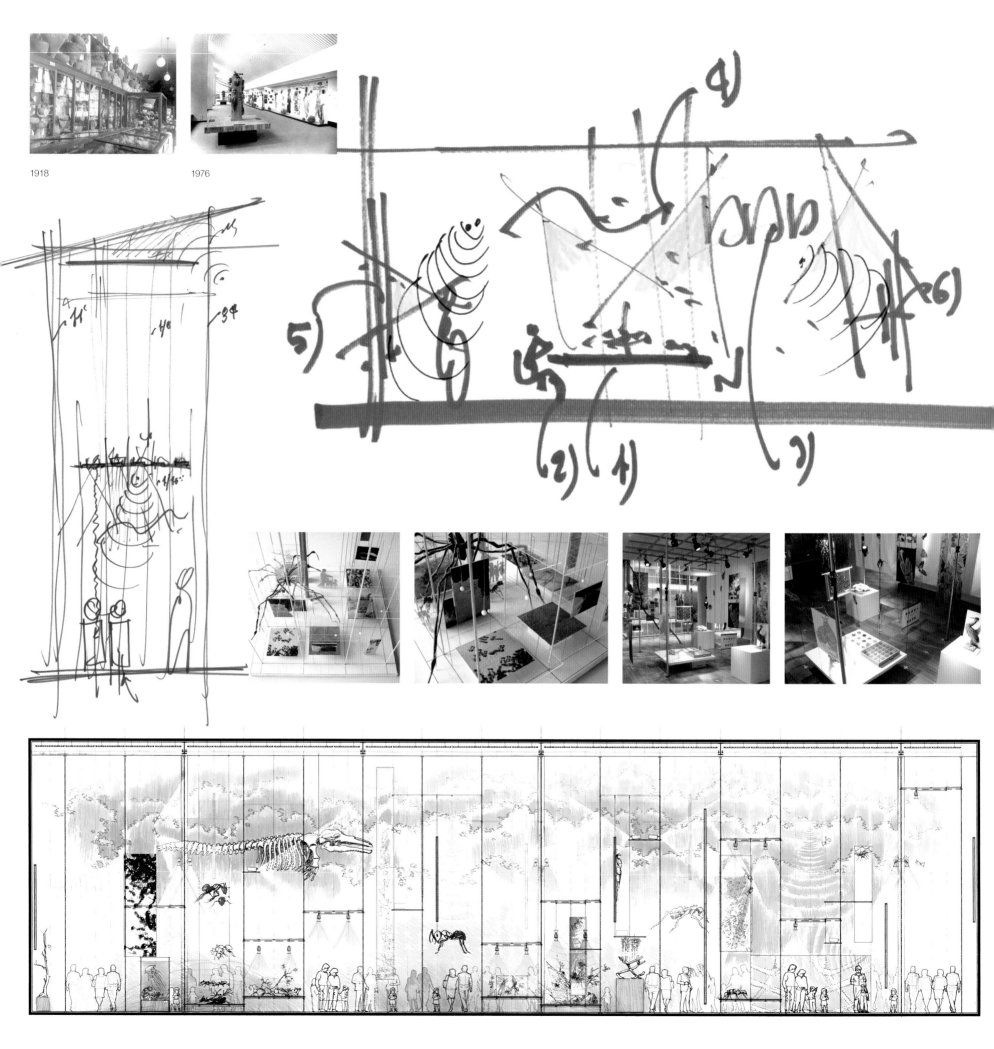

1918

1976

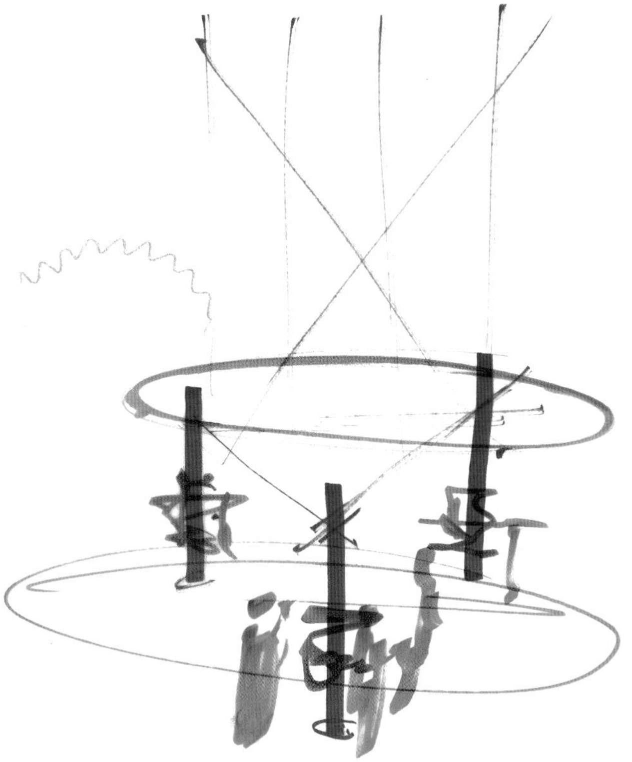

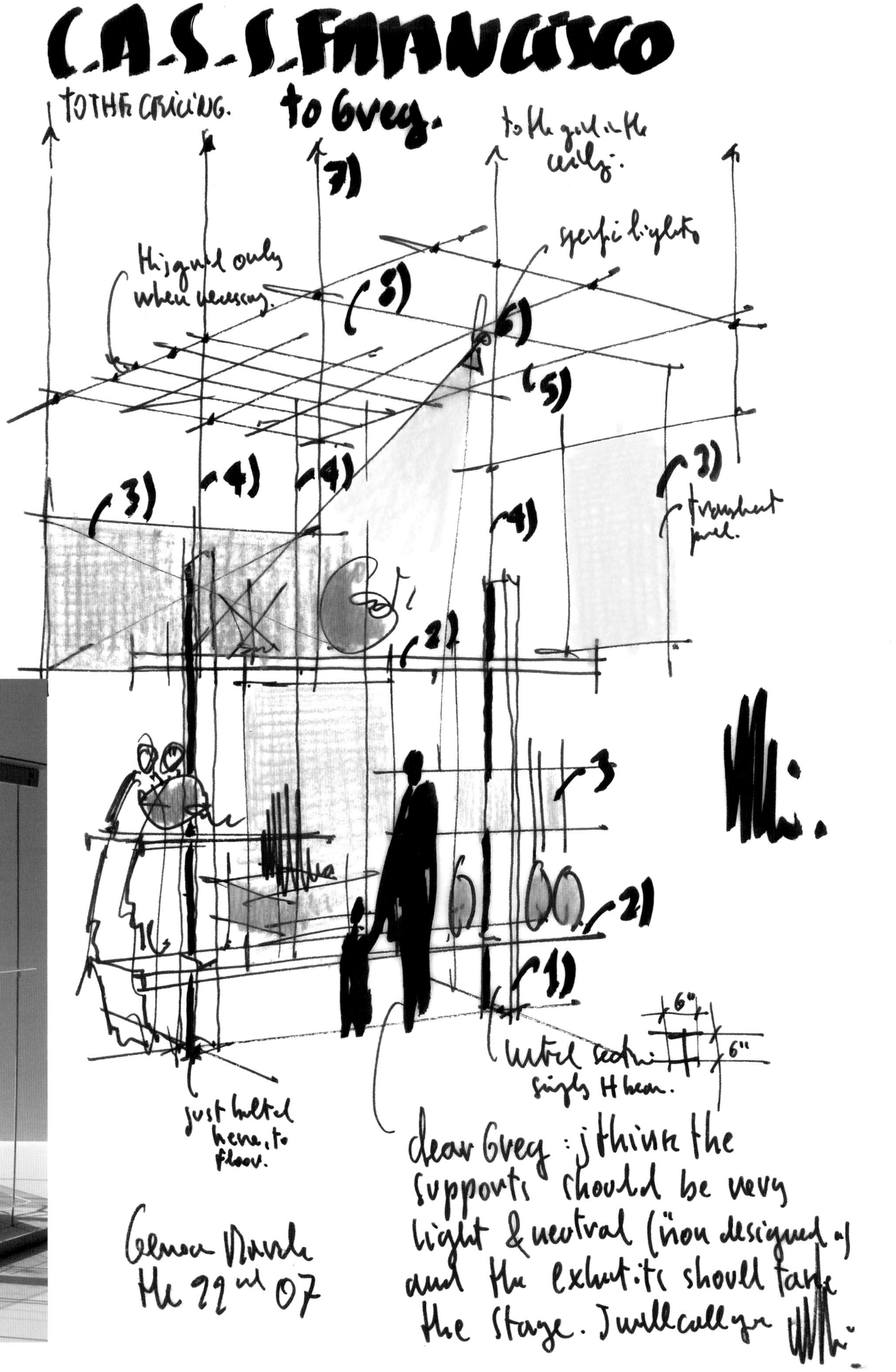

C.A.S. S.FRANCISCO

TO THE CEILING.   to Greg.

to the girl in the ceiling.

specific lights

This girl only when necessary.

(7)

(8)

(6)

(5)

(3)   (4)   (4)   (4)

(3)

transparent panel.

(3)

(2)

(1)

just bolted here to floor.

lateral section single H beam.

6"   6"

Genoa March Me 22nd 07

dear Greg: j think the supports should be very light & neutral (non designed of) and the exhibits should face the Stage. j will call you

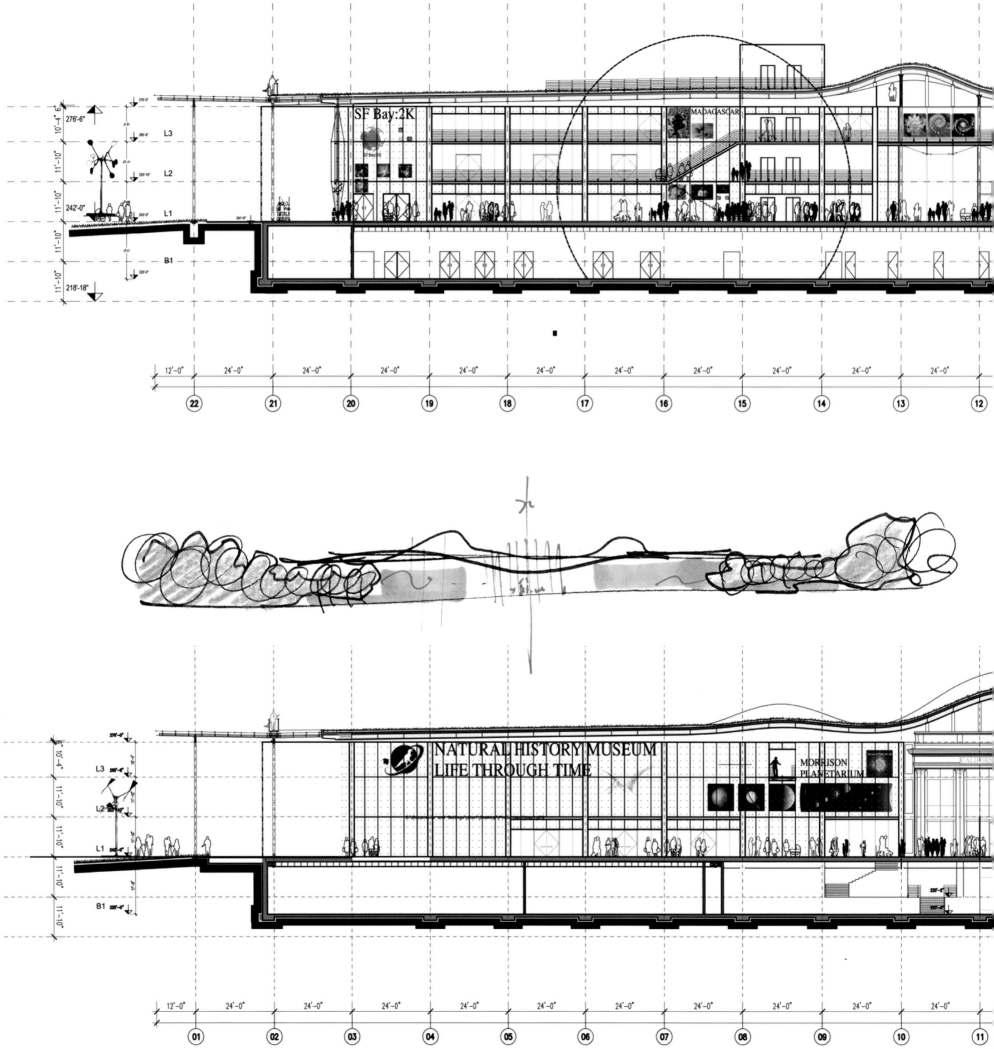

SF Bay:2K

MADAGASCAR

276'-0"
276'-6"
10'-4" 6"
L3
285'-8"
11'-10"
L2
253'-10"
11'-10"
L1
242'-0"
242'-0"
11'-10"
B1
230'-0"
11'-10"
218'-18"
229'-0"

| 12'-0" | 24'-0" | 24'-0" | 24'-0" | 24'-0" | 24'-0" | 24'-0" | 24'-0" | 24'-0" | 24'-0" | 24'-0" |

22 21 20 19 18 17 16 15 14 13 12

NATURAL HISTORY MUSEUM
LIFE THROUGH TIME

MORRISON
PLANETARIUM

CALIFORN

276'-4"
10'-4" 6"
L3
285'-8"
11'-10"
L2
253'-10"
11'-10"
L1
242'-0"
11'-10"
B1
229'-0"
11'-10"

| 12'-0" | 24'-0" | 24'-0" | 24'-0" | 24'-0" | 24'-0" | 24'-0" | 24'-0" | 24'-0" | 24'-0" | 24'-0" |

01 02 03 04 05 06 07 08 09 10 11

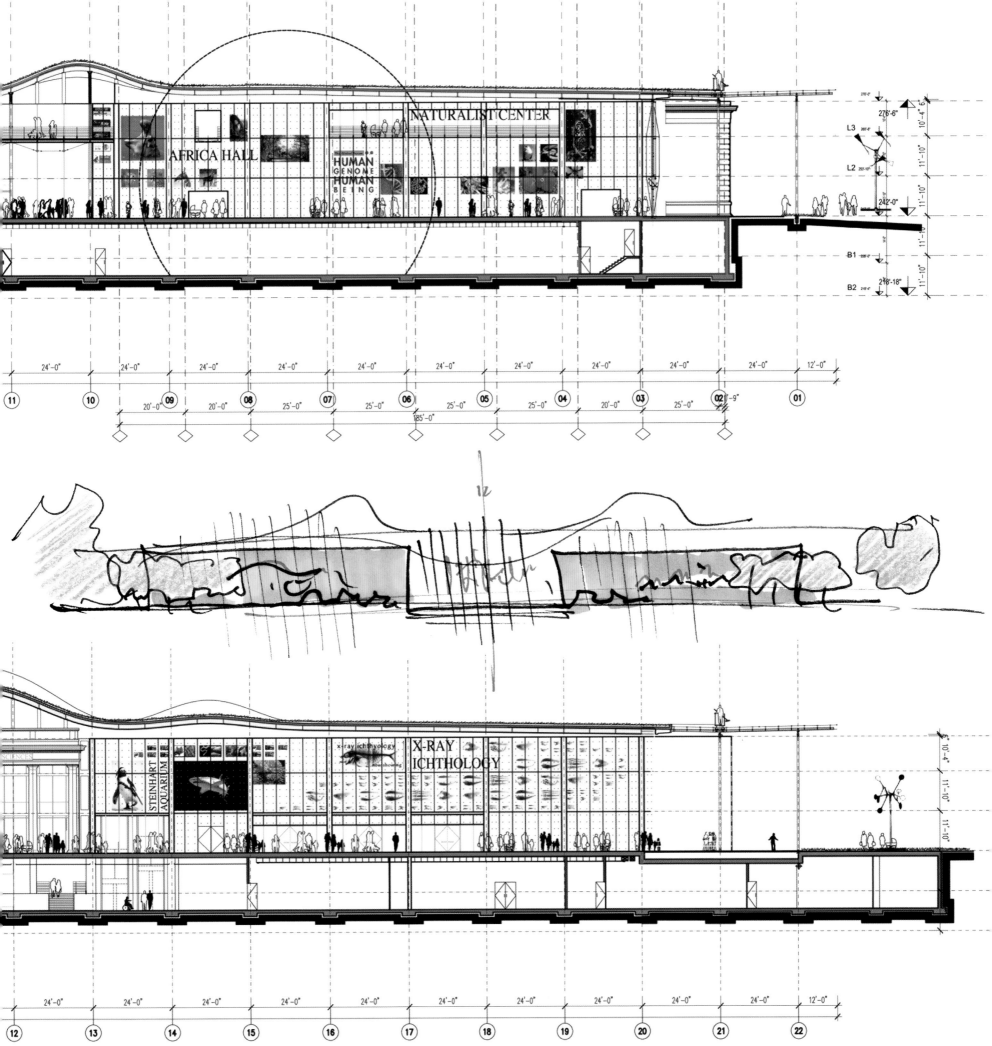

AFRICA HALL

NATURALIST CENTER

HUMAN GENOME HUMAN BEING

L3 267'-0"
L2 257'-10"
242'-0"
B1 228'-0"
B2 218'-6"

276'-0"
276'-6"
10'-4" 6"
11'-10"
11'-10"
11'-10"
11'-10"

24'-0" 24'-0" 24'-0" 24'-0" 24'-0" 24'-0" 24'-0" 24'-0" 24'-0" 24'-0" 12'-0"

11 10 09 08 07 06 05 04 03 02 01

20'-0" 20'-0" 25'-0" 25'-0" 25'-0" 25'-0" 20'-0" 25'-0"
185'-0"
21'-9"

SCIENCES

STEINHART AQUARIUM

x-ray ichthyology

X-RAY ICHTHOLOGY

10'-4"
11'-10"
11'-10"

24'-0" 24'-0" 24'-0" 24'-0" 24'-0" 24'-0" 24'-0" 24'-0" 24'-0" 24'-0" 12'-0"

12 13 14 15 16 17 18 19 20 21 22

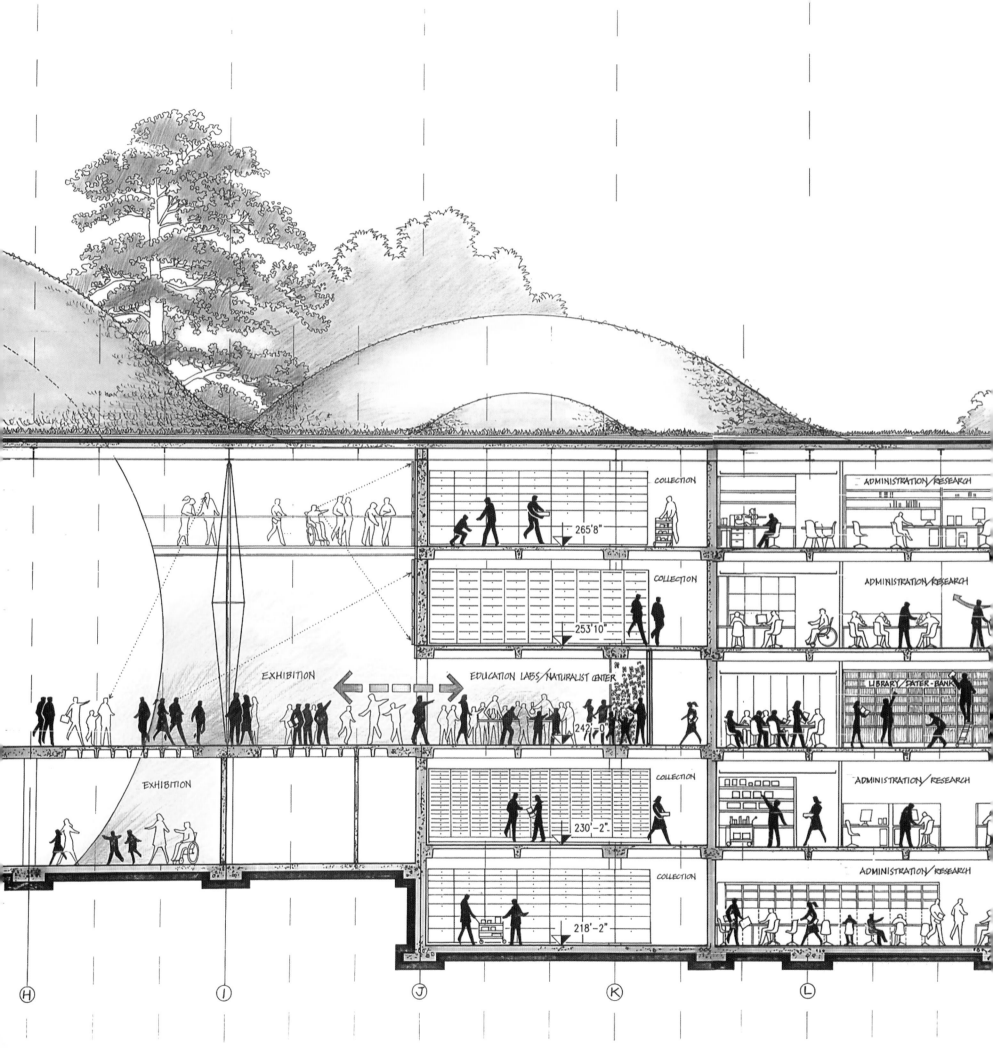

COLLECTION

ADMINISTRATION/RESEARCH

265'8"

COLLECTION

ADMINISTRATION/RESEARCH

253'10"

EXHIBITION

EDUCATION LABS/NATURALIST CENTER

LIBRARY/DATER-BANK

242'0"

EXHIBITION

COLLECTION

ADMINISTRATION/RESEARCH

230'2"

COLLECTION

ADMINISTRATION/RESEARCH

218'2"

H   I   J   K   L

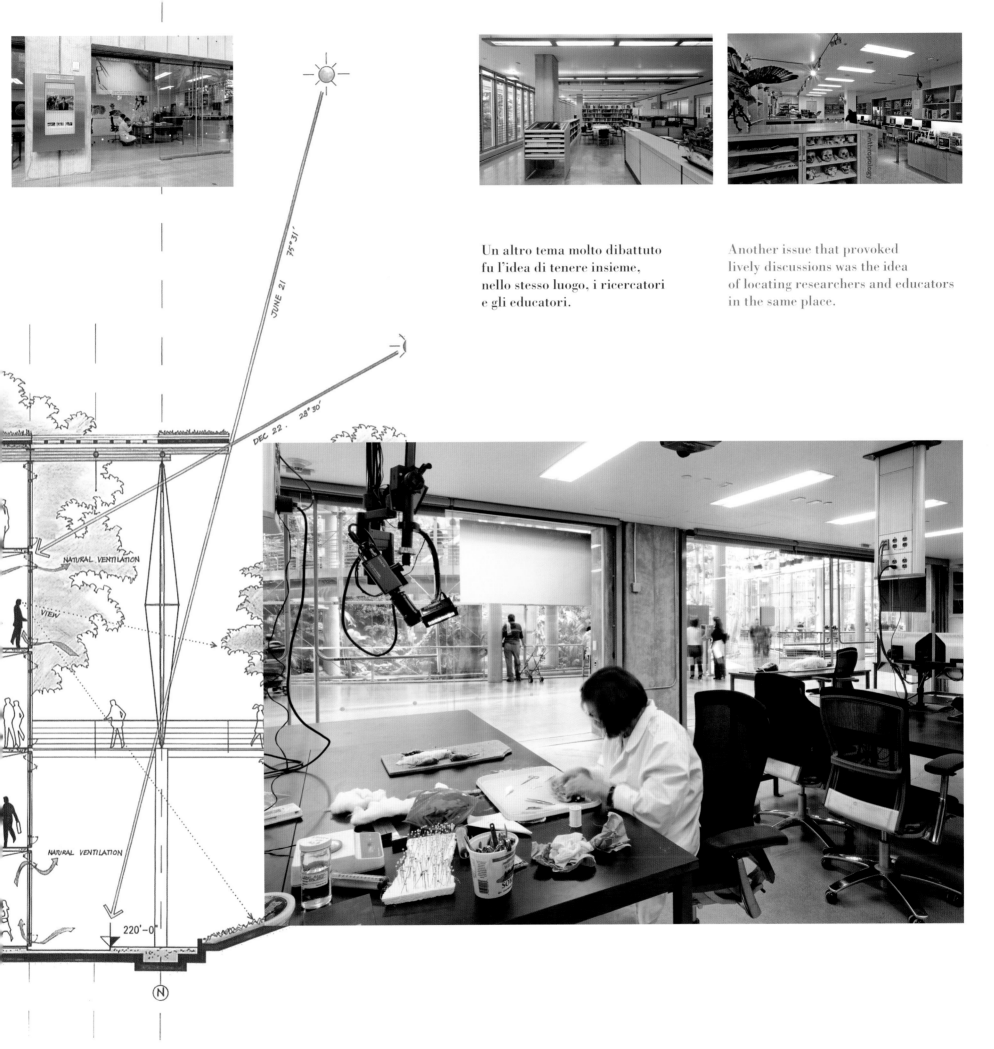

Un altro tema molto dibattuto
fu l'idea di tenere insieme,
nello stesso luogo, i ricercatori
e gli educatori.

Another issue that provoked
lively discussions was the idea
of locating researchers and educators
in the same place.

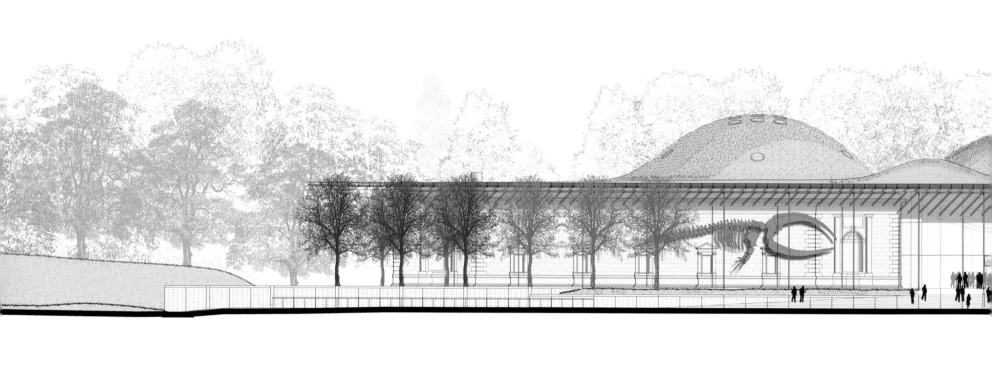

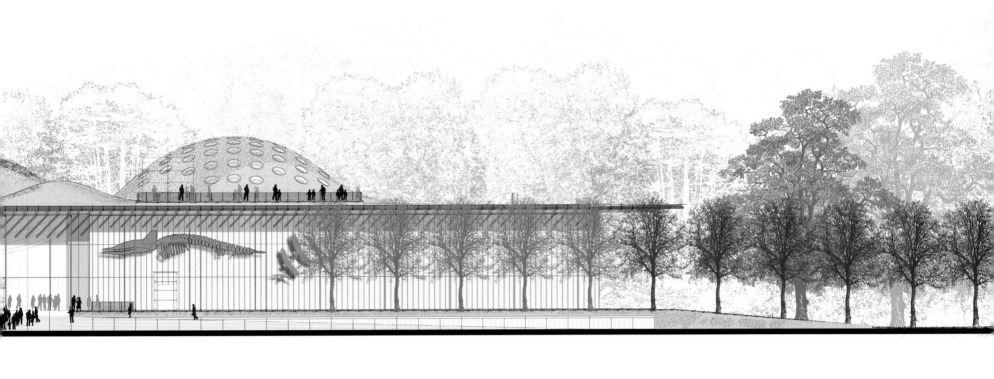

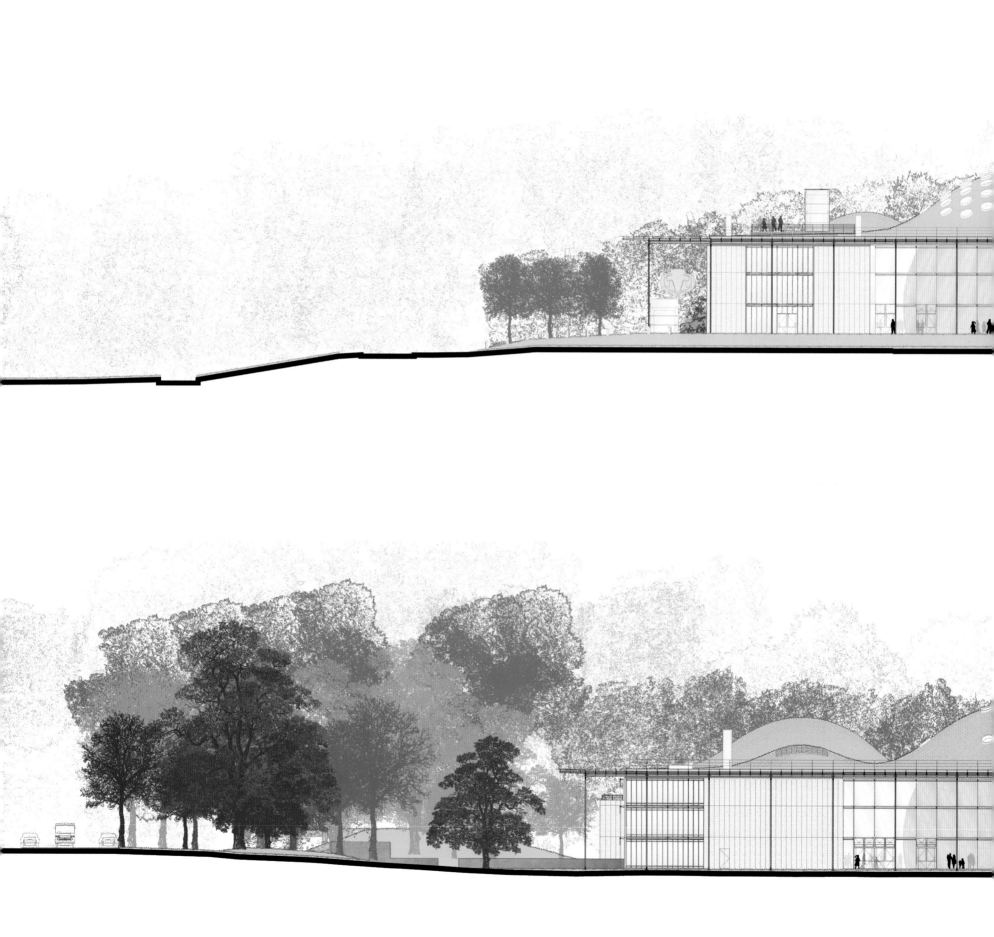

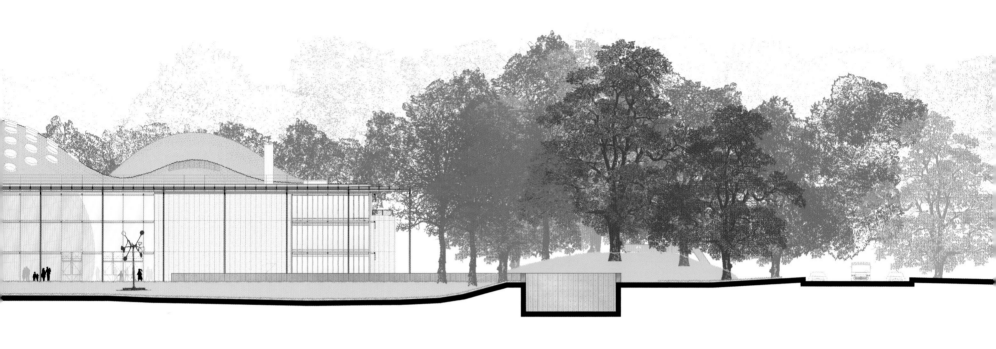

ELEVATION SHAKESPEARE GARDEN

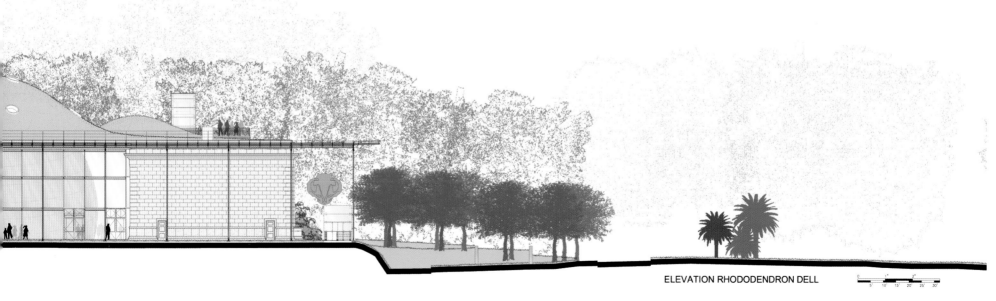

ELEVATION RHODODENDRON DELL

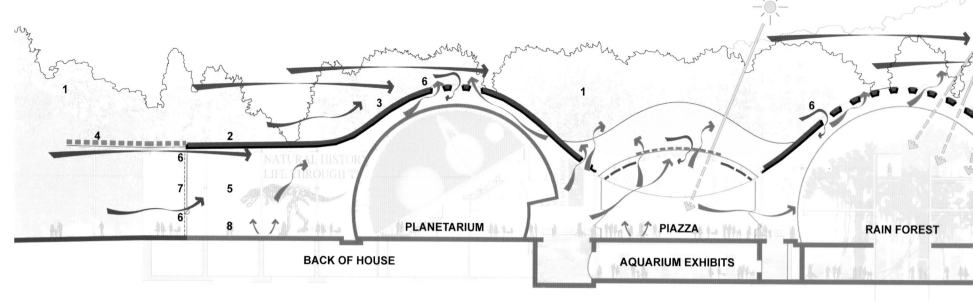

PLANETARIUM

PIAZZA

RAIN FOREST

BACK OF HOUSE

AQUARIUM EXHIBITS

1 RESTORE ADJACENT PARK (NATURAL SHADOW)
2 GREEN ROOF (INSULATION & PASSIVE COOLING)
3 ROOF GEOMETRY FAVORS "VENTURI EFFECT"
4 GLASS CANOPY WITH PHOTOVOLTAIC CELLS
5 CONCRETE WALLS (PASSIVE COOLING)
6 OPERABLE VENTS AND SKYLIGHTS
7 SUNSHADES
8 RADIANT FLOOR
9 NATURAL LIGHT FOR PLANTS

PASSIVE COOLING AND
NATURAL VENTILATION
IN HIGH MASS
RESEARCH SPACES

ALTERNATIVE ENERGY
SOURCES INTEGRATED INTO
ROOF STRUCTURE
• PV CELLS
• SOLAR PANELS

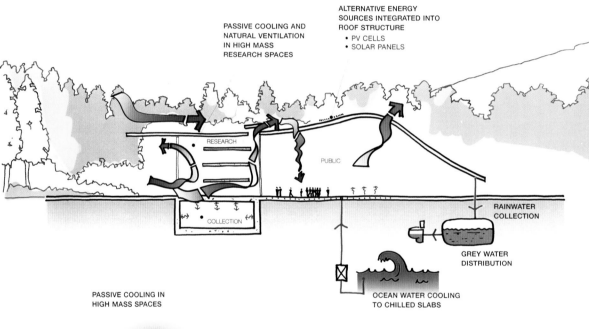

RESEARCH

PUBLIC

COLLECTION

RAINWATER
COLLECTION

GREY WATER
DISTRIBUTION

OCEAN WATER COOLING
TO CHILLED SLABS

PASSIVE COOLING IN
HIGH MASS SPACES

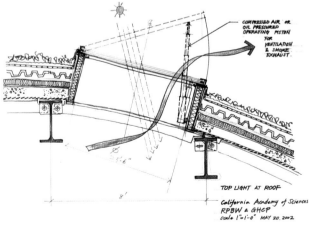

COMPRESSED AIR OR
OIL PRESSURED
OPERATING PISTON
FOR
VENTILATION
& SMOKE
EXHAUST

TOP LIGHT AT ROOF

California Academy of Sciences
RPBW & GHCP
scale 1"=1'-0" MAY 20, 2002

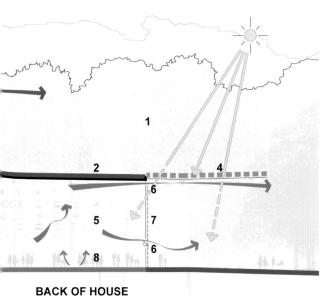

1

2   4

6

5   7

8

6

BACK OF HOUSE

I was very excited when Renzo first talked to me about working with him on the engineering feasibility of this project. My passion is sustainable design and it seemed that right from the outset here was a project that had the potential to be an exemplar in every way. The Academy were keen that the new project would embody ways to use the earths natural resources in a responsible and friendly way so that the building itself would be a living demonstration to its staff and visitors.

In the early workshops we explored how to capture the wind that came across the park from the ocean, how to have a minimal disruption to the ecology of the park, how to reuse the good parts of the existing building and to see if we could incorporate renewable energy sources into the project. We should use the energy from the sun and perhaps the sea.

At one early workshop Renzo produced a beautiful wood model of a sculpted roof which would fly over the whole building. It consisted of a plate flat at the edges but in the centre indented with a number of different size domes. The domes gave me an idea based on the traditional domed roofs of Middle Eastern houses. If we made a hole in the top of the dome it would create suction as the wind blows over it causing the hot air to be sucked out of the space beneath.

We decided to use the shape of the roof to ventilate the main exhibition space using the cool ocean breezes without fans or air conditioning. The holes in the 'hills' could be opened and closed to control the ventilation and would be transparent to let in the light to the exhibition hall and the rainforest below.
As the roof evolved, Renzo imagined that it could become a garden transporting the park to the roof and providing a home for plants, insects and butterflies. The perimeter of the roof overhangs the building protecting the walkways from rain and sun but also contains photovoltaic cells to collect energy from the sun.
The exciting thing for me was that as we worked together this roof which started as a flying carpet became a multiuse, multifunction living space.

The other concept we discussed in the early workshops was the idea that the large central exhibition space should be like a cathedral. It would have solid walls, floor and roof that together with the roof ventilation would keep the space cool in summer. Renzo understood this idea and evolved the exhibition space with fair faced concrete walls and floor which help provide comfort without energy.

Later on when the whole building was assessed according to the LEED criteria it received the highest platinum rating because from the outset we sought to maximise the interaction of the building with the natural environment. This result comes from Renzo not being content to just add sustainable thinking to his design but fully embracing it as a driver for the building making it a truly beautiful sustainable building which I am proud to be associated with.

Alistair Guthrie
Director of Arup's building service
Leader of Global Building Sustainability Network

La prima volta che Renzo mi propose di lavorare con lui agli studi di fattibilità ingegneristica di questo progetto fui davvero entusiasta. La mia passione è la progettazione sostenibile, e sin dall'inizio mi è sembrato che questo progetto avesse il potenziale per essere esemplare da tutti i punti di vista. La California Academy of Sciences aveva a cuore che il nuovo progetto rappresentasse un approccio responsabile ed ecologico all'utilizzo delle risorse naturali della Terra, e che l'edificio stesso ne fosse esempio sia per lo staff che per i visitatori.

Nelle prime riunioni, ci dedicammo a studiare come catturare le brezze dell'oceano che soffiano attraverso il parco, come salvaguardare il parco stesso, e come poter riutilizzare le parti dell'edificio esistente rimaste in buono stato; esaminando la possibilità di sfruttare, all'interno del progetto, fonti rinnovabili di energia. Avremmo potuto utilizzare l'energia del sole ed eventualmente quella del mare. In uno dei primi incontri, Renzo presentò un bellissimo modello del tetto che avrebbe "volato" su tutto l'edificio. Era una lamina di legno dai bordi piatti, sagomata nel mezzo da diverse collinette di varie dimensioni, che mi suggerirono un'idea ispirata dai tetti tradizionali a cupola delle abitazioni mediorientali. Realizzando un foro nella parte superiore della cupola, si sarebbe creata un'aspirazione al passaggio del vento, risucchiando così l'aria calda fuori dallo spazio sottostante.

Decidemmo di utilizzare la forma del tetto per la ventilazione dello spazio espositivo principale, sfruttando le fresche brezze che provengono dall'oceano per fare a meno di ventilatori e aria condizionata. I fori nelle "colline" del tetto potevano essere aperti e chiusi come oblò per controllare la ventilazione, e sarebbero stati trasparenti per lasciare penetrare la luce nello spazio espositivo e nella foresta tropicale sottostante.
Quando il tetto si sviluppò, Renzo immaginò di trasformarlo in un giardino, come se avesse trasferito il parco sul tetto, creando un habitat per piante, insetti e farfalle. Spingendosi oltre il perimetro dell'edificio, esso garantisce oggi un riparo dalla pioggia e dal sole. Contiene inoltre delle cellule fotovoltaiche per catturare l'energia solare necessaria al museo. Questo tetto, che da "tappeto volante" iniziale è diventato uno spazio vivo, un "tetto vivente" versatile e multifunzione, rappresenta per me la parte più entusiasmante della nostra collaborazione.

Un altro concetto preso in considerazione nelle prime riunioni fu l'idea che il grande spazio espositivo centrale assomigliasse a una cattedrale. La ventilazione del tetto, i muri spessi, il pavimento e la copertura avrebbero mantenuto la freschezza durante l'estate. Renzo lavorò su questi temi e sviluppò lo spazio espositivo con facciate e pavimento di cemento a vista, che avrebbero fornito comfort ambientale senza consumare energia.

Più avanti, quando l'intero edificio fu valutato secondo i criteri LEED, conquistò il livello platinum, il più alto, perché si era cercato sin dall'inizio di massimizzare l'interazione dell'edificio con l'ambiente naturale. Questo risultato è stato raggiunto grazie a Renzo, che non si accontentò di aggiungere semplicemente delle teorie sostenibili al suo progetto, ma spostò interamente la sostenibilità in quanto fattore chiave per la realizzazione del museo; oggi sono orgoglioso di affermare che anche io ho contribuito a realizzare questo bellissimo edificio.

Alistair Guthrie
Direttore Gruppo Impianti Arup
Leader del Global Building Sustainability Network

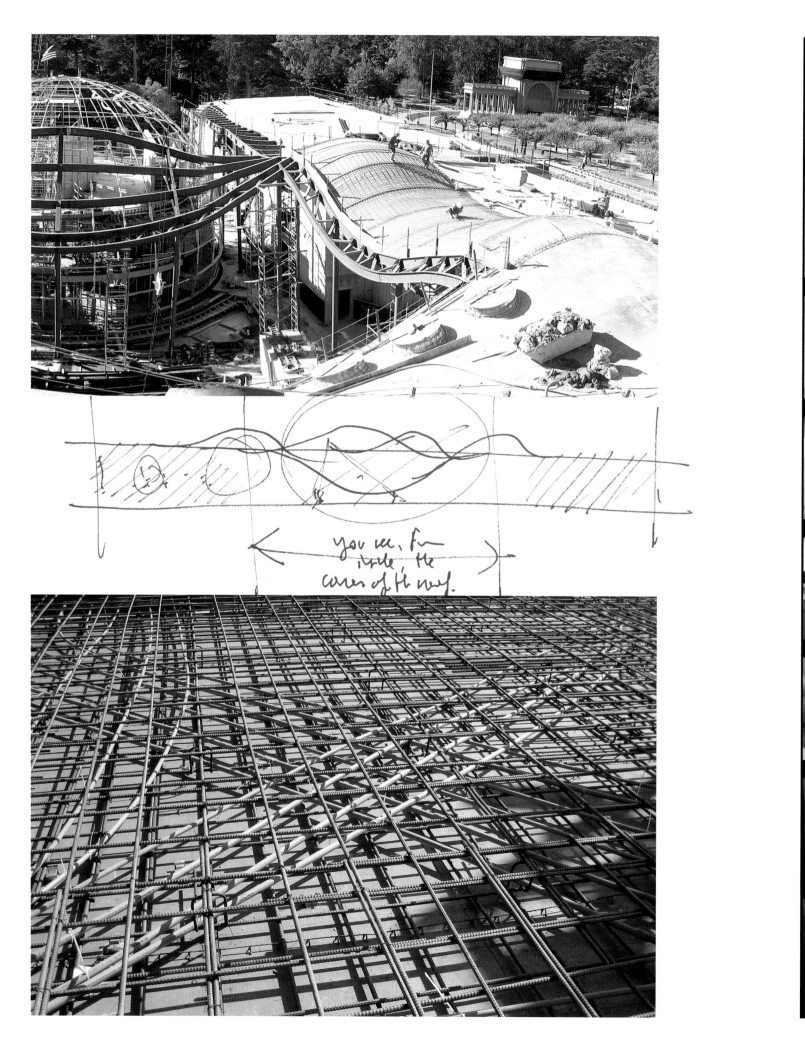

you see, from inside the curves of the roof.

90% of all demolition materials were recycled

Il 90% dei detriti di demolizione sono stati riciclati

32,000 tons of sand from foundation excavation applied to dune restoration projects in San Francisco

32 tonnellate di sabbia, provenienti dagli scavi, sono state utilizzate nei progetti di rifacimento delle dune di San Francisco.

95% of all steel from recycled sources

Il 95% dell'acciao proviene da fonti riciclate

15% fly ash (a recycled coal by-product),

15% di ceneri volatili (sottoprodotto riciclato del carbone)

35% slag in concrete

35% di scorie in calcestruzzo

50% of lumber harvested from sustainable-yield forests

50% del legno proviene da foreste a gestione sostenibile.

68% of insulation comes from recycled blue jeans

Il 68% del materiale di isolamento proviene dal riciclo di blue jeans.

90% of office space will have natural light and ventilation

Il 90% degli uffici hanno illuminazione e ventilazione naturali.

60,000 photovoltaic cells; 213,000 kilowatt-hours

60.000 cellule fotovoltaiche, 213.000 kilowatt-ora

30% less energy consumption than federal code requirement

30% di riduzione del consumo energetico rispetto al fabbisogno previsto dal codice federale.

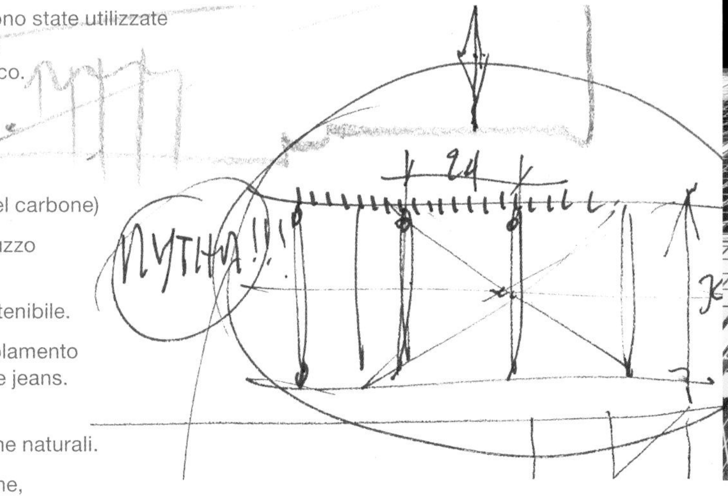

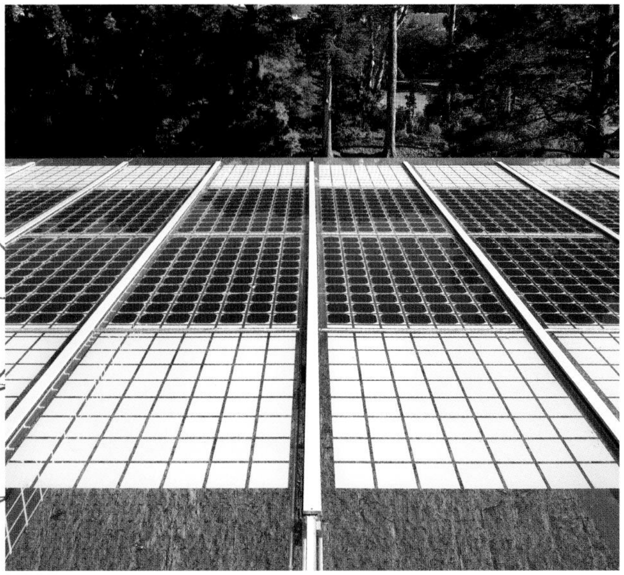

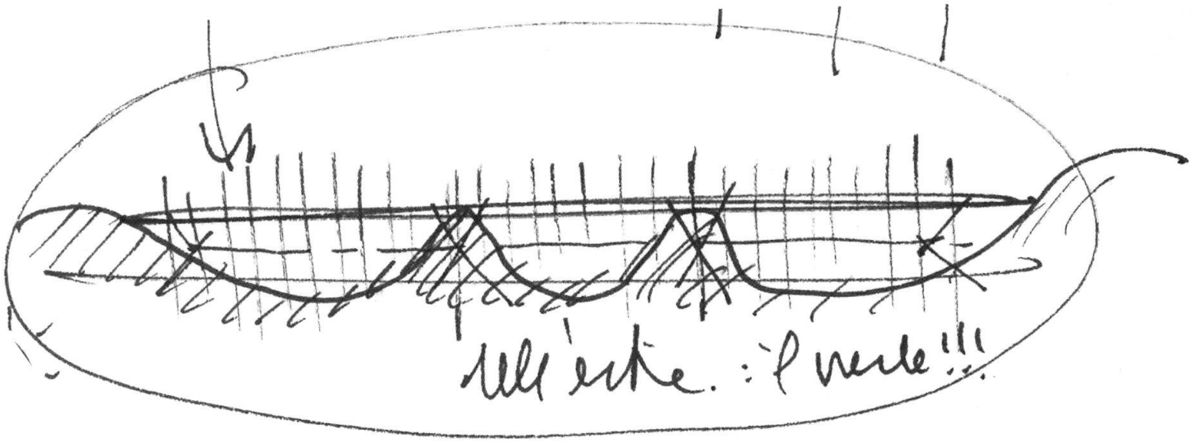

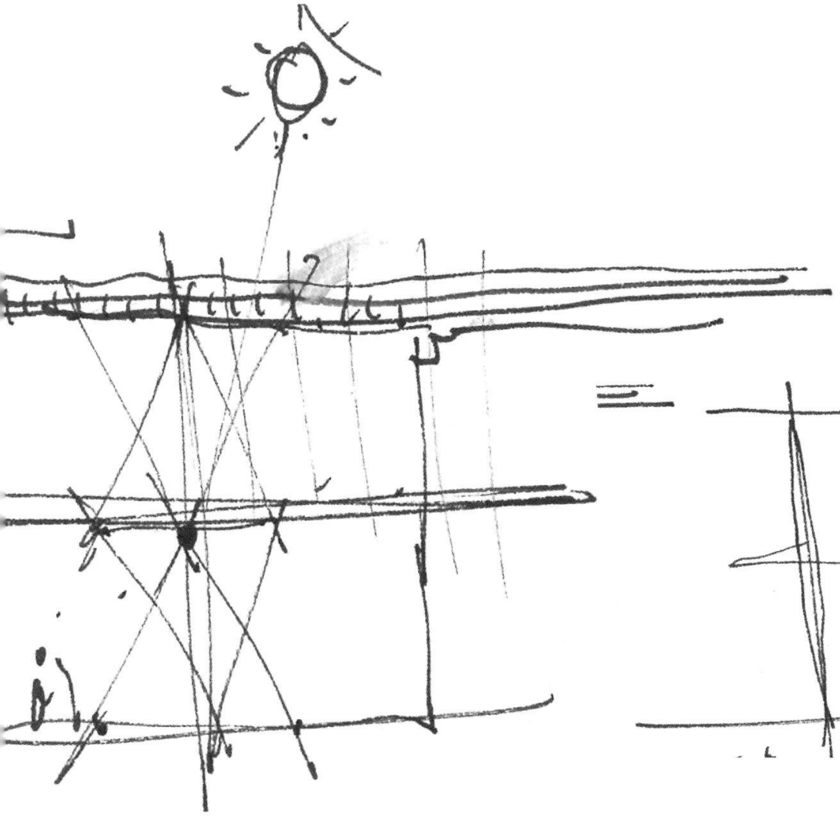

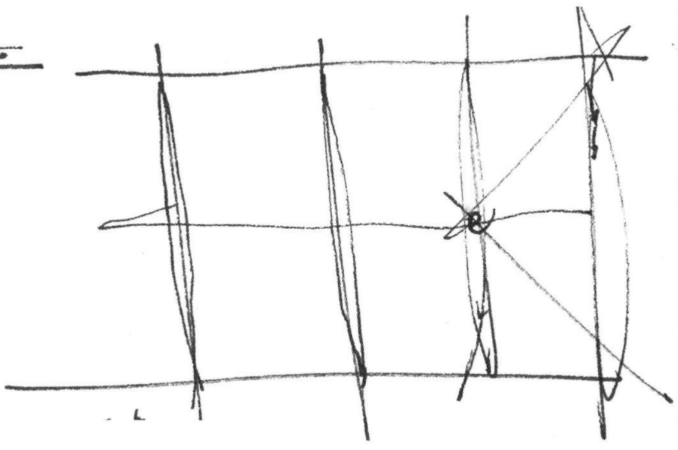

Dear Lia,

I am so happy to hear from you. I would be pleased to tell you a short story. Not many people know how an ecologist came to work with Renzo on the design of the living roof for the Academy of Sciences Museum. He and I had a few brief but meaningful exchanges that I often retell.
Few know he was responsible for inspiring me to invent the biotray planting method and product.
I was first introduced to the architectural team as an ecologist. My idea was to plant the roof with an assemblage of native plants that would mimic and/or simulate natural habitats, attract insects and birds, and be a demonstration of urban ecology. Renzo looked over my test plots, and told me, (Paul, you tell an interesting story, and this is important work, "but is has to be beautiful!")
Renzo inspired me to look at the plants and planting with a refined eye. Then Renzo and our team selected plants that would satisfy the habitat requirements and provide seasonal flowers and beauty. The plants also looked good with the roof topography and form.
Then one day Renzo asked me, "Paul can you develop a method of planting the roof without plastic containers, commonly used in the green roofing industry?"
This simple question inspired me to invent the Biotray, a biodegradable, modular, soil based, fungi inoculated tray made from coconut fiber waste. We grew 1.9 million individual plants and filed the trays with the plants and seeds. This was never done before, and now has become a standard in the living roof industry.
When the Piano Workshop team visited us at our nursery, they were all highly interested in all the facets of horticulture and plant propagation. We threw a party and made a CAS cake, a decorative model cake made to look just like the Academy replete with living roof!
I am very honored to have worked with your father. I can also tell you he inspired the people who worked for him. It was a very collegial working group and all the architects respected and learned from his direction.

Paul Kephart
Executive Director of Rana Creek,
Lead Horticulture and technical Consultant for Living Architecture

Renzo Piano, Paul Kephart

Cara Lia,

Che piacere avere tue notizie! Ti racconto volentieri una storia. Pochi sanno come un ecologista arrivò a collaborare con Renzo alla progettazione del tetto vivente del museo dell'Academy of Sciences. Io e lui abbiamo avuto alcuni scambi brevi ma così significativi che li ricordo ancora oggi.
Pochi sanno che è stato lui a ispirarmi l'invenzione del metodo di semina e del prodotto Biotray.
Venni presentato al team degli architetti come un ecologista. La mia idea era di realizzare il tetto con un mix di piante native che avrebbero imitato e/o simulato gli habitat naturali, attratto gli insetti e gli uccelli, e che sarebbe stato una dimostrazione di ecologia urbana. Renzo esaminò il mio appezzamento di prova e mi disse: "Paul, quello che dici è interessante, ed è un lavoro importante, ma deve essere bellissimo!". Grazie a Renzo, ho guardato le piante e la semina con un occhio più attento. Renzo e l'équipe hanno poi selezionato le piante che avrebbero risposto ai requisiti dell'habitat e che avrebbero fornito dei fiori stagionali e bellezza. Anche le piante erano adatte per lo studio fatto sulla topografia e la forma del tetto.
Un giorno, Renzo mi chiese: "Paul, saresti in grado di sviluppare un metodo per realizzare il tetto senza i contenitori di plastica che si usano solitamente nell'industria dei tetti vegetali?" Questa semplice domanda fu alla base della mia invenzione del Biotray, un "vassoio" biodegradabile, modulare, a base di terra, inoculato con funghi e realizzato con gli scarti della fibra di cocco.
Abbiamo fatto crescere 1,9 milioni di piantine e riempito i vassoi con le piante e i semi.
Questo metodo, che non era mai stato utilizzato prima, stabilisce ora un metodo standard per l'industria dei tetti viventi. Quando il team del Renzo Piano Building Workshop fece visita al nostro vivaio, tutti si mostrarono molto interessati ai diversi aspetti dell'orticoltura e della produzione delle piante. Organizzammo una festa e realizzammo una torta CAS, una torta decorata con la forma dell'Academy e "ripiena" di tetto vivente!
Sono veramente onorato di aver lavorato con tuo padre. Posso anche dirti che ispira le persone con cui lavora. Era un gruppo di lavoro molto collaborativo, tutti gli architetti lo rispettavano e hanno imparato qualcosa da lui.

Paul Kephart
Direttore esecutivo di Rana Creek,
Esperto in orticoltura e consulente tecnico per "Living Architecture"

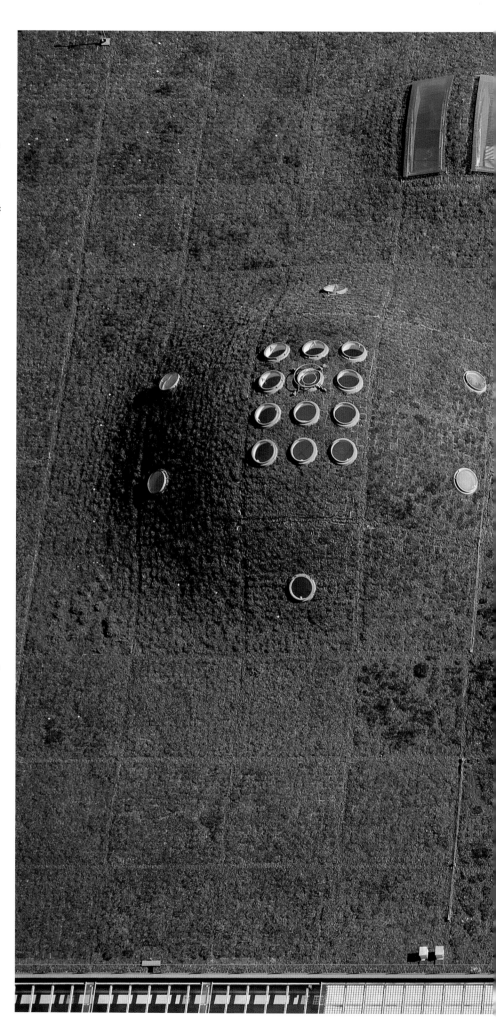

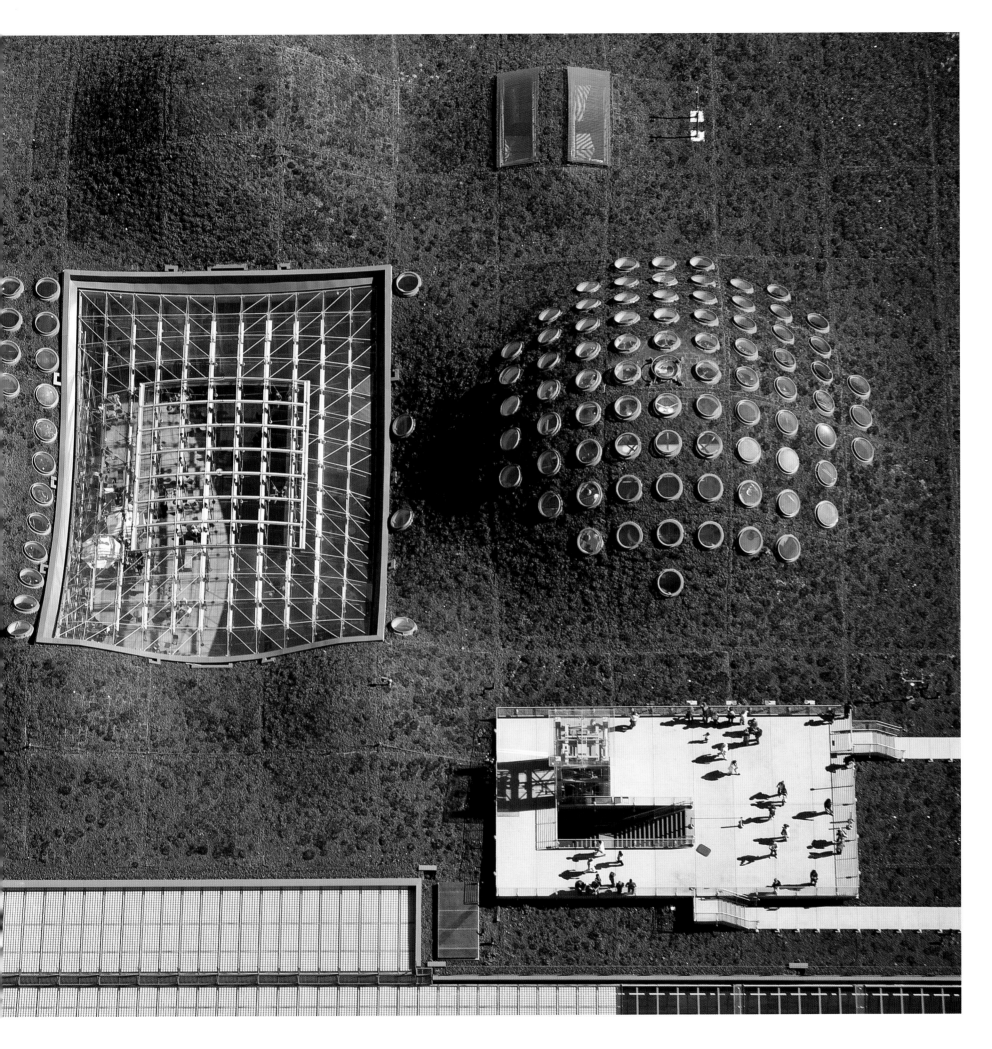

Strawberry - *Fragaria chiloensis*

Self Heal - *Prunella vulgaris*

Sea Pink - *Armeria maritima* ssp. *californica*

Stonecrop - *Sedum spathulifolium*

Tidy Tips - *Layia platyglossa*

Goldfield - *Lasthenia californica*

Miniature Lupine - *Lupinus nanus*

California Poppy - *Eschscholzia californica*

California Plantain - *Plantago erecta*

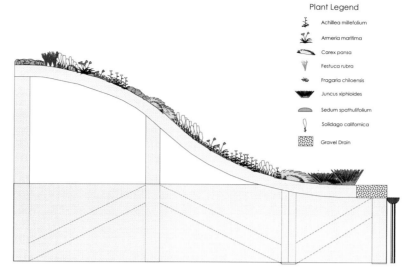

Plant Legend
- Achillea millefolium
- Armeria maritima
- Carex pansa
- Festuca rubra
- Fragaria chiloensis
- Juncus xiphioides
- Sedum spathulifolium
- Solidago californica
- Gravel Drain

North

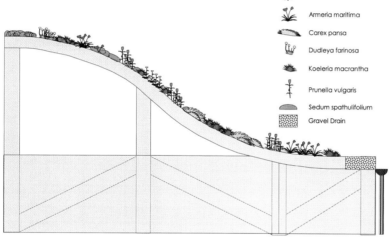

Plant Legend
- Achillea millefolium
- Armeria maritima
- Carex pansa
- Dudleya farinosa
- Koeleria macrantha
- Prunella vulgaris
- Sedum spathulifolium
- Gravel Drain

West

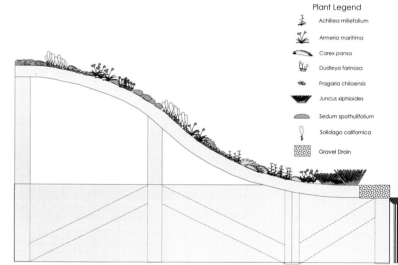

Plant Legend
- Achillea millefolium
- Armeria maritima
- Carex pansa
- Dudleya farinosa
- Fragaria chiloensis
- Juncus xiphioides
- Sedum spathulifolium
- Solidago californica
- Gravel Drain

East

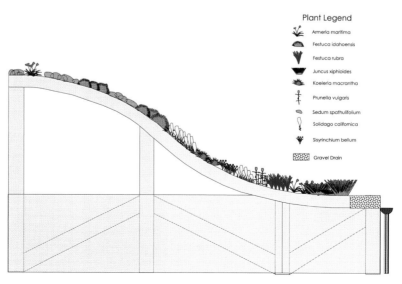

Plant Legend
- Armeria maritima
- Festuca idahoensis
- Festuca rubra
- Juncus xiphioides
- Koeleria macrantha
- Prunella vulgaris
- Sedum spathulifolium
- Solidago californica
- Sisyrinchium bellum
- Gravel Drain

South

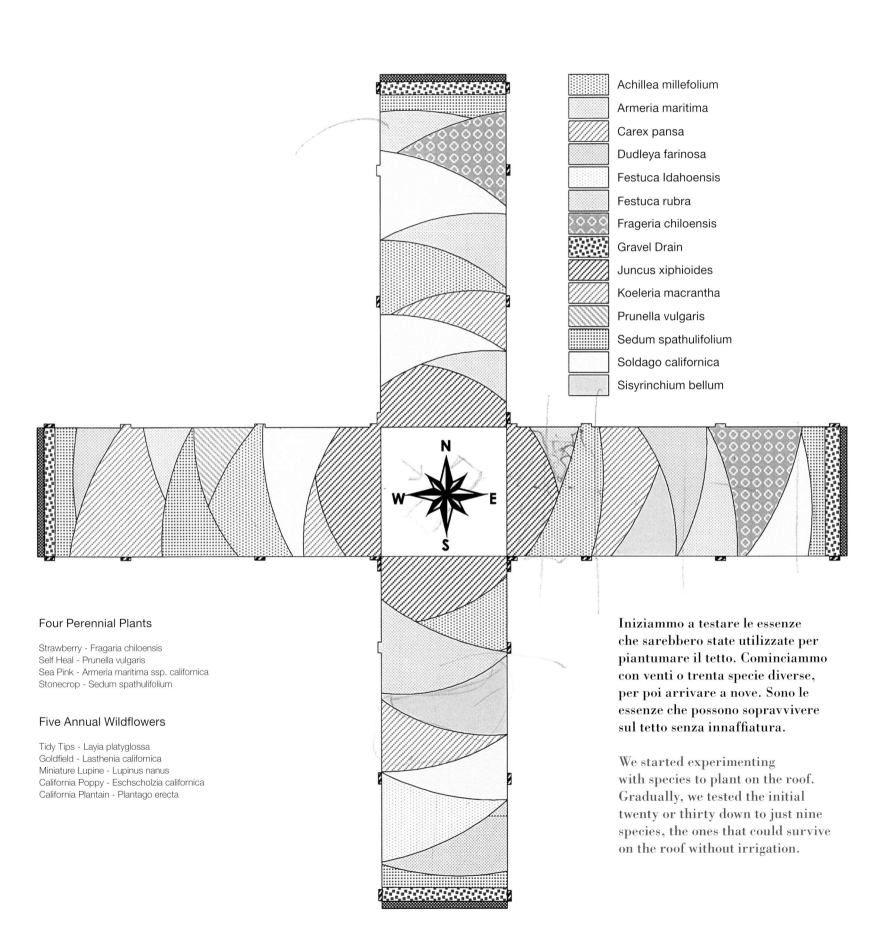

Legend

- Achillea millefolium
- Armeria maritima
- Carex pansa
- Dudleya farinosa
- Festuca Idahoensis
- Festuca rubra
- Frageria chiloensis
- Gravel Drain
- Juncus xiphioides
- Koeleria macrantha
- Prunella vulgaris
- Sedum spathulifolium
- Soldago californica
- Sisyrinchium bellum

Four Perennial Plants

Strawberry - Fragaria chiloensis
Self Heal - Prunella vulgaris
Sea Pink - Armeria maritima ssp. californica
Stonecrop - Sedum spathulifolium

Five Annual Wildflowers

Tidy Tips - Layia platyglossa
Goldfield - Lasthenia californica
Miniature Lupine - Lupinus nanus
California Poppy - Eschscholzia californica
California Plantain - Plantago erecta

Iniziammo a testare le essenze che sarebbero state utilizzate per piantumare il tetto. Cominciammo con venti o trenta specie diverse, per poi arrivare a nove. Sono le essenze che possono sopravvivere sul tetto senza innaffiatura.

We started experimenting with species to plant on the roof. Gradually, we tested the initial twenty or thirty down to just nine species, the ones that could survive on the roof without irrigation.

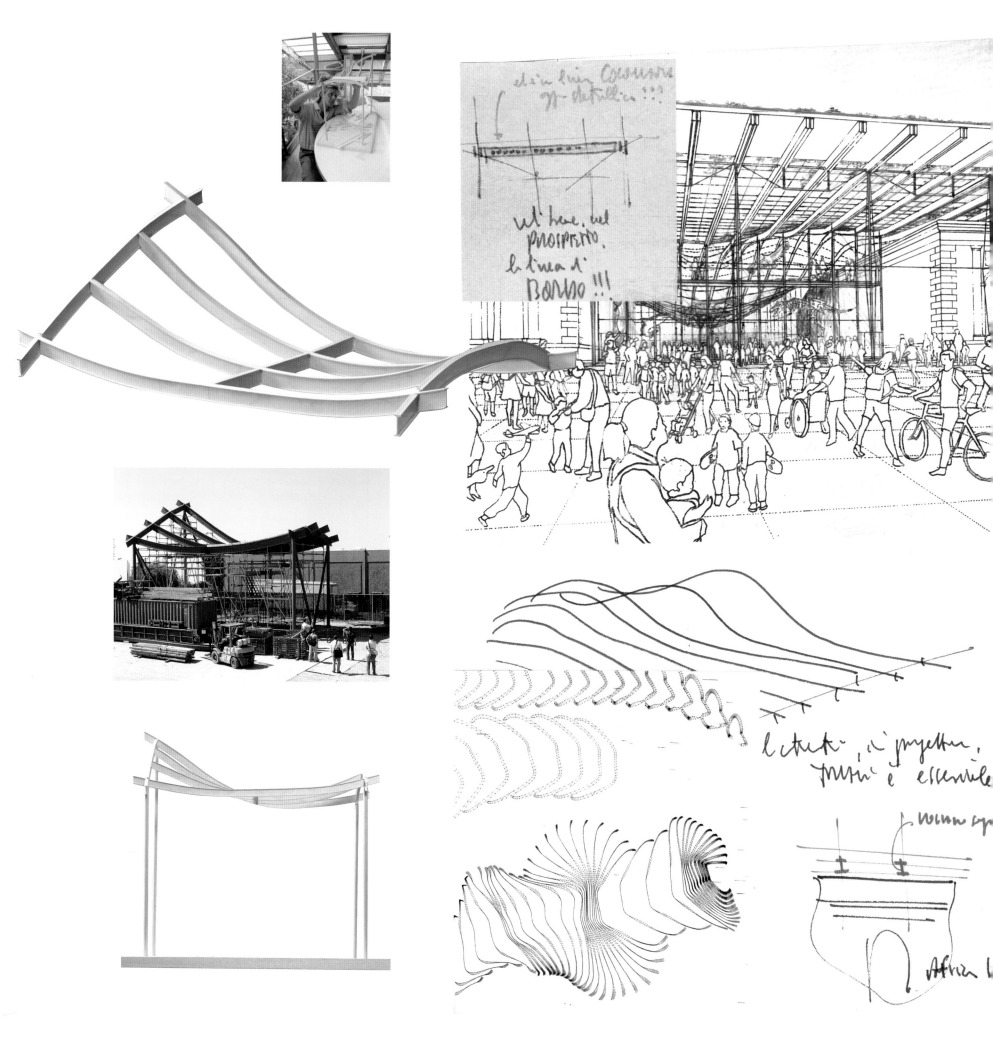

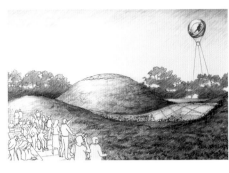

rerfi

nrri'...
louo
ucio, entre
entro !!!

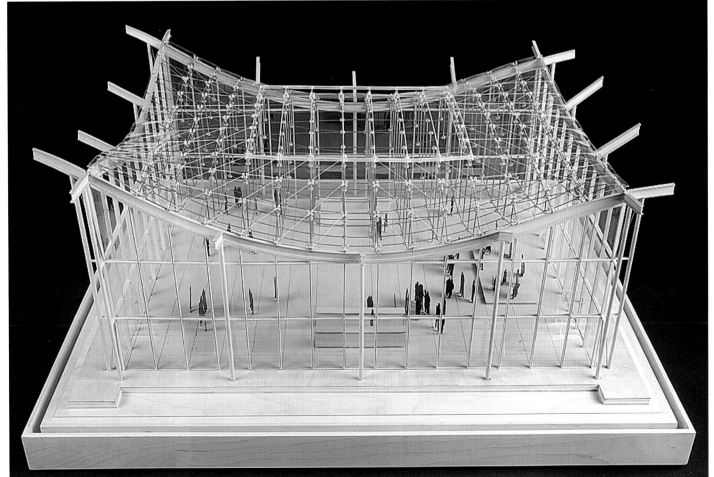

Queste specie furono poi piantate sul tetto
del museo, erano un milione e settecentomila,
tutte messe in "vassoi" di un materiale
organico che dopo la radicazione spariscono
e diventano terra.

One million seven hundred thousand examples
of these species were then planted on
the roof of the museum, placed in biodegradable
organic trays that after rooting, they disappear
and become soil.

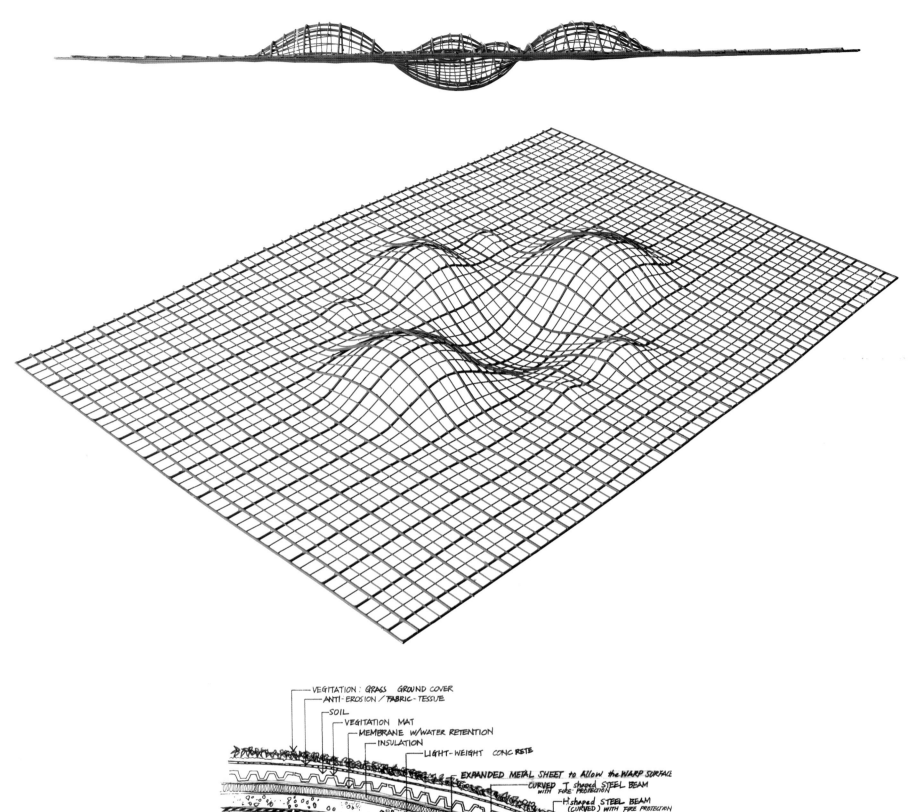

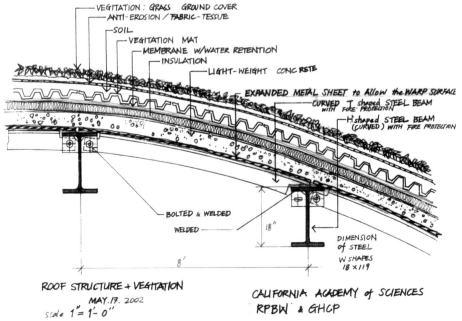

VEGITATION : GRASS GROUND COVER
ANTI-EROSION / FABRIC-TESSUE
SOIL
VEGITATION MAT
MEMBRANE w/WATER RETENTION
INSULATION
LIGHT-WEIGHT CONCRETE
EXPANDED METAL SHEET to allow the WARP SURFACE
CURVED T shaped STEEL BEAM WITH FIRE PROTECTION
H shaped STEEL BEAM (CURVED) WITH FIRE PROTECTION

BOLTED & WELDED
WELDED
18"
8'
DIMENSION of STEEL
W SHAPES
18 x 119

ROOF STRUCTURE + VEGITATION
MAY.17. 2002
scale 1" = 1'- 0"

CALIFORNIA ACADEMY of SCIENCES
RPBW & GHCP

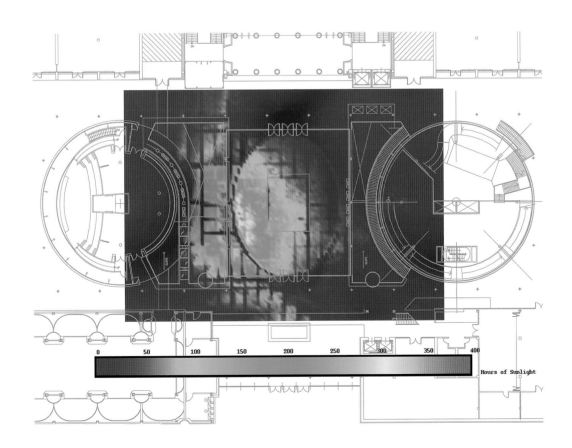

0   50   100   150   200   250   300   350   400

Hours of Sunlight

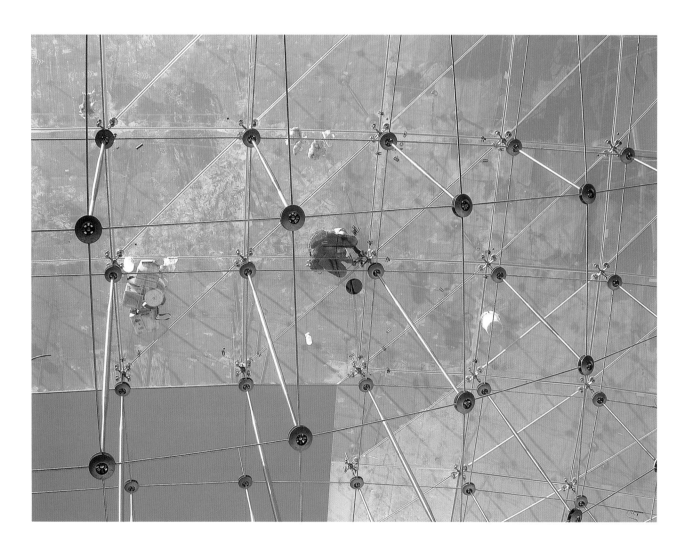

L'idea dello "spider web", una delicata ragnatela d'acciaio
che copre la piazza: una struttura reticolare che di giorno si apre e consente
la ventilazione, mentre di notte, quando la temperatura si abbassa, si chiude.

The idea of the spider's web, a delicate steel structure that covers the Piazza.
During the day, its reticular structure opens to allow the air in for ventilation
and at night, when the temperature drops, the mesh closes.

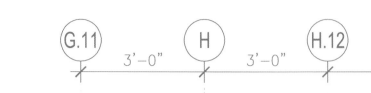

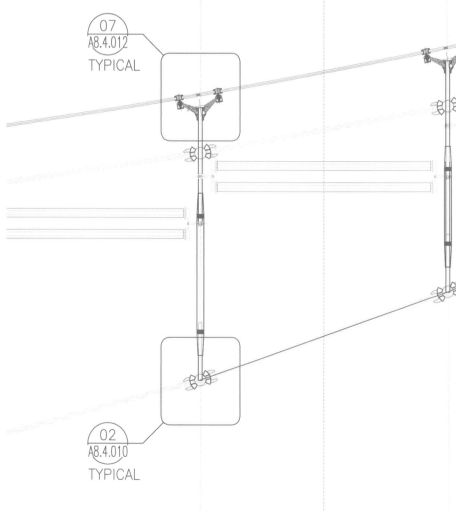

07
A8.4.012
TYPICAL

02
A8.4.010
TYPICAL

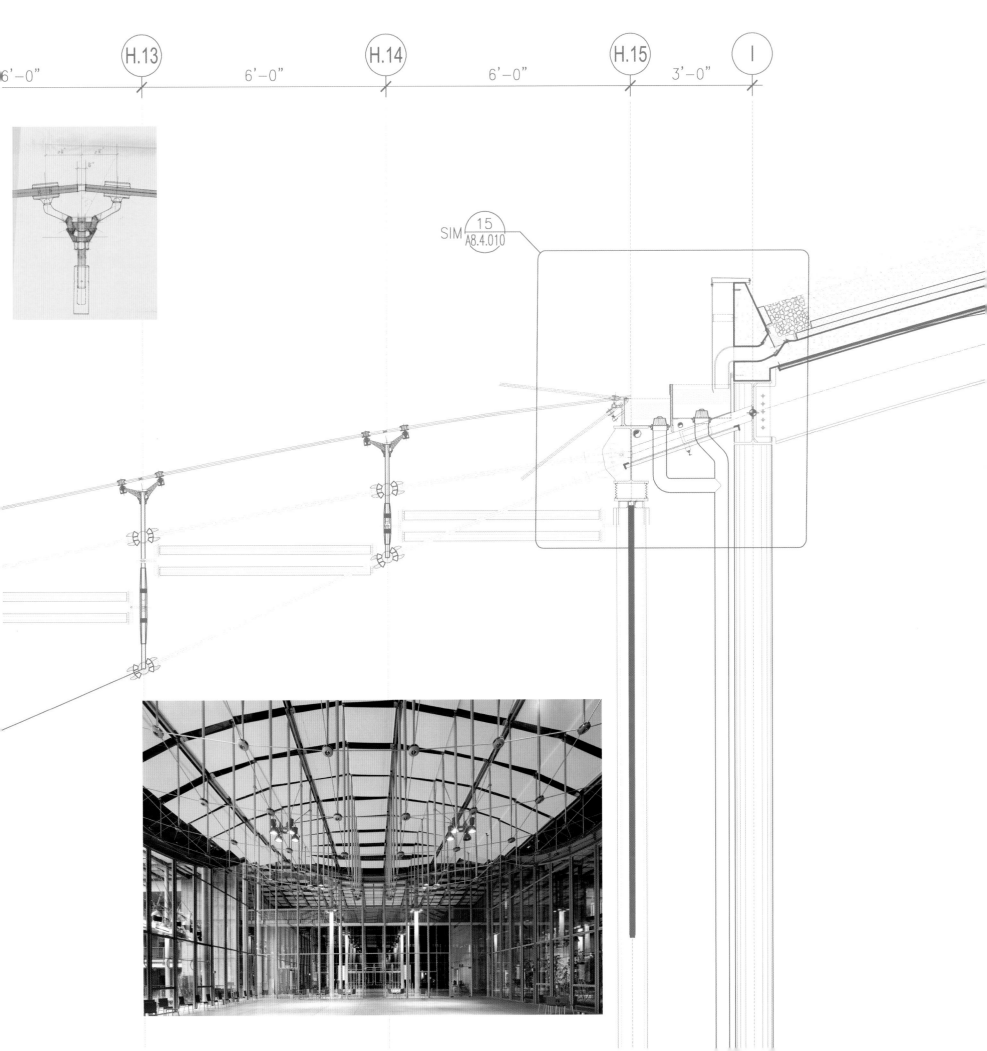

H.13   H.14   H.15   I

6'−0"   6'−0"   6'−0"   3'−0"

SIM 15
A8.4.010

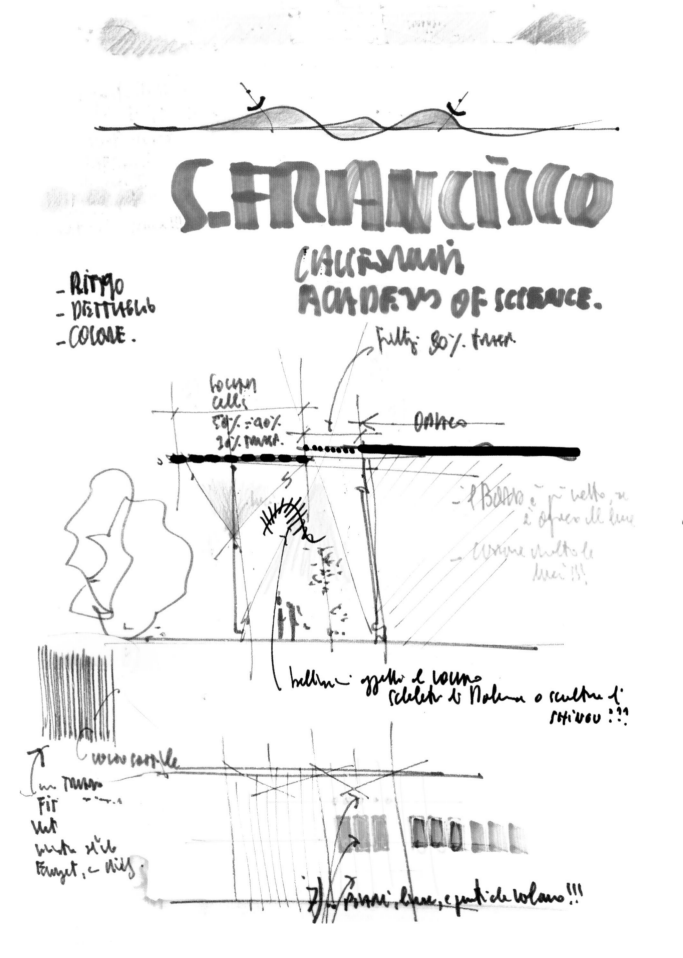

S.FRANCISCO

CALIFORNIA
ACADEMY OF SCIENCE.

- RITMO
- DETTAGLIO
- COLORE.

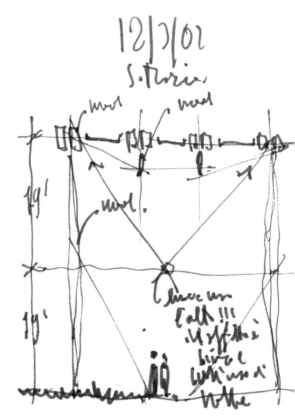

12/3/02
S.Maria

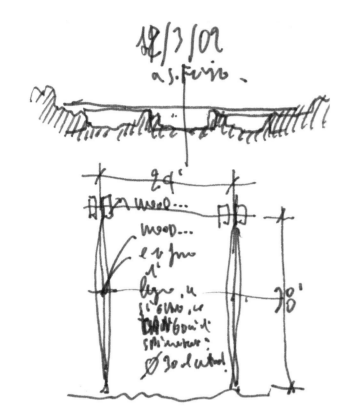

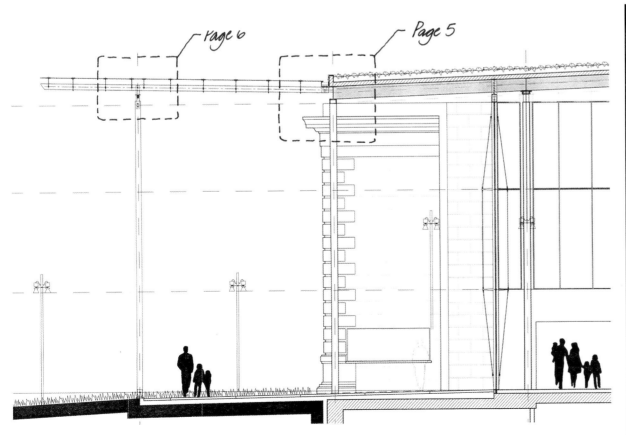

Page 6   Page 5

Section through North Lobby
Approximate Scale 1/8" = 1'-0"

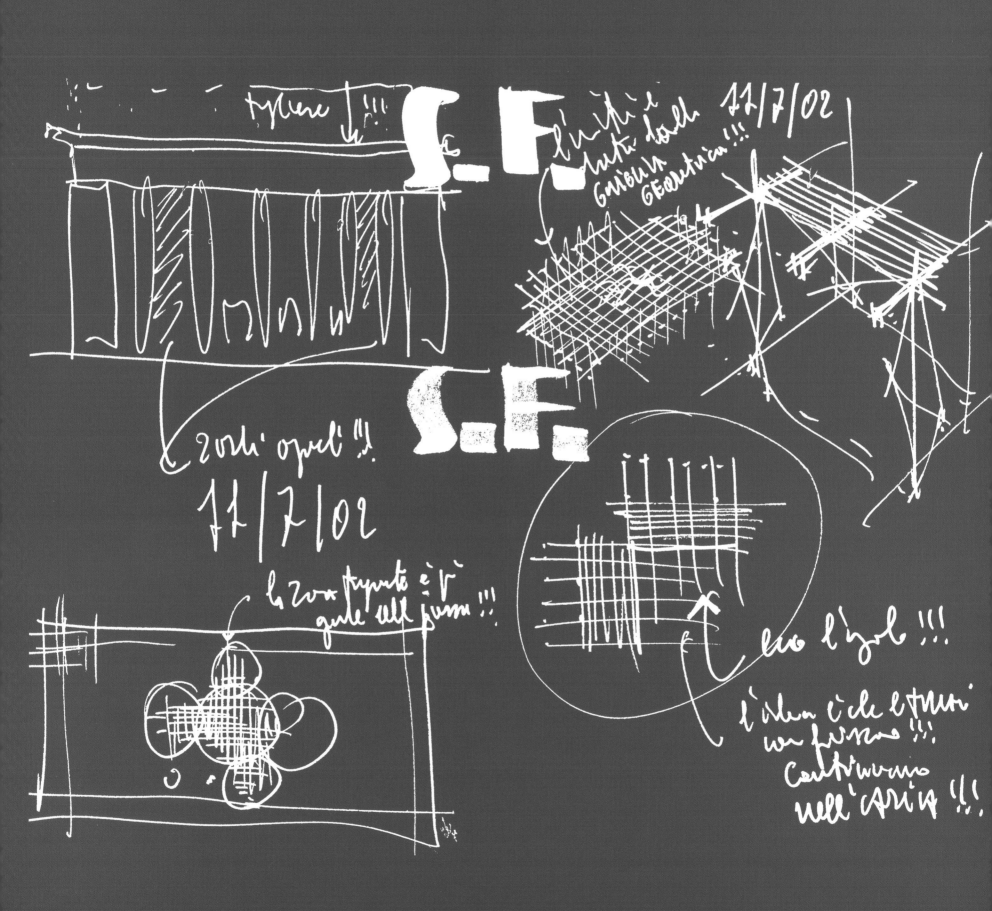

Ed è così che è nata anche l'idea di mettere dei pannelli fotovoltaici tutti intorno all'edificio, che non sono completamente coprenti e quindi permettono che nello spazio fra l'uno e l'altro passi la luce. E questi pannelli, costituiti da 60.000 cellule fotovoltaiche, coprono più del 5% del fabbisogno energetico dell'edificio.

A further development was the idea of setting a canopy of photovoltaic panels round the building. Cover provided by the panels is not total and light can filter through the spaces. These panels, with a total of 60,000 photovoltaic cells, generate more than five percent of the building's energy needs.

In questo modo l'ombra che si crea a terra
è un'ombra vivace e "vibrante", come l'ombra che si crea d'estate
sotto le chiome degli alberi.

What the canopy offers is a "lively", vibrant shade,
much like the shadow provided by trees in summertime.

E quando si alza la nebbia tipica di San Francisco
e nasconde gli alberi si ha l'impressione di essere
in un mondo fantastico.

When the city's signature fog rises and hides the trees,
you feel as if you were in a fantasy world.

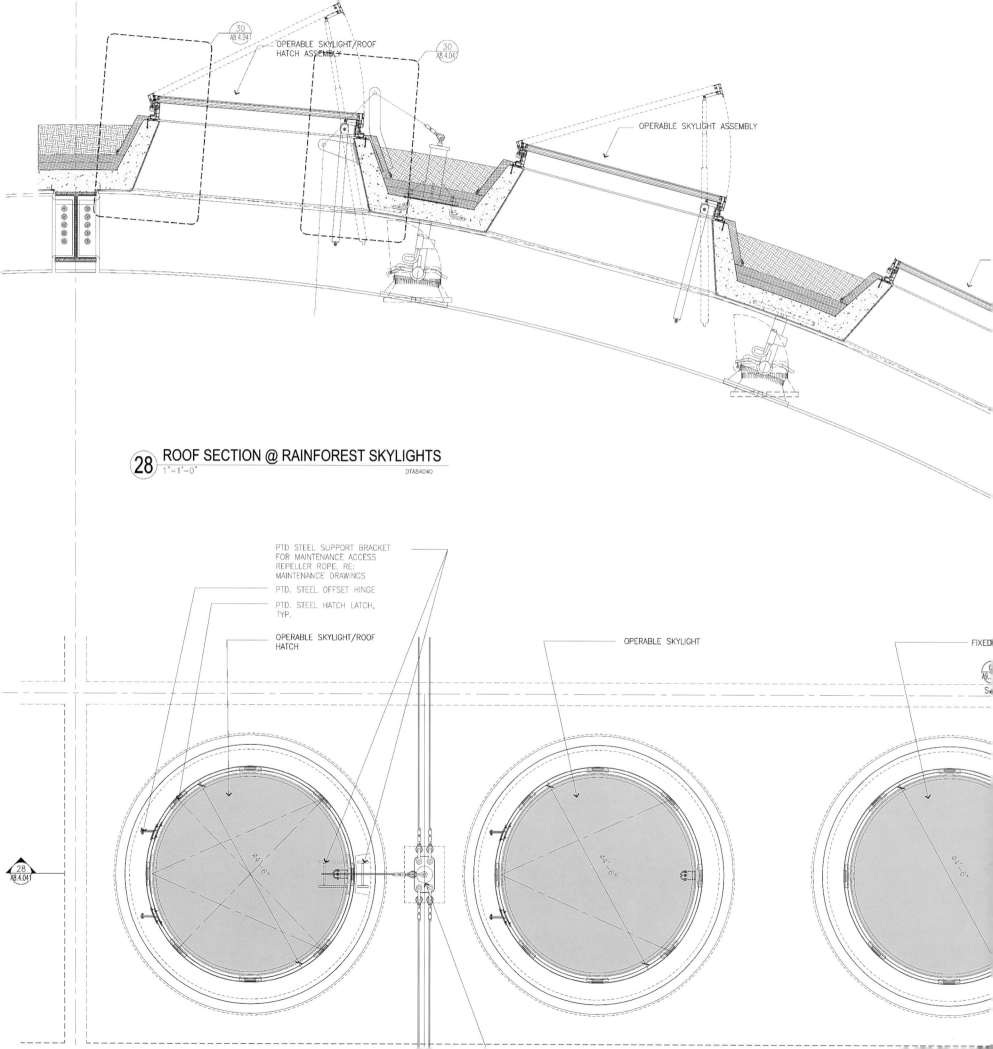

OPERABLE SKYLIGHT/ROOF
HATCH ASSEMBLY

$$\frac{30}{A8.4.041}$$

$$\frac{30}{A8.4.042}$$

OPERABLE SKYLIGHT ASSEMBLY

28 ROOF SECTION @ RAINFOREST SKYLIGHTS
$1"=1'-0"$

DTA84040

PTD STEEL SUPPORT BRACKET
FOR MAINTENANCE ACCESS
REPELLER ROPE. RE:
MAINTENANCE DRAWINGS

PTD. STEEL OFFSET HINGE

PTD. STEEL HATCH LATCH,
TYP.

OPERABLE SKYLIGHT/ROOF
HATCH

OPERABLE SKYLIGHT

FIXED

$\frac{28}{A8.4.041}$

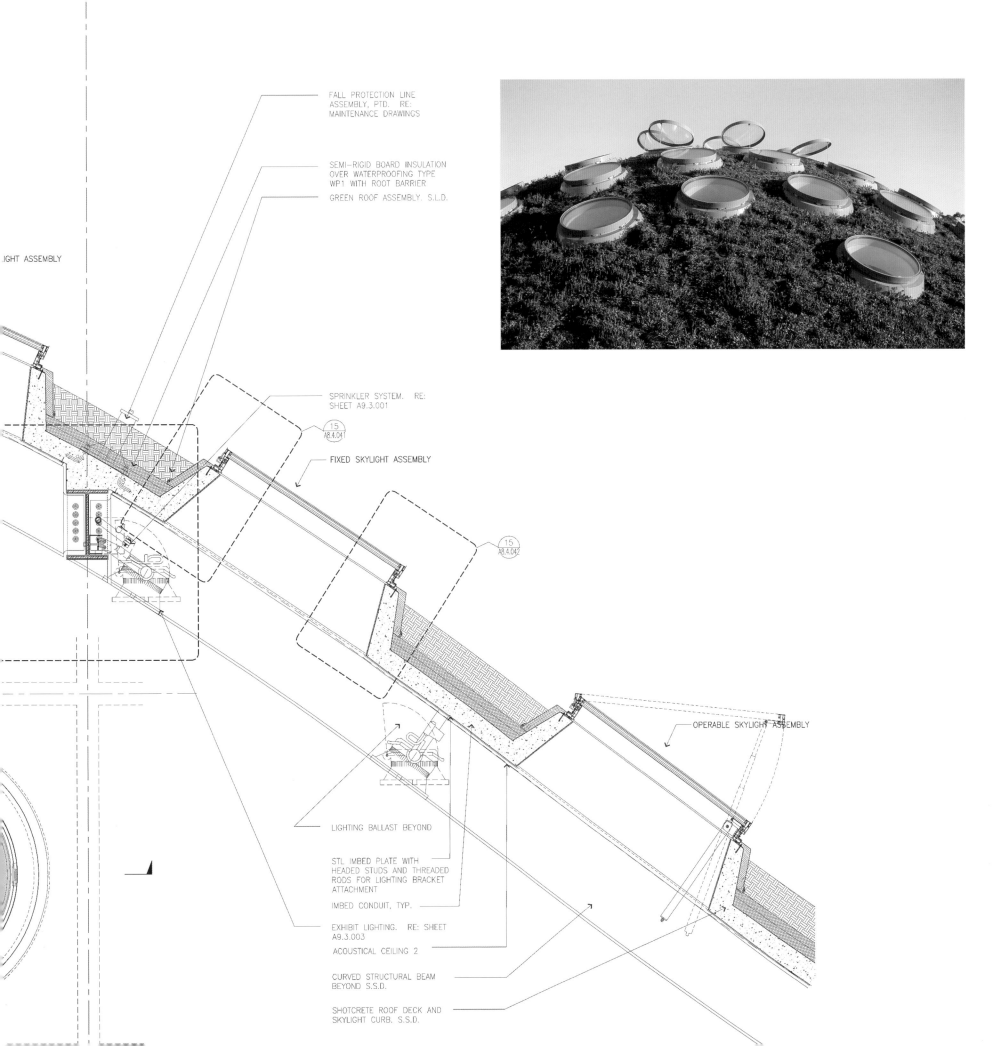

FALL PROTECTION LINE
ASSEMBLY, PTD. RE:
MAINTENANCE DRAWINGS

SEMI-RIGID BOARD INSULATION
OVER WATERPROOFING TYPE
WP1 WITH ROOT BARRIER

GREEN ROOF ASSEMBLY. S.L.D.

IGHT ASSEMBLY

SPRINKLER SYSTEM. RE:
SHEET A9.3.001

15
A8.4.041

FIXED SKYLIGHT ASSEMBLY

15
A8.4.042

OPERABLE SKYLIGHT ASSEMBLY

LIGHTING BALLAST BEYOND

STL IMBED PLATE WITH
HEADED STUDS AND THREADED
RODS FOR LIGHTING BRACKET
ATTACHMENT

IMBED CONDUIT, TYP.

EXHIBIT LIGHTING. RE: SHEET
A9.3.003

ACOUSTICAL CEILING 2

CURVED STRUCTURAL BEAM
BEYOND S.S.D.

SHOTCRETE ROOF DECK AND
SKYLIGHT CURB. S.S.D.

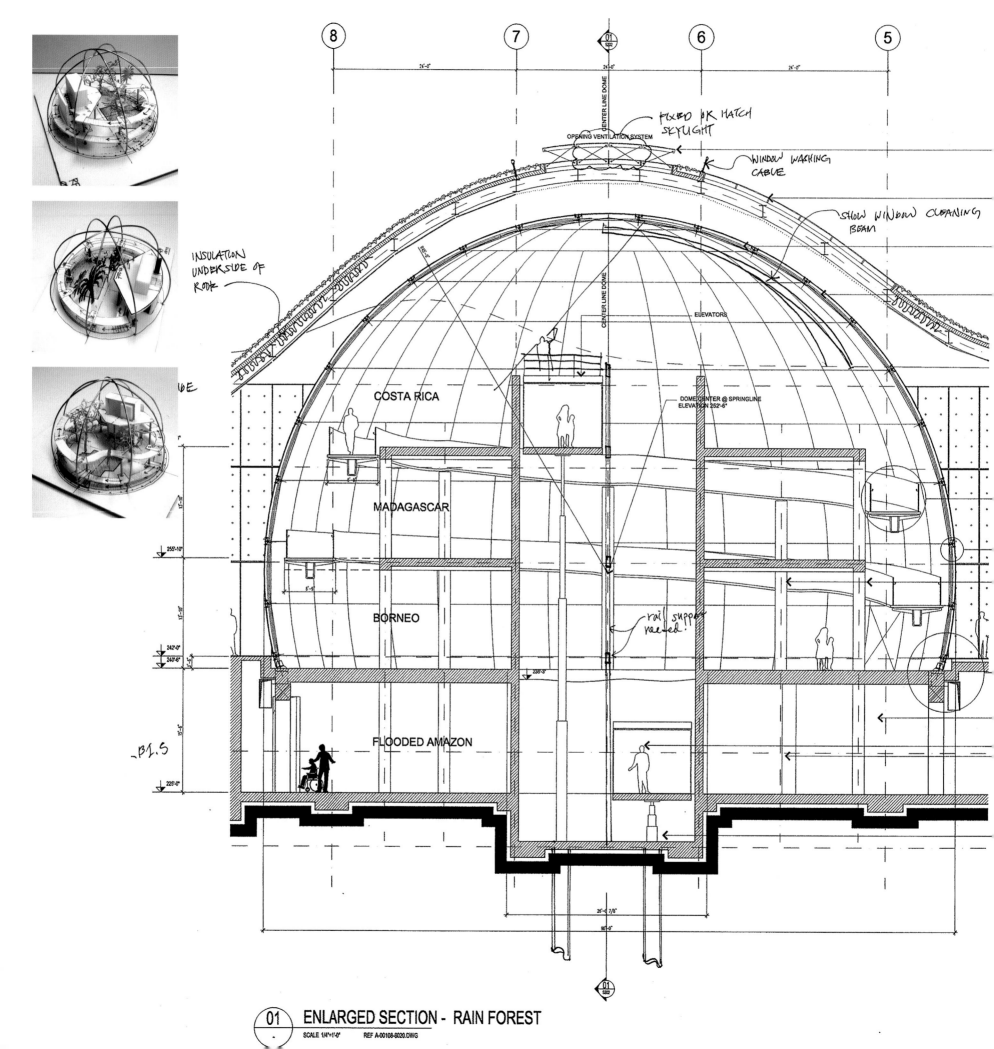

FIXED OK HATCH SKYLIGHT

WINDOW WASHING CABLE

SHOW WINDOW CLEANING BEAM

OPENING VENTILATION SYSTEM

CENTER LINE DOME

ELEVATORS

DOME CENTER @ SPRINGLINE
ELEVATION 252'-6"

INSULATION
UNDERSIDE OF
ROOF

COSTA RICA

MADAGASCAR

BORNEO

rail support
needed!

FLOODED AMAZON

-B1.5

8   7   6   5

01
ENLARGED SECTION - RAIN FOREST

SCALE 1/4"=1'-0"   REF A-00108-8020.DWG

VENTILATION SKYLIGHT
SCALE .   REF A-00108-8440

ROOF SKYLIGHT
SCALE .   REF A-00108-8441

SHADING SYSTEM
SCALE .   REF A-00108-9424.DWG

RAIN FOREST GEOMETR
SCALE .   REF A-00108-9423.DWG

Condensation
mixture.

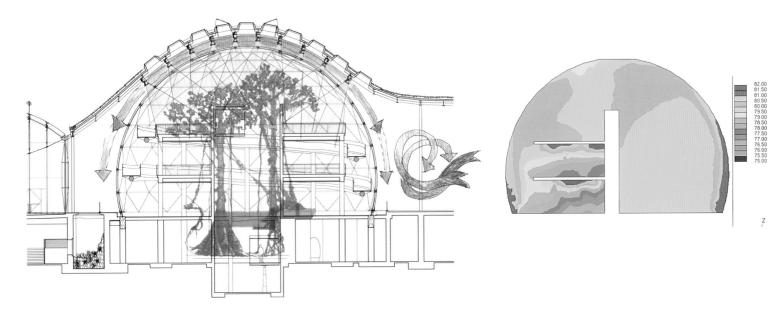

RAMPS DETAILS
SCALE .   REF A-00108-9422.DWG

DETAILED SECTION
SCALE 1"=1'-0"   REF A-00108-9421.DWG

COLUMN

.
SCALE .   REF A-00108-0000.DWG

COLUMN

TANK
ENTRANCE "ACRILIC TUBE"

ELEVATOR PIT

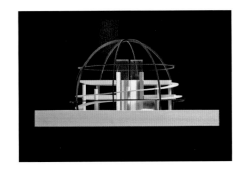

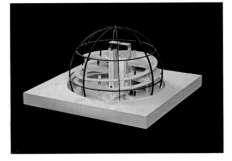

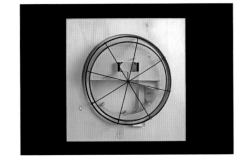

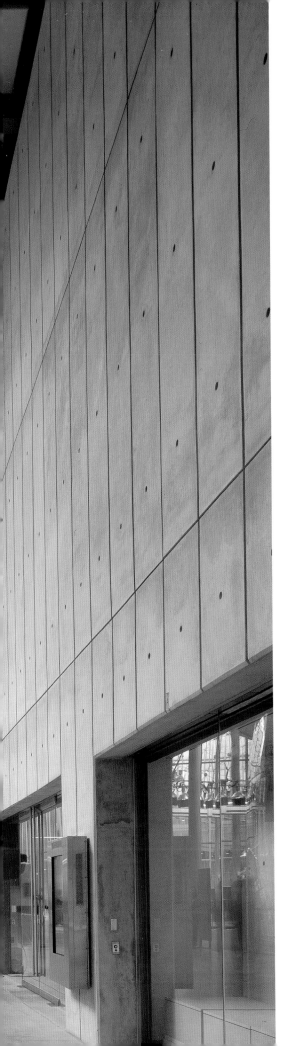

E per realizzare la geometria tridimensionale
delle passerelle sospese abbiamo usato
la tecnologia dei costruttori di montagne russe.

And to achieve the three-dimensional geometry
of the suspended walkways, we used the same
technology of the rollercoasters' manufacturers.

Using Sunlight to the Max

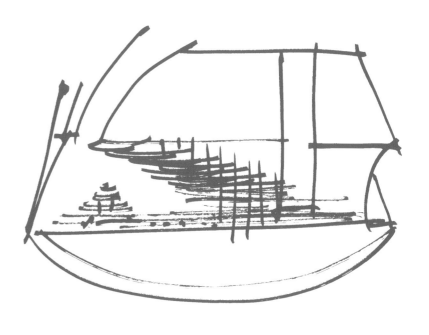

Il nuovo Planetario, a differenza di quello esistente,
non avrebbe avuto un sistema ottico
ma un sistema digitale, che è più attuale.
E non sarebbe servito soltanto a proiettare le stelle,
ma anche a far vedere l'interno del corpo umano,
o la profondità del mare.

1952

The new Planetarium, unlike the existing one,
would have a state-of-the-art digital system.
Also, it would not only be used to project the stars,
but also to show the innards of the human body
and the depth of the oceans.

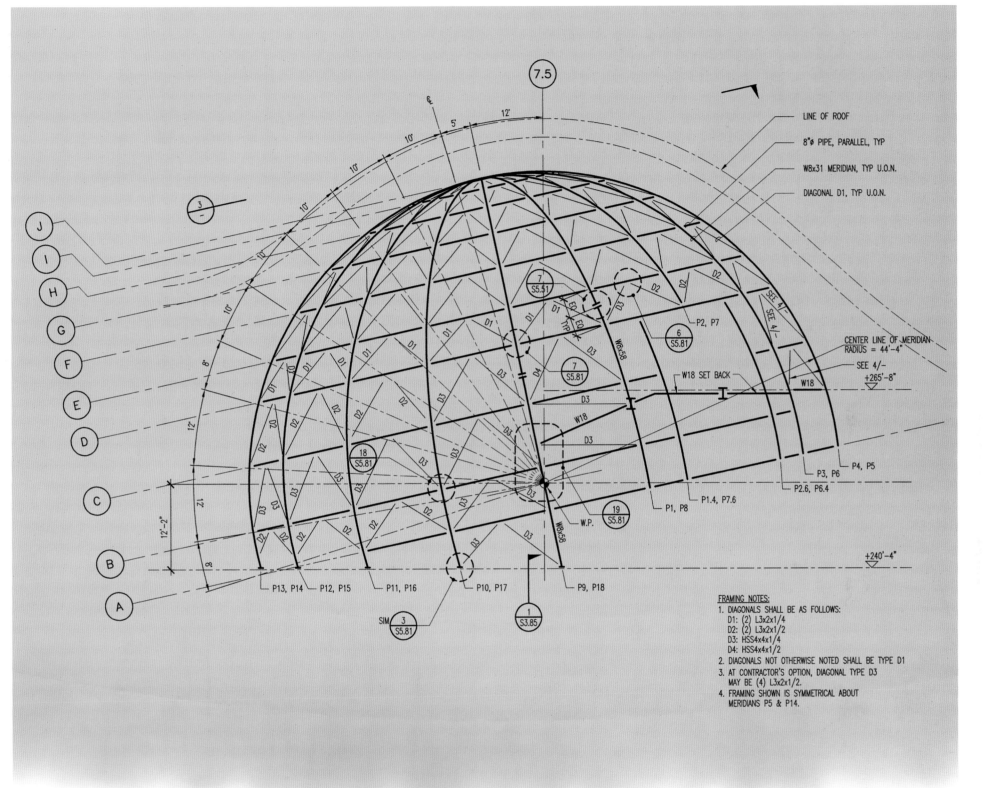

7.5

LINE OF ROOF

8"ø PIPE, PARALLEL, TYP

W8x31 MERIDIAN, TYP U.O.N.

DIAGONAL D1, TYP U.O.N.

CENTER LINE OF MERIDIAN
RADIUS = 44'-4"

SEE 4/-
±265'-8"

±240'-4"

J
I
H
G
F
E
D
C
B
A

12'-2"

7 / S5.51
6 / S5.81
7 / S5.81
18 / S5.81
19 / S5.81
3 / -

P2, P7
P3, P6
P4, P5
P2.6, P6.4
P1.4, P7.6
P1, P8

W18 SET BACK
W18
W8x58
W.P.

P13, P14   P12, P15   P11, P16   P10, P17   P9, P18

SIM 3 / S5.81
1 / S3.85

FRAMING NOTES:
1. DIAGONALS SHALL BE AS FOLLOWS:
   D1: (2) L3x2x1/4
   D2: (2) L3x2x1/2
   D3: HSS4x4x1/4
   D4: HSS4x4x1/2
2. DIAGONALS NOT OTHERWISE NOTED SHALL BE TYPE D1
3. AT CONTRACTOR'S OPTION, DIAGONAL TYPE D3
   MAY BE (4) L3x2x1/2.
4. FRAMING SHOWN IS SYMMETRICAL ABOUT
   MERIDIANS P5 & P14.

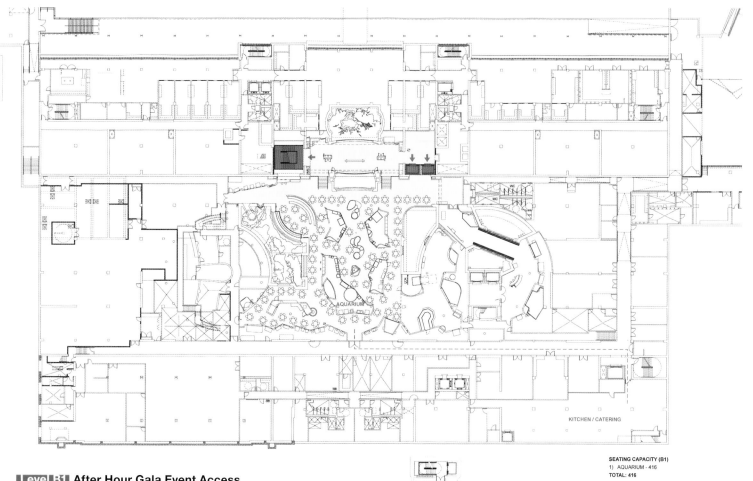

AQUARIUM

WC

KITCHEN / CATERING

Level B1 After Hour Gala Event Access

SEATING CAPACITY (B1)
1) AQUARIUM - 416
TOTAL: 416

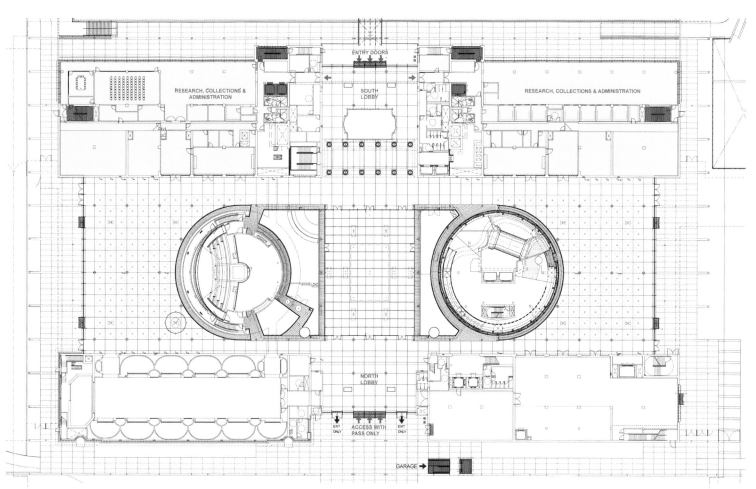

ENTRY DOORS

RESEARCH, COLLECTIONS & ADMINISTRATION

SOUTH LOBBY

RESEARCH, COLLECTIONS & ADMINISTRATION

NORTH LOBBY

EXIT ONLY
ACCESS WITH PASS ONLY
EXIT ONLY

GARAGE →

Level 1 Research, Collections & Administration access

2006.05.23

2006.06.20

2006.07.10

2006.07.30

2006.09.05

2006.09.26

2006.10.01

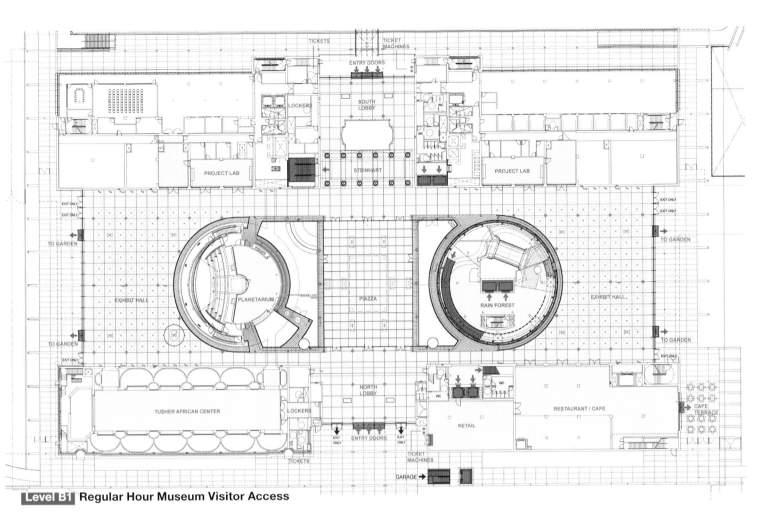

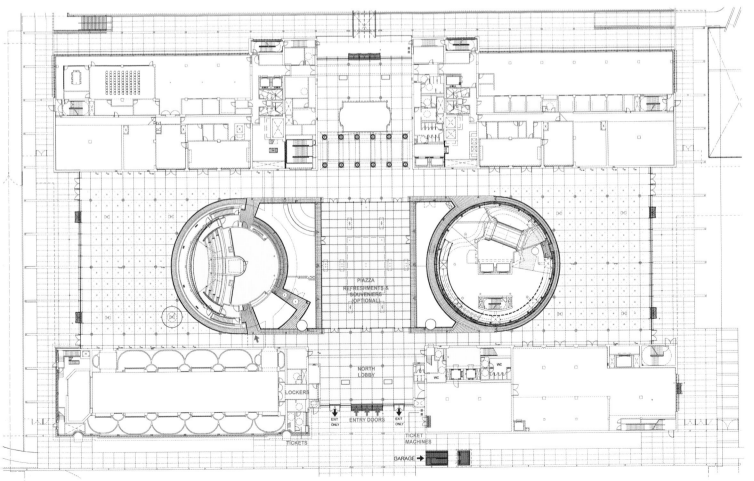

Level B1 Regular Hour Museum Visitor Access

PROJECT LAB
LOCKERS
SOUTH LOBBY
TICKETS
TICKET MACHINES
ENTRY DOORS
WC
STEINHART
PROJECT LAB
EXIT ONLY
EXIT ONLY
TO GARDEN
EXHIBIT HALL
PLANETARIUM
PIAZZA
RAIN FOREST
EXHIBIT HALL
TO GARDEN
TO GARDEN
EXIT ONLY
TUSHER AFRICAN CENTER
LOCKERS
NORTH LOBBY
WC
WC
RETAIL
RESTAURANT / CAFE
CAFE TERRACE
EXIT ONLY
ENTRY DOORS
EXIT ONLY
TICKETS
TICKET MACHINES
GARAGE

Level B1 After Hour Planetarium Access

PIAZZA
REFRESHMENTS & SOUVENIERS (OPTIONAL)
NORTH LOBBY
WC
WC
LOCKERS
EXIT ONLY
ENTRY DOORS
EXIT ONLY
TICKETS
TICKET MACHINES
GARAGE

2006.10.05

2006.11.06

2006.11.10

2006.11.22

2006.12.01

2006.12.04

2006.12.13

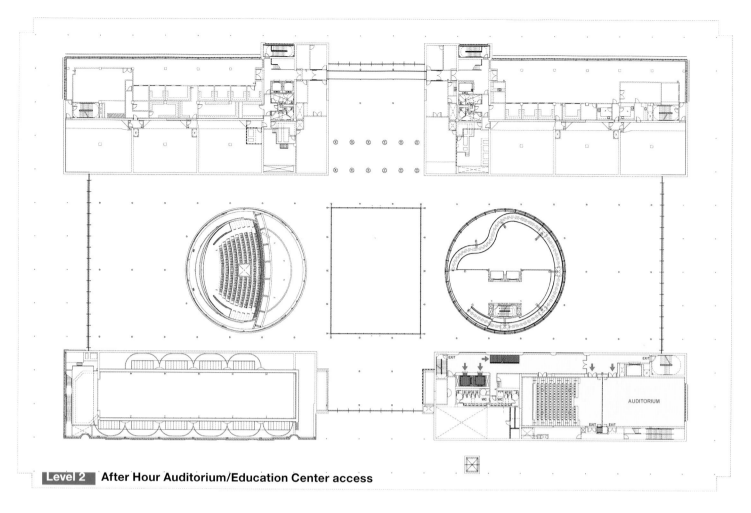

Level 2 After Hour Auditorium/Education Center access

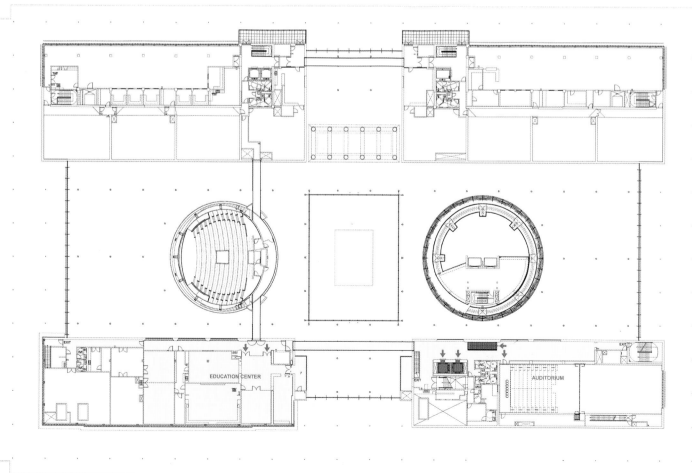

Level 3 After Hour Auditorium/Education Center access

2006.12.21

2007.01.07

2007.01.11

2007.01.15

2007.01.22

2007.02.05

2007.02.07

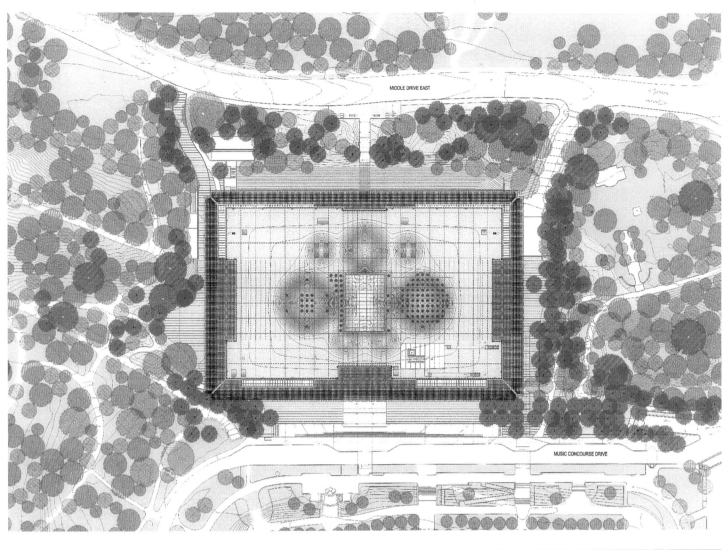

MIDDLE DRIVE EAST

MUSIC CONCOURSE DRIVE

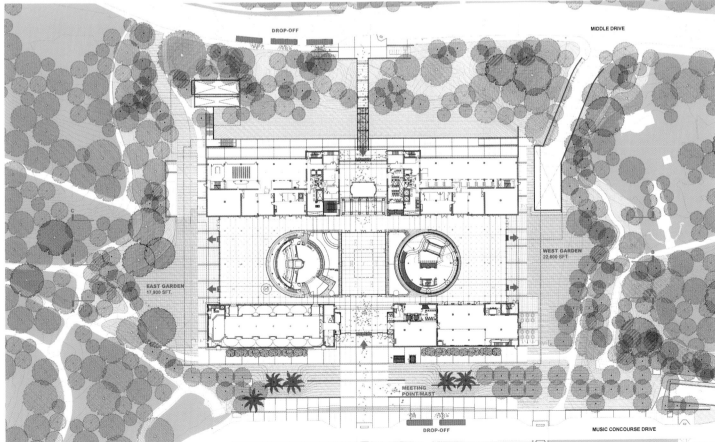

DROP-OFF

MIDDLE DRIVE

EAST GARDEN
17,900 SFT.

WEST GARDEN
22,600 SFT.

MEETING
POINT/MAST

DROP-OFF

MUSIC CONCOURSE DRIVE

2006.03.01

2007.05.07

2007.06.07

2007.06.25

2007.07.10

2007.07.28

2007.09.21

La California Academy of Sciences
è una "macchina gentile"
pensata per esplorare il rapporto
tra l'edificio e la natura, l'ambiente.

The California Academy of Sciences
is a soft machine designed to explore
the building's relationship with nature
and environment.

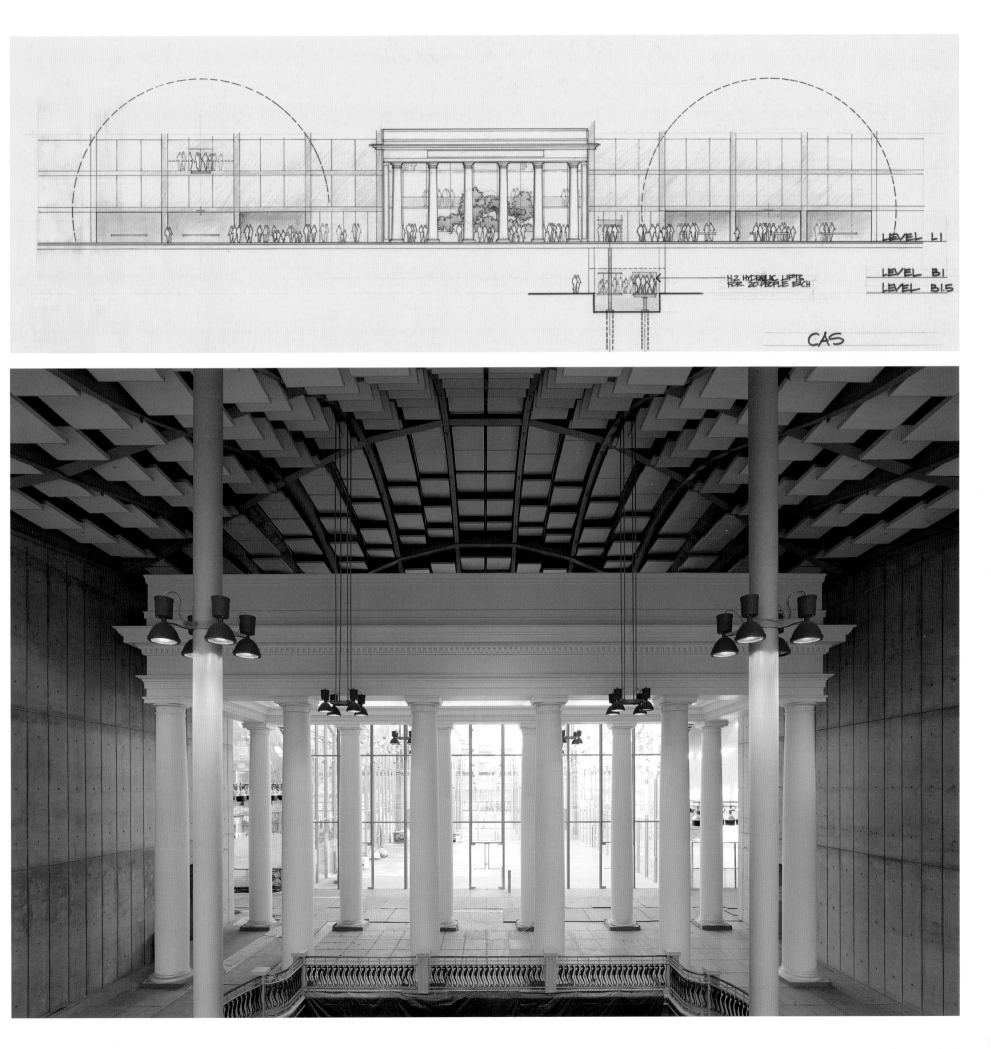

Il tema della memoria non era solo un tema
di convenienza pratica e pragmatica, ma aveva
anche a che fare con la ritualità di questo luogo.
Perché tutti a San Francisco, da quelli che hanno
sei anni a quelli che ne hanno novanta,
ricordano gli alligatori nella palude dell'acquario.

Memory was not merely just practical
or pragmatic issue. It also had to do with
the rituals of this special place.
Everyone in San Francisco between the ages
of six and ninety has seen the alligators
in the aquarium swamp.

Aquarium
Restrooms 🚹🚺

Rainforest

African
Center
Dining 🍴
Education
Center
Forum
Living Roof

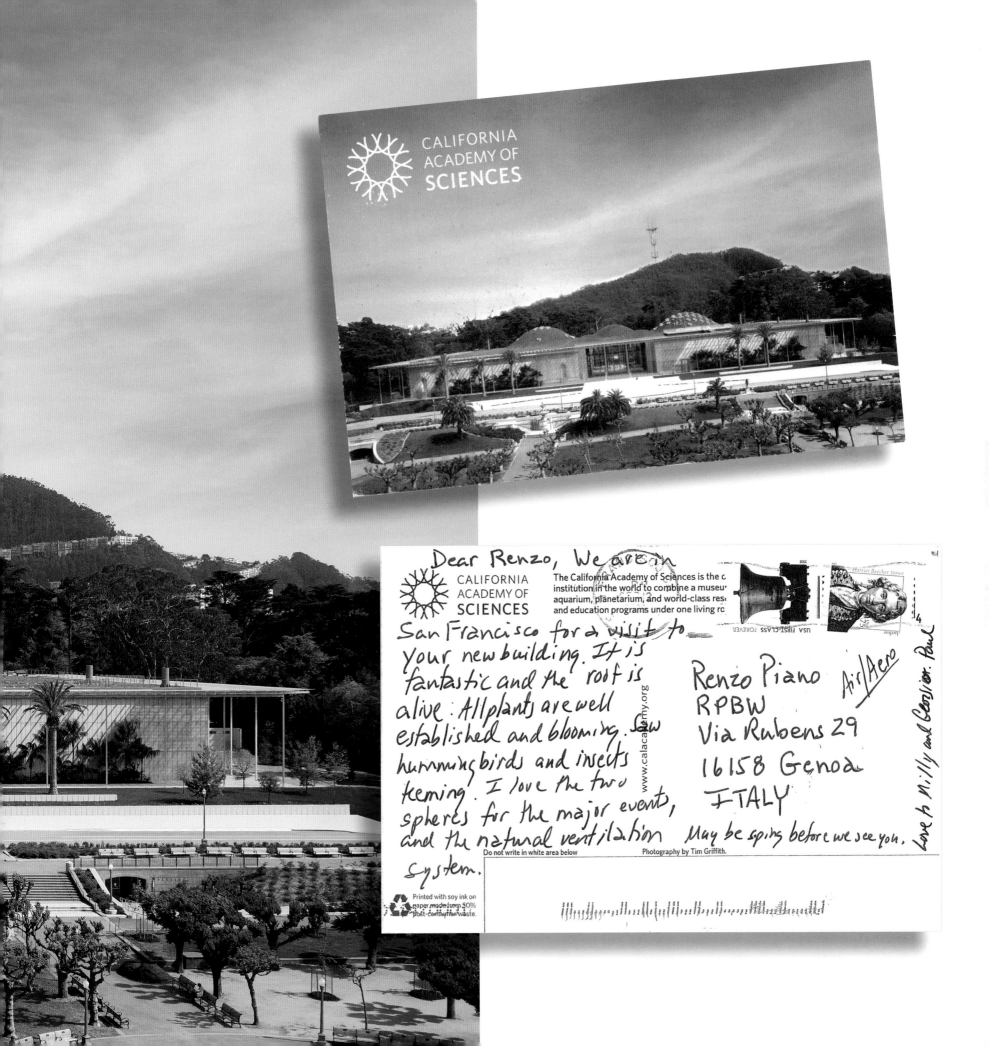

CALIFORNIA ACADEMY OF SCIENCES

Dear Renzo, We are in

The California Academy of Sciences is the o
institution in the world to combine a museu
aquarium, planetarium, and world-class res
and education programs under one living ro

San Francisco for a visit to
your new building. It is
fantastic and the roof is
alive. All plants are well
established and blooming. Saw
hummingbirds and insects
teeming. I love the two
spheres for the major events,
and the natural ventilation
system.

www.calacademy.org

Do not write in white area below

Photography by Tim Griffith.

Printed with soy ink on
paper made from 50%
post-consumer waste.

Renzo Piano
RPBW
Via Rubens 29
16158 Genoa
ITALY

Air/Aero

May be spring before we see you.

Love to Milly and Carolier. Paul

USA FIRST-CLASS FOREVER

The Bad News About Green Architecture

Sustainable buildings are virtuous, but they can be ugly. Only a few designs are truly great.

GREAT DESIGN AS WELL AS GREEN: *The rainforest exhibit at the California Academy of Sciences*

PHOTOGRAPH BY DWIGHT ESCHLIMAN FOR NEWSWEEK

By CATHLEEN MCGUIGAN

I HATE GREEN ARCHITECTURE. I CAN'T stand the hype, the marketing claims, the smug lists of green features that supposedly transform a garden-variety new building into a structure fit for Eden. Grassy roofs? Swell! Recycled gray water to flush the toilets? Excellent! But if 500 employees have to drive 40 miles a day to work in the place—well, how green is that? Achieving real sustainability is much more complicated than the publicity suggests. And that media roar is only getting louder. The urge to build green is exploding: more than 16,000 projects are now registered with the U.S. Green Building Council as intending to go for a LEED (Leadership in Energy and Environmental Design)—or sustainable—certification, up from just 573 in 2000.

Among those are various plans to build at least 50 million square feet of new green resorts in Las Vegas, where ecoconsciousness is suddenly as hot as Texas Hold 'Em. The largest LEED-rated building in the country is the 8.3 million-square-foot Palazzo Resort Hotel and Casino, which opened there last January. As it happens, the state of Nevada offers developers property-tax rebates—up to 35 percent—for LEED certification. Don't worry about the tons of jet fuel that will be used to deliver millions more tourists to Vegas each year—those visitors can help make up for that by reusing the towels in their hotels.

When it comes to green, people don't want to hear that size matters. We keep building not just bigger entertainment complexes but bigger houses. "Green McMansion" is one of my favorite oxymorons. Currently the average new house is 2,500 square feet, up 1.5 percent in size from last year—though the shock of this winter's fuel bills may finally slow the trend. Building green houses—or at least advertising them as green—is on the rise, though there are no national standards about what constitutes a green home. People are attracted to sustainable houses partly as a cool novelty, when in fact green dwellings have been around for eons. Think of igloos, tepees or yurts—they took advantage of readily available local materials and were designed to suit their specific environments. Shelters around the world tend to be situated to benefit from the sun in the winter or to shield their inhabitants from chilling winds. But we forgot those basic principles when we plunked down every possible style of house into our sprawling American suburbs.

If you want to understand what makes sustainable sense, check out the classic old shotgun houses of New Orleans that best survived Katrina (and just got a pass from Gustav): these modest homes are built high off the ground to resist flood damage; they are made of local wood that dries out; they have high ceilings and cross ventilation to deal with the stifling summer heat. But the houses that were ruined—whether in the Lower Ninth Ward or more-affluent neighborhoods—tended to be low-slung ranch houses, a style originally developed for the climate of California.

What bugs me most about the fad for green architecture is the notion that virtue makes for better design. OK, I suppose an ugly green building is better than an ugly

THE LARGE AND THE SMALL OF IT: *The retail mall in America's biggest green building, the Palazzo resort in Las Vegas; a Louisiana shotgun house*

Sustainability is about the practical systems of building; it doesn't always make for great architecture.

nongreen building—but it's still ugly. So when I come upon a beautiful sustainable building that doesn't scream green, it cheers me up. The California Academy of Sciences, opening later this month in San Francisco, is a perfect example. It replaces the old science museum that was damaged in the 1989 Loma Prieta earthquake. Its design is sensitive to its place and history: the new building doesn't gobble up more space on its spectacular site in Golden Gate Park, and its architect, Renzo Piano, was careful to go no higher—36 feet—than the original structure. The most obvious ecofeature of his elegantly simple glass-sided pavilion is the green roof: a rolling 2.5-acre terrain, inspired in part by the surrounding hills, it cleverly disguises, under its two biggest bumps, the domes of the planetarium and of the rainforest exhibit underneath. The roof is planted with 40 native species (unlike Golden Gate Park itself, which was created out of a sand pit and includes such glamorous nonnatives as palm trees). The plants are kind of low and scrubby—though they bloom at various times—but they were chosen less for prettiness than hardiness, and the fact that they won't need irrigation.

There are lots of examples of innovative green technology in the building, but perhaps the most surprising is in the museum's offices where, says the executive director, Gregory Farrington, you can see hardware that's rare in today's buildings: handles to open the windows. That's because, amazingly, there's no artificial cool air. The only air conditioning is provided free of charge by the breezes that blow off the Pacific—including those that are naturally pulled down by that curvy roof into a lovely open piazza at the center of the museum. "It's a building that breathes with nature," says Piano. And all the gizmos that make this building even greener—the weather sensors that dim or brighten the artificial lights; the thousands of little solar cells tucked into the roof overhangs; the old denim jeans recycled as insulation—are so carefully integrated into the overall architecture that you hardly notice them. Of course, the green features will be explained in the museum's education programs—each year, 50,000 San Francisco schoolkids will visit its aquarium, alligator pool and other exhibits of the living and the dead. But personally, I like that Piano's trademark gifts for inventive design and great craftsmanship seem to make the sustainable elements disappear. "Making green buildings is a practical answer," he says in the accent of his native

For more of NEWSWEEK's Project Green coverage, go to xtra.Newsweek.com

Italy. "But architecture is about desire; it's about dreams."

Spoken like a true romantic, but the point is right-on: sustainability is about the practical systems of building, not the beauty of great design. Established architects like Piano—he's 71—have learned to integrate green into their practices, depending on where they're working (the rules are strict in many countries of Europe, where Piano is based). But for the next generation of architects, sustainability will be second nature—they're learning in architecture schools how to incorporate green into design, and some of them will become the innovators who'll devise ever more efficient ecological solutions. And the U.S. Green Building Council is continuing to evolve its suggested standards: access to mass transit, rather than the necessity of cars, gets credit, as does adapting to a specific climate—a principle central to the sustainability of the California Academy of Sciences. It's expected to score a LEED platinum rating, making it the greenest museum in the United States. But I wish we didn't have to trumpet that achievement in the same breath as praising its design. I look forward to a future when green architecture won't be discretionary but required of every architect and builder. Then we could all shut up about it. Sustainable features would become as exciting as the plumbing systems and as essential as a roof that keeps out the rain.

With DANIEL STONE

STEVE MARCUS—REUTERS-LANDOV (LEFT); MARIO TAMA—GETTY IMAGES

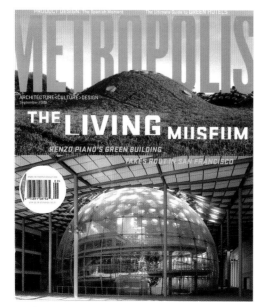

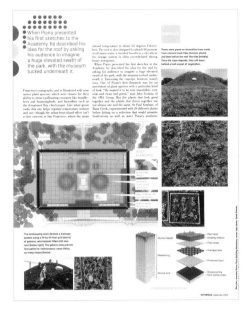

ArtsArchitecture

In pictures
View more photographs of Piano's California
Academy of Sciences guardian.co.uk/architecture

Second nature

Home to alligators, penguins, a coral reef, rainforests and an amazing living roof, Renzo
Piano's Academy of Sciences is an environmental marvel, says **Jonathan Glancey**

How invisible should a major public building be? How invisible *can* a major public building be? These thoughts must have crossed Renzo Piano's mind when he made his first sketch for the newly opened California Academy of Sciences in San Francisco. That drawing revealed nothing more than an energetic and undulating, pencil-thin roof, yet this was to be the key to this special design.

Beneath this hypothetical roofline, the building that now houses a planetarium, several slices of rainforest, a colony of seabirds, giant reptiles, classrooms, bats, 18 million pickled animal specimens, chameleons, temporary exhibition spaces, geckos, auditorium, frogs, cafeteria, lungfish, and millions of visitors each year was initially left undrawn. The roof would determine the whole. The main body of the academy was to be as immaterial as technically possible. The details would be filled in later.

Why was this? Because the whole point of the California Academy of Sciences, founded in 1853, is its research into and celebration of the natural world, and especially of biodiversity. What better way to highlight these endeavours than to build a new home that does as little as possible to obstruct the trees and lawns surrounding it in the Golden Gate Park, a home that touches the ground with the delicacy of a ballerina?

The steel columns that support the enchanting green roof of this parkland pavilion are so thin, they must be held in tension by long wire cables. These not only permit the interior of the museum to be as transparent and as free from structural intrusion as possible, but, in the event of an earthquake, should allow the building to sway safely like a ship weathering a storm at sea.

It was, in fact, the Loma Prieta earthquake of 1989 that determined the academy's need for a new home in the first place. Until then it was housed in 11 buildings in Golden Gate Park, dating from between 1912 and 1976. Some were badly damaged by Loma Prieta. Since then, several much-loved old buildings in the park have been restored, including the late 19th-century Conservatory for Flowers — the biggest building of its type in North America — while such dazzling new designs as Herzog and De Meuron's copper-clad De Young Museum have added fresh charms to this vast outdoors space, claimed from Pacific dunes in the 1870s.

Facing the De Young Museum across the park's open-air music concourse, the Academy of Sciences has been an instant crowd-pleaser. Its clear glazed walls reveal some of the attractions inside, notably the two great spheres of its planetarium and artificial rainforest. From the outside, you can see straight through the building into the park from almost any angle.

Inside, the academy is as bright and airy as it is generously proportioned and clearly planned. The central lobby is lit by a over-storey whose windows actually open (far rarer than it should be), and protected from the sun by automatic blinds. Throughout most of the year, the building fills with ocean breezes sped up and slowed down, deliberately and to subtle effect, by the roof's artificial hillocks. Sunlight casts shafts of light and shadows across walls and floors.

"You can say that the building is made of shadows," says Renzo Piano. "Being inside is like being under a tree in summer. The green roof with its bubbles is like foliage wrapping itself over branches. And Pacific breezes make sure you don't feel trapped inside some heavy institutional building.

"This is a complex building, but we wanted it to feel natural and relaxed as well as easy to get around. Here you have scientists busy at very slow work, researching, and visitors who consume the experiences the academy has to offer in a few hours. But this was a good starting point for thinking about the design. When the academy started in the 1850s, there was always a kind of dualism at work. In summer, the scientists sailed on voyages of research and discovery, bringing their finds back to San Francisco. In winter, they were teachers, showing an eager public what they had found. So we have tried to create a building that balances the world of the scientist and the visitor, of science and nature, of technology and wildlife, all under one roof."

The roof really is an extraordinary thing. Fortunately, there is a viewing platform from which visitors can watch it grow. Here Piano and Frank Almeda, the academy's botanist, have planted 1.7m native California plants. Beach strawberries, self heal, sea pink and California poppies are already attracting hummingbirds, bees and endangered species such as Bay Checkerspot and San Bruno Elfin butterflies.

"It seems strange," says Piano, "but here on top of the new building we've recreated a patch of the original natural landscape of this part of California. At the opening, an American Indian, whose great-great-grandfather once owned the site, lit a pipe and blew smoke in an act of blessing across the roof. He told us he was happy that the spirit of the place had been reborn. Below us, 50 schoolchildren released 30,000 butterflies. They were attracted to the roof, too."

The roof does more than attract wildlife; it also helps to keep the building's interior 6C (10F) cooler than a conventional covering would, while dampening noise in the galleries. And because it is surrounded by a band of 60,000 photovoltaic cells, the academy will use around a third less energy than the maximum allowed by San Francisco's strict laws.

"We could have thought of a different solution for the roof without plants and birds," says Piano, "but the green roof is about a new spirit for 21st-century buildings. We are learning to develop an aesthetic, as well as a practical technique to save energy, that demonstrates a concern for the fragility of biodiversity and the need to care for nature. This doesn't mean we have to go back and live in mud huts with green roofs. We can work with both new technology and nature to find the right balance."

Seventy-one-year-old Piano, who made his name internationally with the design of Paris's Pompidou Centre with Richard Rogers in the 1970s, has made great strides in the US in recent years. As well as the California Academy of Sciences, he is currently working on, or has recently completed, buildings for the Art Institute of Chicago, the Los Angeles County Museum of Art, the Whitney Museum of American Art in New York, the Isabella Stewart Gardner Museum in Boston and the Morgan Library and Museum, New York. He has also designed a new headquarters for the New York Times in Manhattan. A man who, in his own words, was once one of the "bad boys" of architecture has become a kind of patrician figure among high-minded American cultural institutions.

This latest building is an adventure on any level. The planetarium offers the thrill of journeys to the stars, while the rainforest sphere delights with four different habitats on four different levels. Elsewhere in the

An adventure on any level . . . you can see through the building into the park from almost any angle

building, there is a swamp of alligators and a deep tank nurturing a living coral reef. A colony of Cape penguins can be found in a reconstruction of the 1934 Africa House. The scientists themselves can be seen at work through glass partitions.

This is, I think, an important building. Built of recycled steel, 90% of it recovered from the old academy pavilions damaged in the 1989 earthquake, and locally sourced concrete, it is exceptionally "green" even before one takes account of its special roof. It is somehow classical, modern and organic in one and the same green breath. Schoolchildren and scientists are at home here, as are the thousands of living exhibits, those millions of rooftop plants and the winged visitors they attract.

When Piano was designing his first major building in the US — the Menil Collection in Houston, completed in 1987 — I remember discussing the notion of "soft machine" buildings with him. How could truly modern buildings using the latest technology and materials be more gently related to our senses and with nature?

There is a long way to go before architects, and their clients, strike the right balance, yet here in Golden Gate Park is an enjoyable, elegant and environmentally friendly building that should be recognised as a key staging post ⊙

The appliance of science . . . the academy's roof is planted with nearly two million native California plants

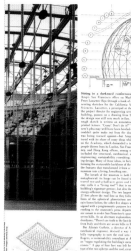

The Engineering

Part 3

By Michael Silverberg

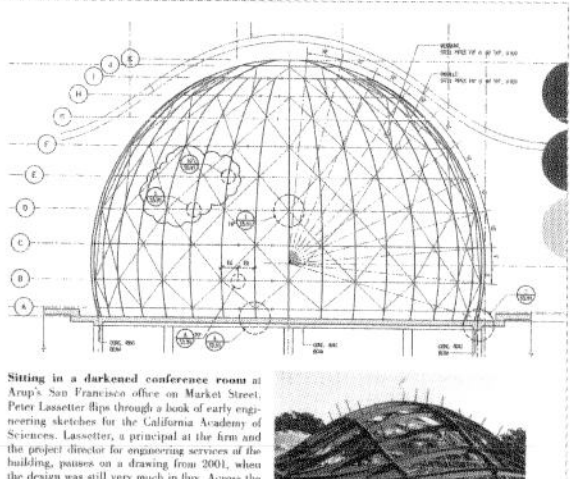

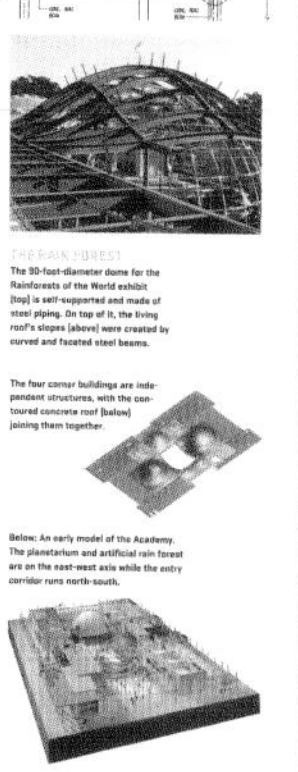

San Francisco Chronicle

★★★ | Printed on recycled paper | SUNDAY, OCTOBER 28, 2007 | sfgate.com | 415-77

ACADEMY OF SCIENCES: Officials getting keys to new $484 million structure, which is ready to be filled with 20 million research specimens and 38,000 live animals in preparation for its fall 2008 opening

BREATHTAKING SNEAK PEEK

Photos by MICHAEL MACOR / The Chronicle

Jamie Perez walks through a tunnel that leads to the four-story living rain forest dome at the new museum.

> "The biggest challenge to building this place was visualizing what it would look like, with so many curves and structures stacked on top of each other."
>
> JES PEDERSEN, senior vice president of Webcor Builders

By Kevin Fagan and David Perlman
CHRONICLE STAFF WRITERS

Take a deep breath, science buffs — and get ready to be blown away.

The newly built $484 million California Academy of Sciences was officially turned over to academy officials on Friday, and the promise of things to come was as palpable in the air of Golden Gate Park as the smell of new paint inside the building itself.

The first thing that overwhelms the senses is the very entryway, which is essentially a huge wall of glass revealing the contents of the building as if it were presenting an intellectual feast. From the door, you can see two huge, exotic-looking domes, a glassed-in piazza with a roof so high it's tough to see the top, and enough aquatic pools to fill an entire shoreline.

Taking possession of the building simply means the two-year-long construction job is virtually done, and the exhibits and collections must now be installed. But it's easy to see what's coming by looking at the structures that sit ready for stocking.

And what's to come will essentially amount to a massive,

SFGate.com

▶ To see what's shaping up at the new Academy of Sciences at Golden Gate Park, take a video tour with Chronicle Science Editor David Perlman at sfgate.com.

working display case for the public. Newly renamed the Kimball Natural History Museum, the sprawling edifice takes the musty old, dark-halled concept of natural history museums and blows it wide open.

It is full of airy, glassily transparent galleries and research labs, and everything from the "living roof" of plants and birds and butterflies already at home there, to the heat-recycling systems, is aimed at making it one of the most environmentally friendly museums on the planet. The exhibits being readied push the old paradigm forward several expensive steps in many ways — from adding bubble-shaped observation windows for viewing coral reefs and sharks to presenting the nation's largest planetarium, with digital film quality so precise it will make visitors feel like they're flying through space.

▶ **MUSEUM:** Page A8

Rigger Leighton Hill joins electricians Mike Hurley (top left) and Eugene Garcia (top right) working on the dome.

ACADEMY OF SCIENCES

BREATHTAKING BUILDING

▶ **MUSEUM**
From Page A1

The plans for every room, every glass-walled tank, and every exhibit of rain forest trees will bespeak the museum's basic mission: to tell the world how life evolved on planet Earth, how its diversity has spread across all the seas and continents, and how every visitor must come away newly committed to protect and sustain these infinitely varied life forms that are now threatened everywhere.

It was easy to see, during a preview walk-through this week, where all those 484 million dollars went. Even the construction workers were impressed.

"I've worked on a lot of construction jobs, but this one is special," carpenter Salvador Gonzalez said, awe in his voice. He was polishing a Brazilian Ipe wood rail, and the reverential care he took in the rubbing was reflected in the equally mindful finishing work going on all around him. The crews knew they were having a once-in-a-lifetime experience.

"There are so many different parts here. It's going to be a great museum," Gonzalez said. "I feel like it's a privilege to work on it."

The academy will ceremonially receive the keys to the new building on Thursday, and filling the 410,000-square-foot space — 40,000 square feet larger than the old, seismically unworthy one —

> "It's going to be a great museum. I feel like it's a privilege to work on it."
> SALVADOR GONZALEZ, carpenter

with 20 million research specimens and 38,000 live animals will continue well into next year.

Opening day for the public is scheduled for the fall of 2008, but within the next few weeks the first of the Kimball museum's exhibits will begin moving in, and the academy's scientists will start toting their equipment and precious

Photos by MICHAEL MACOR / The Chronicle

Touring the new structure are Matt Rossie (left), Susan McComb and J.D. Durst. Four rain forests will be installed in this area.

> The African exhibit hall "will hopefully look very familiar to our visitors. It has been a favorite for many, many years, and people wanted it to look the same as much as possible."
> STEPHANIE STONE, museum spokeswoman

At the eastern end of the wing will stand an old friend from the previous academy building: the 30-foot-high Foucault pendulum, which illustrates the Earth's rotation by swinging steadily while the planet rotates beneath it.

Early childhood center

Every parent with a hands-on, active toddler will wind up in this spacious room on the east end of the museum, and be happy for it.

A replica of the good ship Academy, the schooner that undertook the academy's first, groundbreaking expedition to Galapagos in 1905-06, will stand in the middle for energetic youngsters to crawl upon.

An artificial tree with treehouse and burrows will also produce eyeready stuffed knees, and on the opposite side of the room will be an underwater-themed exhibit with dress-up costumes.

"This whole room was designed to capture the active energy of young children and give them a nature-themed space to play in," said Stone.

It is also sure to give parents a few moments of breathing space while they watch their tots frolic.

Coral reef

At a depth of 25 feet, the living coral reef will be the deepest such museum reef in the world. It consists of a long, narrow trench in the floor of the museum. It is studded with fake stone — made, like much of the fake stone in the building, of Shotcrete that is sprayed in place — acrylic observation windows have been cut into the trench's base. One that is sure to be a favorite is a bubble window that visitors will have to crawl into through a cement tunnel for a view of the reef's fish swimming by. Visitors will also be able to peer into the reef from that open top.

Some 1,500 colonies of coral, in a dizzying variety of colors from pink to green, are being grown right now at the academy's temporary downtown Howard Street labs on artificial rocks that were specially aged in the sea off Fiji for a year. Coral is a living animal, with algae embedded into its skeleton for nourishment, and moving it requires trucking the entire rock onto which each coral has glued itself.

Scientists will begin transporting the academy's 1,000 square feet of coral to the new building in December, and it will take some months to install all the 4,000 live coral stingrays and turtles.

Morrison Pl

This wild has been Now a 90-foot screen as big Observatory which was, a planetarium rion will sp precise digit not only pre plays, but al from NASA' and other sp

This museum to watch in gl front of the sterlingly acc Mars town, t elibles and ar my managers capsule while.

"It really v a space flight here," Stone love it until

The old pl rangement h 11 steep rises ers will have shot at what well as the t through to the si

Living rain

Perhaps the ning feature will be the dome that wi four rain fore a constant 82

This dome palm and cr feet high, and an elevator w four different

The first the imitate the r with a live c alongside sna os, frogs and floor will ho and channel floor will le butterflies co

Above: Angie Arias and Jamie Barajas install a walkway of Brazilian Ipe wood that leads to the new planetarium.

Left: Robin Allen works on the coral reef lagoon, where 1,000 square feet of coral will be home to 4,000 fish.

Expeditions wing

This is where visitors will get to see a continuously changing exhibit of the specimens and displays the academy's scores of working scientists bring back every year from the globe-spanning expeditions the organization has conducted throughout its 154-year history.

The wing covers most of the eastern half of the main floor, and on opening day, exploration crews will roll out findings from trips to the Galapagos Islands and Madagascar, both historic and recent.

The idea of this initial display will be to contrast the development of life on these two very different islands.

Galapagos is a fairly new volcanic formation that rose abruptly from the sea, so the species that evolved there did so independently. Madagascar, on the other hand, broke off from Africa a millennium ago, so it nurtured species that had already existed on its mother continent but have evolved ever since.

and tortoise shells dating back to the turn of the last century still join thousands of other treasures brought back by academy expeditions.

ACADEMY OF SCIENCES

IS ACADEMY'S NEW HOME

▶ **MUSEUM**
From previous page

ting through the canopies of the dome's gigantic trees.

Finally, the basement will take visitors beneath a living mockup of a flooded Amazonian rain forest floor. To save visitors the trouble of swimming through heated muck, there is a long, acrylic tunnel that will allow them to stroll through and gaze directly into the bottom of the forest with its mangroves, soggy tree roots and freshwater fish.

Central piazza

This is a huge square in the middle of the museum, and it is breathtaking, with an abundance of natural light pouring in from its high glass roof and nothing but ceiling-to-floor glass walls on all sides, giving a 360-degree view of the museum's attractions.

Dinners and special events will be held here when the piazza is not giving regular visitors a well-lit respite.

The glass roof is cleverly vented, in the interest of green-conscious air circulation, at the very top.

Living roof

The entire top of the museum, with the exception of the piazza's glass ceiling, consists of the biggest sustainable roof in the world. It is essentially a planted garden stretching to all four walls, supporting 1.7 million plants, including California

MICHAEL MACOR / The Chronicle

Workers walk through the lobby, which opens onto a huge atrium in the center of the Academy of Sciences' new structure.

poppies and strawberries.

Counting the tops of the two domes — Morrison Planetarium and the living rain forest — the roof sports a total of seven soil hills, mimicking the seven hills of San Francisco. This serendipitously also echoes the seven hills of Rome — capital of the home country of the man who designed the museum, Italian architect Renzo Piano.

California and climate change wing

The entire west end of this hall will highlight the wonders of the Golden State through exhibits

the famed grizzly bear who served as the model for the bear on the California state flag.

The rest of the hall will feature video footage, models and other displays designed to generate discussion of California's wildfires, shrinking snowpack and other natural events that are marks of global climate change.

Steinhart Aquarium

The academy's old, familiar Steinhart Aquarium will be a very different kettle of fish in its new incarnation. Instead of row after row of small, static tanks and a few big ones, life in the water world will be on display everywhere, said Christopher Andrews, the aquarium's new director.

"It's all about diversity," Andrews said, "and we'll show it in diverse ways — with fish and reptiles and amphibians and jellies and birds and even bats. We'll show how aquatic life varies in the varied environments of this water planet: saltwater fish in their tanks next to freshwater ones, fish that love warm water next to those that like it cold.

"And active researchers and docents will be everywhere, so people can get up close and really personal with the animals they're looking at."

ranging from Sierra Nevada gold and the skeleton of a long-extinct saber-toothed cat to a 75-foot-long blue whale hanging from the ceiling. The hall will also be home to the stuffed remains of Monarch,

E-mail the writers at kfagan@sfchronicle.com and dperlman@sfchronicle.com.

★★★★★
SECTION
A
PAGE 13
Wednesday,
July 10, 2002

Living roof tops Sciences Academy plan

Design will be revealed today

By John King
CHRONICLE URBAN DESIGN WRITER

Golden Gate Park could get four acres of greenery added to it in the most unlikely location: atop a new home for the California Academy of Sciences.

The environmentally friendly roof — complete with undulating contours meant to evoke San Francisco's fabled topography — is the most startling element of the design being disclosed today as the academy begins a drive to build a new $220 million facility to replace its current home on the south edge of the park's Music Concourse.

The academy, one of the nation's leading natural history museums and research centers, has been in Golden Gate Park since 1916. It has sought a new home for years, both because of a desire for a more efficient facility and because the m...
structures doe...
seismic codes...
quirements.

If San Fra...
prove the p...
would close...
open its new...
between, the...
and 18 milli...
mens — rangi...
ic plants to fi...
would move to...
tion.

The archite...
Renzo Piano c...

recipient of the Pritzker Prize, architecture's equivalent of the Nobel, and among the handful of international architects courted by image-conscious institutions. His current projects range from an expansion of the Art Institute of Chicago to a 1,000-foot-high skyscraper in London.

Academy officials say the design's villagelike cluster of spaces under a contoured roof took shape in two years of discussions.

"We didn't seek an architect's particular 'look.' We wanted someone who would be responsive to our needs," said executive director Dr. Patrick Kociolek, explaining the desire to go with Piano rather than one of his flashier peers. "We wanted a building that is appropriate and blends in."

The project would be larger and costlier than the new M.H. de Young Memorial Museum, which will start construction later this...

Arts

MOVIES ■ MUSIC ■ BOOKS ■ EXHIBITIONS ■ FASHION ■ ARCHITECTURE

Landscape design
Piano's Academy building is topped by a green roof

ARCHITECTURE
King of the Hill. Italian architect Renzo Piano is changing the face of America, one inventive building at a time

BY RICHARD LACAYO

IT'S JUST TWO DAYS BEFORE ITS OFFICIAL reopening, and the new California Academy of Sciences in San Francisco looks like the old ones but less when they used to shoot five pictures at one time. Caterers hauling pumpkins are brushing past construction workers sweeping out the manmade rain forest. Divers in wet suits are

TIME October 13, 2008

49

A Building That Blooms and Grows, Balancing Nature and Civilization

NICOLAI OUROUSSOFF
ARCHITECTURE REVIEW

SAN FRANCISCO — Not all architects embrace the idea of evolution. Some, fixated on the 20th-century notion of the avant-garde, view their work as a divine revelation, as if history began with them. Others pine for the Middle Ages.

But if you want reaffirmation that human history is an upward spiral rather than a descent into darkness, head for the new California Academy of Sciences, in Golden Gate Park, which opens on Saturday. Designed by the Italian architect Renzo Piano on the site of the academy's demolished home, the building has a steel frame that rests amid the verdant flora like a delicate piece of fine embroidery. Capped by a stupendous floating green roof of undulating mounds of plants, it embodies the academy's philosophy that humanity is only one part of an endlessly complex universal system.

This building's greatness as architecture, however, is rooted in a cultural history that stretches back through Modernism to Classical Greece. It is a comforting reminder of the civilizing function of great art in a barbaric age.

The academy building is the last in a series of ambitious projects to be conceived in and around the park's Music Concourse since the devastating 1989 Loma Prieta earthquake.

Herzog & de Meuron's mesmerizing de Young Museum, enclosed in perforated copper, opened three years ago. Scaffolding is to come down at the concourse's neo-Classical band shell this week after a loving restoration.

Glimpsed through the concourse's grove of sycamores, the science academy gives the impression of weightlessness. A row of steel columns spanning 36 feet high along the facade lends the building a classical air; the sense of lightness is accentuated by a water-thin canopy above that creates the illusion that the roof is only millimeters thick. It's as if a section of the park carpeted in native wildflowers and

Continued on Page 5

California Academy of Sciences Designed by Renzo Piano, the San Francisco museum's new building, top and above, opens on Saturday.

PHOTOGRAPHS BY TIM GRIFFITH

The new building incorporates the 1930s African Hall, lined with dioramas.

A Building That Blooms, Balancing Humanity and Nature

From First Arts Page

beach strawberries had been lifted off the ground and suspended in midair.

The idea is to create a balance between public and private, inside and out, the Cartesian order of the mind and the unruly world of nature.

A glass lobby allows you to gaze straight through the building to the park on the other side. Other views open into exhibition spaces with their own microclimates. The entire building serves as a sort of specimen case, a framework for pondering the natural world while straining to disturb it as little as possible.

Mr. Piano's building is also a blazingly uncynical embrace of the Enlightenment value of truth and reason. Its Classical symmetry — the axial geometry, the columns framing a central entry — taps into a lineage that runs back to Mies van der Rohe's 1968 Neue Nationalgalerie and Schinkel's 1828 Altes Museum in Berlin and even further, to the Parthenon.

Just as Mies's glass-and-steel museum reworked Classical precedents, Mr. Piano's design invokes Mies's model, though with a sensitivity that makes the muscularity of the 1968 museum look old-fashioned. The roof of the academy's lobby, supported by a gossamerlike web of cables, swells upward as if the entire room were breathing. Views open up to the landscape on all four sides, momentarily situating you both within the building and in the bigger world outside. A narrow row of clerestory windows lines the top of the lobby. One of the building's many environmental features, these windows let warm air escape and create a gentle breeze that reinforces the connection to the natural setting.

From here you can proceed into the exhibition halls, delving deeper into the universe's secrets. Two enormous 90-foot-tall spheres — one housing a planetarium, the other a rain forest — beckon from either side of the lobby. They are the most solid forms in the building, yet seem to hover in the space. The base of the planetarium sphere floats in a pool; a broad ramp snakes around the rain-forest sphere. Enveloped in gnarled branches,

the ramp seems to have been swallowed up by the jungle landscape over millenniums.

Once you reach this point, the genius of the green roof's design becomes apparent. The mounds of earth visible on the exterior turn out to be hollow: their forms, punctured by round skylights, bulge upward to make room for the giant spheres underneath. It's as if a lush protective rug has been gently draped over the entire building.

Additional exhibition spaces just beyond the spheres are designed with movable walls that give them a tentative quality. Large windows open up onto park views.

The museum has preserved its African Hall, a gorgeous vaulted ceiling with oramas of somnolent grazing antelopes, into the new design. In addition to the Academy, museums in Dallas, Atlanta and Los Angeles carry his stamp. So do an agile reconfiguration of the Morgan Library in New York City and a 52-story headquarters for The New York Times. Still to come are an addition to the Art Institute of Chicago, new buildings for the Kimbell Art Museum in Fort Worth, Texas, and the Los Angeles County Museum of Art; a makeover of the Harvard University Art Museums; and a satellite facility in Manhattan for the Whitney Museum of American Art. It's Renzo Piano's world. We're just living in it.

In particular, Piano has become the go-to guy for any institution about to undertake a tricky expansion. "I'm not looking for trouble," he says, laughing. "But I never

find myself in an easy space, where they say to me, 'O.K., here's a piece of land—do it.'" At 71, he's well known for the clarity of his problem-solving in complicated spaces. "Today," he says, "the discussion of architecture is based too often on how funny you can be with making new shapes. We all know that making new shapes is not very difficult. What is more difficult is to make new shapes that make sense."

This would not have been the position most people would have predicted for Piano in 1977, when he became suddenly famous for one of the funniest buildings of all time: The Georges Pompidou Center in Paris, which he co-designed with the British architect Richard Rogers, a museum that's been disemboweled, its brightly colored ventilation tubes, pipes and escalators draped along the exterior in a riot of externalized eccentricities.

After the Pompidou became a hit with tourists, Piano might have been expected to go on to a career length succession of wild and crazy schemes. But lurking with in him was a closet classicist. The barium obvious in 1987 with the opening of his Menil Collection in Houston—another startling building, but this one startling in its simplicity. A subdued, low rise museum, the Menil is a machine for delivering light, which it coaxes indoors in just the right amounts through an ingenious roof system of louvers.

What the Menil made clear was that light was going to be one of Piano's chief materials. His best buildings are elegant variations on the idea of transparency. His Nasher Sculpture Center in Dallas just five adjacent bays with travertine walls, is one of the most gratifying art exhibition spaces in the world. But not everything Piano touches turns out as nicely. In pre-construction models, his New York Times headquarters looked delicate almost to the point of evanescence—quite a trick for a Manhattan sky scraper. But in the execution, the ceramic rods decided to screen the glass walls are bulky, and the battleship gray exterior looks anything but weightless.

With the California Academy, a combination research institute, natural history museum, planetarium and aquarium,

The new California Academy of Sciences is capped

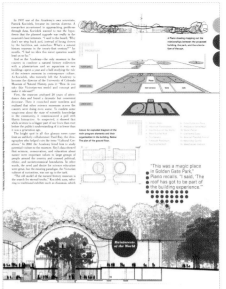

Karen E. Steen

The new California Academy of Sciences, in San Francisco's Golden Gate Park, is a building of applex proportions. At 410,000 square feet, it's expected to be the largest public building ever to receive a LEED Platinum rating. And, with a $488 million price tag, it also represents the largest fund-raising effort for a cultural institution in San Francisco history. How did this low-profile natural history museum and research facility become a half-billion-dollar marquee project by a Pritzker Prize-winning architect, not to mention a landmark in sustainable design?

According to an oft-told origin story, it all started on the roof. In late 1999, architect Renzo Piano visited the site, climbed up on top of the Academy's former building, and—there amid the canopy of trees—declared that the roof itself needed to become an exhibit of the museum. "This was a magic place in the middle of Golden Gate Park," Piano recalls. "I said, 'The roof has got to be part of the experience of the building, part of the itinerary.'"

But that was only nine years ago—the lifted at one eye in the world of architecture, and even less in the world of science. If you reach further back, there's another precipitous event—appropriately enough, an event of the natural world. When the Loma Prieta earthquake struck the Bay Area in October of 1989, the venerable museum, which dates back to 1853, sustained severe damage and was forced to close one building and retrofit several others. At first, the Academy had modest hopes for the shattered building and by up modest; but the beloved Steinhart Aquarium. But then the institution decided to turn the lens of scientific inquiry upon itself, and that's when everything changed.

A section drawing shows how the planetarium and the rain forest are integrated into the building.

Il Sole 24 Ore
Venerdì 26 Settembre 2008 - N. 266

Con

Un museo firmato dall'ecologia

Renzo Piano: «Una Ferrari a zero consumi e zero emissioni» - Hi-tech e vivibilità

di Fulvio Irace

Acrobati cinesi e suonatori di tamburo nigeriani, ballerini e artisti del circo: con le loro esibizioni, domani al Golden Park di San Francisco, apriranno un lungo weekend dedicato al rispetto ambientale e ai segreti della natura. Scelta obbligata nello Stato dell'Unione più convintamente ambientalista, e quanto mai opportuna per il battesimo di quello che già la stampa definisce il "museo più verde degli Stati Uniti", la California Academy of Sciences.

L'edificio ospita in un'unica sede dodici edifici costruiti a varie tappe in circa ottanta anni di vita, alcuni dei quali seriamente danneggiati dal terremoto del 1989 che distrusse anche i padiglioni in stile coloniale del vicino De Young Museum, ricostruito l'anno scorso su progetto degli svizzeri Herzog&deMeuron.

L'autore in questo caso è un italiano, anzi l'italiano più famoso in America visto che ha firmato in poco più di dieci anni tutte le più prestigiose istituzioni culturali del Paese, dalla sede del New York Times e della Morgan Library a New York, dal Kimbell Art Museum di Forth Worth alla Columbia University di New York: Renzo Piano.

Una «Ferrari a zero consumi e zero emissioni», la definisce Piano con ironia: un gioiello di alta tecnologia al elevato gradiente poetico, dove per la prima volta in maniera convincente la sostenibilità esce fuori dal gergo degli ecologisti e dei costruttori ediliz per entrare organicamente nell'arte del costruire. Visto da lontano, infatti, il segno distintivo del museo è una sorta di prato sospeso al posto del tetto: una leggera ondulazione di colline erbose alta circa dieci metri sul suolo, come se un lembo di parco fosse

PANNELLI SOLARI

Circondato da un bordo di vetro con 60 mila cellule fotovoltaiche (che forniscono il 5% dell'energia per illuminare) il tetto è rivestito da uno spessore di terra di un metro e mezzo e garantisce un abbassamento della temperatura all'interno di circa 10 gradi più efficiente di un normale tetto

TETTO GIARDINO

È il tratto distintivo: il tetto-giardino è parte integrante del museo perché è una serra sperimentale all'aria aperta per la coltivazione e la conservazione di specie originarie della flora californiana. La forma delle colline e modellata sui grandi volumi del Planetarium e dell'Acquarium

STRUTTURE METALLICHE

L'85% delle strutture metalliche utilizzano materiali riciclati. Persino gli scarti dei jeans sono stati impiegati con successo come materiale isolante. Uno dei motivi per cui l'edificio è stato subito definito il museo più verde degli Stati Uniti: e insignito del riconoscimento più alto in materia di sostenibilità

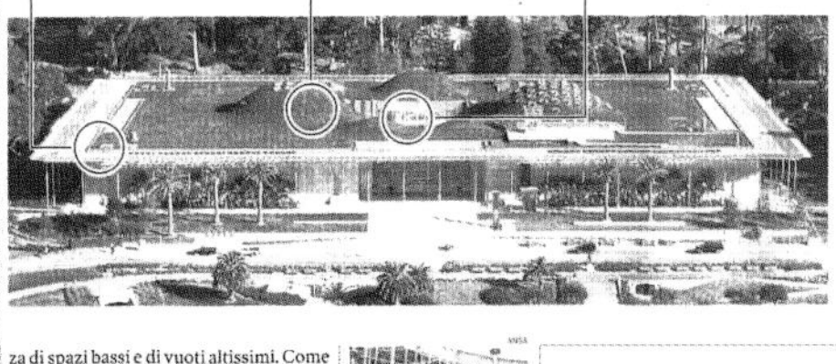

DODICI EDIFICI A EMISSIONI ZERO

L'edificio ospita in un'unica sede dodici diverse strutture costruite in circa ottanta anni e danneggiate dal terremoto del 1989. La ristrutturazione è stata commissionata a Renzo Piano dopo i danni causati dal terremoto del 1989

za di spazi bassi e di vuoti altissimi. Come al solito per Piano, l'idea di progetto non nasce mai da una forma precostituita, ma da un processo di interpretazione del luogo e di individuazione dell'anima dell'architettura.

Quando nel 1999 fu invitato a un colloquio con i curatori e il direttore del Centro, fu l'unico ad arrivare senza una presentazione del futuro lavoro: davanti allo sguardo perplesso dei suoi interlocutori, raccattò dal tavolo dei fogli di carta e, ammettendo che non aveva nessuna idea del nuovo museo, si mise a tracciare con pochi segni a matita le idee di base di un

della California, prima che l'uomo intervenisse per trasformare il suolo arido della baia in un giardino.

Nell'architettura di Piano il tetto è sempre stato una componente essenziale per la definizione degli spazi e dei volumi: nella Fondazione Bayler di Basilea, ad esempio, le sale delle collezioni sono distribuite in un vuoto interrotto, coperto da una lastra sottile di metallo e di doghe mobili, che come palpebre di un occhio si aprono e chiudono al riverbero del sole. A San Francisco il tetto è però vivente, metafora costruita di un'architettura che si presenta come un organismo capace di respirare e di trasudare: rifiutando la pratica moder-

Piano is back in stride. What he has produced is a fascinating hybrid of classicism and a romantic view of nature that stretches back to the 18th century. The original museum, a complex of 11 buildings constructed over decades in Golden Gate Park, was badly damaged by the earthquake that hit the Bay Area in 1989. While keeping some of the original Beaux Arts structure, Piano has wrapped it in a finely detailed package of glass and steel.

But what appears from the outside as a serene Cartesian box gives way inside to something ever more complicated. On either side of the building's interior "piazza" are two giant spheres, both sliced at the bottom. One is an opaque steel ball that encloses the 90-seat planetarium. The other, a glass globe, holds a multistory recreation of a rain forest. This globe, in turn, sits against a wide glass wall that looks onto the cultivated woodlands of Golden Gate Park, mingling views of rain forest and parkland until this very rational building seems just about overtaken by the natural world. "As in music," says Piano, "in architecture you always need a kind of precision, clarity, but with one condition—that you have the freedom then to destroy the whole thing."

And on its roof the Academy really is overtaken by nature. It's topped with a 2.5-acre (1-ha) field of native California plants, a "green roof" that aids in heating and cooling efficiency. The roof comes with its own topography of seven grassy humps, including two perforated by circular skylights. It's a normal terrain, full of dreamlike, fertile swells. If Antoni Gaudí had been a hobbit, he might have designed something just like it.

What all this means is that the Academy doesn't contain the world of nature. It's penetrated by it. That's good metaphor for the cooperative dealings with the environment that Piano wants his building to symbolize. He sees the project as a step toward developing what he calls "the aesthetics of sustainability," a new vocabulary of forms for a future in which green buildings will be the norm. "The 19th century was about new kinds of construction," he says. "Steel and so forth. And the 20th century created a language for that. Now architects must develop an aesthetic for our discovery about the fragility of nature." And as they do, one of the places they'll study most closely is this inspired academy—not a temple to nature but a hill that's a hill on a temple.

Renzo Piano

TIME October 13, 2008

51

La California Academy of Sciences

Lia, oggi ti racconto della California Academy of Sciences
a San Francisco. È un progetto recente, inaugurato a
settembre del 2008 dopo nove anni di lavoro. Ogni volta,
quando si inaugura un edificio, ripenso per un attimo a
quanto tempo c'è voluto per realizzarlo.
Nove anni non è male: quando va tutto bene ce ne vogliono
cinque o sei, ma quando va male possono diventare anche
venti, quindi direi che nove è un'ottima media.
Come spesso accade, tutto cominciò con una telefonata.
Era il settembre del 1999, e la telefonata mi sorprese,
come sempre, mentre facevo qualcos'altro.
Quasi tutti i miei progetti cominciano così, con un sospiro,
che sarebbe la traduzione del "ci manca anche questa!"
che penso ogni volta. Perché quando sto facendo qualcosa
ne sono preso completamente. E in questa specie di
"lunga infanzia" che è il mio mestiere mi trovo spesso a
lavorare su un progetto, ad esserne completamente assorbito,
e a reagire con diffidenza alle nuove proposte.
Si trattava di una selezione tra più architetti, fra i quali
avrebbero poi scelto a chi affidare il progetto.
"Selezione" significa che, a differenza che nel caso di
concorso, gli architetti chiamati a partecipare non devono
presentare un progetto, ma sono valutati in base ai lavori già
svolti e ad una serie di incontri preliminari.
In questo caso, ad accompagnare il dossier con la proposta di
partecipare alla selezione, arrivarono delle immagini terribili
del museo com'era allora: un insieme di 12 diversi edifici,
costruiti fra il 1916 e il 1991 all'interno del Golden Gate Park.
Appariva come una serie di blocchi posizionati malamente,
in gran parte distrutti o molto danneggiati dal terremoto
del 1989, che poi fu la ragione che spinse le istituzioni ad
occuparsi del museo.
Il 17 ottobre 1989, San Francisco fu colpita da un terribile
terremoto che prese il nome dal luogo dell'epicentro, Loma
Prieta, una montagna a pochi chilometri da Santa Cruz.
La maggior parte degli edifici che costituivano l'Academy
era danneggiata, e la scena del Goden Gate Park,
con al centro il museo, devo dire che appariva disperata.
La proposta non era quella di rifare completamente il museo,
ma era piuttosto una sfida a porsi il problema di cosa fare
in una circostanza del genere, di come reagire.
Insomma, il progetto cominciò così, con un certo distacco,
e con la consapevolezza che in quel momento in studio c'era
troppo da fare; stavamo già lavorando molto e non ci sarebbe
stato il tempo per un altro progetto.
Poi quello che cambiò tutto fu un fatto completamente
estraneo al progetto.

The California Academy of Sciences

Lia, today I am going to tell you about
the California Academy of Sciences in San Francisco.
It is a recent project, inaugurated in September 2008
after nine years' work. Every time I inaugurate a building,
I think for a minute about how long it took to complete.
Nine years is not bad. It takes five or six when
everything goes smoothly but that can rise to twenty.
I'd say nine years is a good average.
As so often happens, it started with a phone call. It came
in September 1999 and as always, I was busy with something
else. Almost all my projects start with a sigh of resignation,
an outward manifestation of the "that's all we need!"
running through my mind. When I am busy doing something,
I get completely wrapped up in it. In the extended childhood
that is my craft, I am often working on a project I get so caught
up in that I am very reluctant to entertain new proposals.
This one was a selection process involving a number of
architects, one of whom would then be entrusted with the
project. A selection, as opposed to a competition, means that
the architects invited do not have to present a project.
Instead, they are evaluated on the basis of work they have
already done, and on a series of preliminary meetings.
In this case, the dossier with the invitation to take part in the
selection was accompanied by a number of alarming photos
of how the museum looked at the time. The twelve separate
buildings, constructed in the Golden Gate Park between 1916
and 1991, looked like blocks put together randomly.
Many had been badly damaged during the 1989 earthquake,
which was in fact what had prompted the local authorities
to turn their attention to the museum.
On 17 October 1989, San Francisco was hit by a terrible
tremor that was named after the site of its epicentre, Loma
Prieta, a mountain a few kilometres from Santa Cruz.
Most of the Academy buildings had been damaged and the
Golden Gate Park, with the museum at its heart, was a
depressing spectacle. It was not so much a proposal to rebuild
the entire museum as a challenge.
What should be the response in these circumstances?
In any case, we went into the project with a certain air of
detachment and the knowledge that we had too much to do in
the studio just then. There was a lot of work; we were already
working hard and we really couldn't handle another project.
But that soon changed thanks to an event that had nothing to
do with the project.
At the time, I was organising a trip with you. You will
remember that we had been toying with the idea of a trip
round the world and a visit to San Francisco slotted neatly in.

In quel momento stavo organizzando un viaggio con te, se ti ricorderai avevo già da un po' di tempo l'idea di fare un giro del mondo insieme, e ci stava bene una tappa a San Francisco. Spesso le storie cominciano così, in maniera abbastanza casuale. Non è che avessimo elaborato un piano straordinariamente intelligente: i tempi coincidevano, e San Francisco era più o meno sulla rotta per poi procedere verso altri luoghi: l'Australia, la Nuova Caledonia, il Giappone.

E poi devo dire che andare a curiosare mi attirava, anche se le foto mi avevano spaventato. Così siamo partiti e ci siamo fermati a San Francisco per due o tre giorni.

C'erano anche altri invitati alla selezione: ricordo benissimo che la sera del nostro arrivo cenammo con Richard Rogers, che è uno dei miei più cari amici, e il giorno successivo andammo a fare un giro sul sito.

Mi sembra che fosse una domenica; siamo andati al museo in incognito, come visitatori qualsiasi, guardandoci intorno, osservando e cercando di capire.

Allora io non lo sapevo, ma era sottinteso che gli invitati a questo incontro portassero qualcosa, tanto è vero che il giorno dopo venni a sapere che le altre équipes arrivarono con dei progetti, con delle proposte. Forse non è esatto dire che non lo sapevo: più esattamente facevo finta di non saperlo.

Ho sempre avuto una certa diffidenza verso l'idea di fare schizzi come in un concorso di bellezza, e sono sempre stato resistente all'idea di fare un progetto senza aver visto il sito. Quindi noi ce ne andammo semplicemente in giro, visitando, guardando, facendo delle osservazioni magari anche abbastanza epidermiche.

Innanzitutto osservazioni sul tempo: San Francisco nel quadro del microclima californiano è particolarmente fortunata, perché ha un clima mite, non freddo d'inverno e non troppo caldo d'estate, con un tasso di umidità piuttosto elevato soprattutto di notte. L'escursione termica tra il mese più freddo e quello più caldo è di 8°, quella giornaliera varia da 6 a 8 gradi. Gli inverni sono miti e piovosi, le estati secche, fredde e nebbiose. E il cuore verde di San Francisco è il Golden Gate, un bellissimo parco lussureggiante.

Ma è così verde perché estrae l'acqua dalla falda freatica sotterranea. In California non c'è molta acqua in superficie, è sostanzialmente un deserto, e se c'è la vegetazione è perché l'acqua viene estratta dal sottosuolo.

Questi dati sono molto importanti, perché senza i capricci del clima di San Francisco un edificio come la California Academy of Sciences non si sarebbe neppure potuto ipotizzare.

Quando arrivai al Golden Gate Park scoprii anche, ma in effetti c'era da aspettarselo, che l'idea di lavorare alla nuova Academy era affascinante. Intanto perché un museo di scienze è sempre un luogo straordinario.

E poi per la storia di questa istituzione, nata più di 150 anni fa. Nella bella stagione gli scienziati navigavano su una goletta, che si chiamava proprio Academy, e raccoglievano le specie vegetali e animali; d'inverno invece tornavano a San Francisco, attraccavano al molo e la goletta diventava un museo. Gli scienziati che durante l'estate erano stati esploratori si trasformavano, durante l'inverno, in educatori, in divulgatori delle scienze naturali.

That's the way it is sometimes. Things happen in a fairly random fashion. It is not as if we had drawn up a particularly well thought-out plan but the timing matched and San Francisco was more or less on our way to other destinations, like Australia, New Caledonia and Japan.

And I have to say that I was curious, although the photographs had looked intimidating. In the end, we left and stopped over at San Francisco for a couple of days.

Other architects had been invited. I can clearly remember that on the evening we arrived, one of my dearest friends, Richard Rogers, was with us for dinner. The next day, we went to visit the site together. It must have been a Sunday and we went to see the museum like ordinary visitors, looking around us, observing and trying to understand.

I did not know it at the time but the architects invited were supposed to bring something with them. The next day I found out that the other groups had come with plans and proposals. Or rather, it was not really true that that I did not know. I was pretending not to know.

I have always had mixed feelings about doing sketches for beauty contests and I have always hated the idea of drafting a project without visiting the site. So we just went around visiting, looking and making our probably rather superficial observations.

Especially about the weather. In the Californian context, San Francisco is blessed with a particularly mild climate, which is not too cold in winter and warm in summer with high humidity, particularly at night. The temperature variation between the coldest month and the warmest is 8 °C and fluctuations during the day are 6-8 °C. Winters are mild and rainy and the summers are dry, cool and foggy.

The green heart of San Francisco is the Golden Gate, a wonderfully luxuriant park. But the Golden Gate is lush because it draws water from the aquifer. There is not a lot of groundwater in California, which is basically a desert, and what vegetation there is exists because it sucks moisture from below ground. All this is important because without the particularities of San Francisco's climate, a building on the lines of the California Academy of Sciences would have been inconceivable. When I finally went to Golden Gate Park, I discovered that the idea of working on a new Academy was intriguing, although I should have realised this in advance. A science museum is always a fantastic place.

Then there was the history of this museum, founded 150 years ago. In the summertime, the scientists took to the high seas on board of a schooner called Academy, to collect plants and animals. Back in San Francisco in winter the schooner became a floating dockside museum. Scientists who were explorers in the summer months turned into educators and popularisers of scientific knowledge.

In the late 19th century, the first museum premises were built on the corner of California and Dupont Streets, in what today is Chinatown, moving to Market Street soon afterwards. It was then in 1906 that the first of the two earthquakes that have changed the history of the Academy struck. The museum was destroyed in a catastrophic tremor and the exhibits were lost.

Alla fine del 1800 costruirono la loro primissima sede, all'angolo tra California and Dupont Streets, quella che è oggi Chinatown, e poco dopo si trasferirono in Market Street. E qui compare il primo dei due terremoti che hanno cambiato la storia della Academy: nel 1906 il museo venne distrutto da un terribile sisma, e la collezione andò perduta.

Il museo ricostruì la straordinaria raccolta di specie proprio grazie alla nave Academy e alle spedizioni alle Galapagos che si succedettero negli anni seguenti.

Ed è a questo punto che il museo si trasferì nel Golden Gate Park: i primi edifici, la North American Hall e lo Steinhart Aquarium, furono costruiti fra il 1910 e il 1920, e fu in qualche modo l'organizzarsi a terra della nave. Nei decenni successivi si aggiunsero prima l'African Hall e il Morrison Planetarium, poi tutti gli edifici che andarono a costituire la "little town" della California Academy of Sciences.

Ma lo spirito era ancora quello, i ricercatori che diventavano divulgatori. Mi ricordo che anche quella domenica, durante la nostra prima visita, attraverso i vetri delle classrooms si vedevano i laboratori pieni di persone intente a discutere.

E poi l'indomani, nella discussione con il board, scoprii che questa era una delle abitudini della Academy: gli scienzati ogni tanto si trasformavano in insegnanti e parlavano delle proprie scoperte. E lo facevano in modo semplice e naturale, senza troppa prosopopea.

Il primo incontro con il board, che avvenne il giorno seguente, fu un momento memorabile. Mi ricordo che arrivai da solo, ed entrai in questa sala molto grande (è un luogo che poi imparai a conoscere molto bene perché lì si tennero tutte le riunioni nel corso del progetto).

C'erano i tavoli messi in circolo, come ad un esame, ed io avrei dovuto sedermi nel mezzo ed esporre le mie idee. Cominciai subito con il chiedere se si poteva cambiare la disposizione, e unire i tavoli per sederci tutt'attorno a lavorare. Questo mio debutto divenne, nel corso del progetto, un aneddoto molto raccontato e forse anche un po' mitizzato. Devo dire che fui subito piacevolmente sorpreso dal capire che il capo del board era Patrick Kociolek, uno scienziato che poi ha seguito il progetto per quattro o cinque anni. Patrick è uno specialista in diatomee – che sono minuscole alghe, microrganismi unicellulari – ed è significativo che fosse uno scienziato ad essere incaricato del progetto, e non un esperto di pubbliche relazioni, o un uomo d'affari. Infatti aveva la capacità di concentrazione tipica degli scienzati, ed era inoltre un formidabile difensore naturale della commistione tra ricercatori ed educatori.

Perché il rischio sempre in agguato è quello di separare le funzioni: da una parte coloro che vivono la dimensione della ricerca, con i suoi tempi lunghissimi, e dall'altra quelli che si occupano solo di mettere questo sapere in mostra.

È il destino di molti musei di storia naturale o di scienza, che sono spesso istituzioni in cui i ricercatori vivono altrove, lavorano nelle università o nei centri di ricerca, e lasciano al museo un ruolo statico.

Una dicotomia particolarmente pericolosa nel caso della Academy, perché rischiava di distruggere la ragione stessa per cui questa istituzione è stata grande.

Thanks to the voyages of the Academy to the Galapagos Islands in subsequent years, the museum was able to rebuild its marvellous collection.

The next move was to Golden Gate Park. First, the North American Hall and the Steinhart Aquarium were built between 1910 and 1920 to recreate the Academy's ship-borne collection on dry land. Over subsequent decades, they were joined first by the African Hall and the Morrison Planetarium, and then by all the other buildings that made up "the little town" of the California Academy of Science.

But the spirit of the place remained unchanged: the scientists continued to be popularisers.

I remember looking through the windows on the Sunday of our first visit and seeing laboratories packed with people engaged in passionate discussions.

The following day, which was when the interview with the board of trustees was scheduled, I found out that one of the Academy's traditions is for the scientists to put on a teacher's hat every so often and talk about their discoveries. They were doing so unaffectedly and quite naturally, without a trace of self-importance.

That first meeting with the board the next morning was memorable. As I recall, I arrived on my own and walked into this huge room, a space I would come to know very well because during the project all our meetings were held there. The tables had been arranged in a circle and I was supposed to sit in a chair in the middle and explain my ideas, like an examination candidate. The first thing I did was to ask if we could move the tables so we could sit round them and work together. As the project went on, this story did the rounds and might even have become part of the museum's mythology.

I have to say that I was pleasantly surprised to discover that the board was chaired by Patrick Kociolek, who then monitored the project for four or five years.

Patrick specialises in diatoms, which are minute unicellular organisms, and it is significant that a scientist, not a PR expert or a businessperson, was put in charge of the project.

He had the scientist's trademark powers of concentration and was also a formidable champion of scientists' dual role as researchers and educators.

There is always a risk of separating the two functions, putting researchers and their extended schedule on one side, and those whose main concern is presenting the researchers' findings to the public on the other one.

This is the dilemma of many museums of natural history or science, which are often institutions whose researchers live somewhere else, work in universities or research centres and leave the museum with only a static role.

Such a rift would be particularly dangerous for the Academy, where it would undermine the very characteristics that made it such a great institution. This was one of the things that attracted me: having as my interlocutors scientists who were also involved in kindling the scientific curiosity of young people. As we know, natural science museums are very popular with youngsters. But they are not the only fans for I could also see lots of elderly people through the classroom windows that Sunday morning.

Per me questa fu una delle ragioni di interesse: il fatto di avere come interlocutori scienziati che si occupassero anche di far nascere la curiosità scientifica nei giovani, nei ragazzi. Com'è noto i musei di scienze naturali sono molto amati dai giovani, dai bambini. Ma non solo, tanto è vero che dietro i vetri di quelle classrooms, quella domenica, mi ricordo di aver visto anche numerose persone anziane.

Uno scienziato "vero" sa quanto è importante, dopo la ricerca, il trasferire questa passione per la conoscenza della natura anche nei giovani. La mattina della riunione, prima ancora di iniziare il colloquio, si fece una visita guidata del museo. Fui molto colpito dai depositi in cui, lungo corridoi infiniti, erano custodite le venti milioni di specie che costituiscono la collezione.

Venti milioni!

E mi ricordo che Patrick Kociolek, di fronte al mio stupore per quella cifra immensa, mi disse che rappresentava circa il 5% delle specie viventi sulla terra, e che quindi era ancora piuttosto lungo il cammino degli scienziati.

A dire il vero mi spiegò anche che le specie di cui ancora non si sa niente sono per la maggior parte quelle invisibili all'occhio umano, o che vivono nelle profondità degli oceani.

Questa breve visita dell'edificio, prima giù nei meandri del sottosuolo e poi su fino al tetto, fu ispiratrice, intanto perché fece nascere in me la consapevolezza che questa grande istituzione dovesse continuare a vivere in maniera "combinata". Cioé combinando la lentezza metodica e sistematica tipica della ricerca – che è un po' la lentezza del guardare l'erba crescere, e non può essere essa stessa l'oggetto dell'insegnamento – con la dimensione educativa, che è naturalmente più rapida, è un lavoro di sintesi che non manca di fascino, quando non è didascalica o noiosa.

Questa cosa fu subito chiara, anche se non la razionalizzai immediatamente.

Le due scoperte più importanti, ripensando oggi a quella prima visita, furono proprio queste: la discesa nelle riserve sotterranee, con le venti milioni di specie che mi guardavano dai corridoi, e la salita sul tetto. Perché camminando sul tetto capii come il nuovo museo, comunque lo si fosse fatto, avrebbe dovuto volare sul parco, mantenendo più o meno la stessa quota del tetto esistente.

La media degli edifici del sito era intorno agli 11, 12 metri, con alcuni elementi che uscivano fuori, ad esempio il Planetario, che pur essendo piuttosto piccolo era troppo grande per essere contenuto nell'edificio.

Ricordo che dal tetto si capiva la magia potenziale di quel luogo, anche se gli edifici erano danneggiati e l'insieme appariva piuttosto sconclusionato. Gli alberi del Golden Gate Park sono altissimi, arrivano a trenta, quaranta metri; quindi, nonostante fossimo sul tetto, eravamo immersi nel verde, ed in lontananza si vedevano le colline e buona parte della città di San Francisco.

E quando si alza la nebbia tipica di San Francisco e nasconde gli alberi si ha l'impressione di essere in un mondo fantastico.

La riunione fu molto rivelatrice.

Come ho già accennato io non avevo preparato niente, e non per una decisione consapevole, presa a tavolino, ma perché mi

The true scientist knows that transmitting a passion for exploring nature to young people is only second in importance to research. Before the meeting began that Sunday morning, there was a guided tour of the museum. I was very impressed by the storage areas, the endless corridors lined with rooms where the collection's twenty million species were kept. Twenty million!

When I expressed amazement at this staggering number, Patrick Kociolek told me that they represented about five per cent of all the species living on the planet, and that science still had plenty more to discover. Actually, he also told me that most of the species we still know nothing about are either invisible to the human eye or live in the depths of the oceans.

The brief tour of the building, from its underground passageways up to the roof, was a revelation. It inspired in me the conviction that this great museum had to continue to be a twofold institution. Combining the slow, methodical pace of research, (like watching grass grow, for example, which is not suitable for teaching) with the dimension of education which is of course more accelerated.

This labour of synthesis has a fascination of its own, if it can avoid becoming over-didactic or boring. I grasped this at once, although it was some time before I worked out the details.

When I think back to that first visit, my two most important discoveries were going down to the underground storage areas, with twenty million species peering at me from the corridors, and (going up onto the roof. As I walked across the roof, I realised that the new museum, no matter how it was designed, would have to float over the park at more or less the same height as the existing roof. The average height of the buildings in the complex was eleven or twelve metres but some features stood proud. The relatively small Planetarium, for example, was too tall to fit inside the building.

From the roof, you could feel the magical potential of the place, even though the buildings were damaged and the complex as a whole looked pretty shapeless. The trees in Golden Gate Park are very high, standing to thirty or forty metres tall, and even up on the roof we were in the midst of trees. In the distance, I could make out the hills and much of the city of San Francisco.

When the city's signature fog rises and hides the trees, you feel as if you are in a fantasy world.

The meeting was a revelation. As I said, I hadn't prepared anything. It wasn't a conscious decision I had made in advance; it just seemed the right thing to do. I started to think out loud, mulling over what I had found out during the visit, and in particular looking at my interlocutors and asking them what they had in mind.

The first thing they told me was that they hadn't yet decided whether to rebuild the whole complex or only some of the buildings. The board had a dozen or so members, some of whom thought that everything should be demolished while others favoured an almost surgically precise intervention on individual buildings. An architect might help them also understand what would the implications of each position actually were. Straight away, I said that they should conserve as many buildings as possible.

sembrava che fosse giusto fare così. Cominciai a ragionare a voce alta, dicendo le cose che avevo capito durante la visita, e soprattutto guardando ed interrogando i miei interlocutori su cosa avessero in mente.

La prima cosa che mi dissero è che non avevano ancora deciso se rifare tutto o intervenire solo su alcuni edifici.

Nel board, che era costituito da una dozzina di persone, c'era chi pensava che si dovesse distruggere tutto, e chi invece credeva che fosse meglio intervenire quasi chirurgicamente su ciascuno degli edifici.

Un architetto serviva anche a capire meglio le conseguenze di quelle loro posizioni. Io dissi subito che si sarebbe dovuto tentare di mantenere quanti più edifici fosse possibile, perché da buon europeo portavo avanti un discorso di difesa della memoria.

Ricordo una persona piuttosto anziana che mi disse di avere l'abitudine di portare al museo il nipotino, ma di essere stato al museo anche da padre, e molti anni prima, da bambino.

Qualcuno cominciò a capire che il tema della memoria non era un argomento accademico, ma era reale, legato al ruolo rituale che il museo ha sempre avuto nella città di San Francisco.

L'ipotesi di mantenere alcuni edifici e non demolirli aveva a che fare con l'idea di una città che si trasforma, che muta e che cresce non distruggendo completamente, ma stratificando.

Sto parlando di un edificio isolato, nel mezzo del Golden Gate Park, e non di una intera città, ma in qualche modo il museo stesso era una piccola città, costituita da 12 edifici separati, tanto è vero che aveva una piazza al centro.

Proprio così: tutti questi edifici erano cresciuti lentamente attorno ad un quadrato, che era una specie di piazza a cielo aperto. Il tema della memoria non era solo un tema di convenienza pratica e pragmatica, ma aveva anche a che fare con la ritualità di questo luogo.

Perché tutti a San Francisco, da quelli che hanno sei anni a quelli che ne hanno novanta, ricordano gli alligatori nella palude dell'acquario.

Insomma, la riunione era stata organizzata per interrogarmi, ma è finita che fui io ad interrogare loro.

Un altro tema molto dibattuto fu l'idea di tenere insieme, nello stesso luogo, i ricercatori e gli educatori. Io senza neppure pensarci su dissi: "ma certamente!".

Capii solo dopo che almeno la metà delle persone che erano lì la pensava esattamente all'opposto, ma ormai l'avevo fatta…

Poi cominciai a dire che, almeno per i primi sei mesi, avrei voluto concentrare il lavoro sulla valutazione di cosa si sarebbe dovuto tenere, attraverso un procedimento molto pragmatico. Gli edifici dopo il terremoto del 1989 erano stati divisi in 5 categorie a seconda del livello di danneggiamento subito. Gli edifici del gruppo 1 erano solo leggermente rovinati, ma quelli del gruppo 5 erano completamente persi, e andavano assolutamente demoliti.

La maggior parte degli edifici che componevano il museo andavano dalla classe 3 alla 5. Una cosa che capii subito è che avrei tenuto la piazza, "the Piazza", così poi battezzata in italiano, che è il punto dove si raccordano tutti i padiglioni che compongono il museo. È l'elemento fondatore di tutto, il vuoto che conta più dei pieni.

As a good European, I nailed my colours to the mast in defence of memory. One rather elderly gentleman told me he liked to bring his grandson to the museum and that many years before, his own father had brought him. Gradually, the members began to realise that memory is not just an academic concept. It is real and bound up with the role the museum has always played in San Francisco's urban rituals. Conserving some of the buildings instead of knocking everything down ties in with the idea of a constantly changing city that grows layer upon layer, not by destroying the past.

I am talking about an isolated building in the middle of Golden Gate Park, not a whole city, but in a sense the museum itself was a little town of twelve separate buildings.

That's right. And all these buildings had grown up around a square, a sort of open-air Italian-style piazza.

Memory was not merely just practical or pragmatic issue. It also had to do with the rituals of this special place.

Everyone in San Francisco between the ages of six and ninety has seen the alligators in the aquarium swamp.

To put it another way, the meeting had been organised so that the board could quiz me, but in the end it was me who asked the questions. Another issue that provoked lively discussion was the idea of locating researchers and educators in the same place. Almost without thinking, I said: "Absolutely!"

Only later did I realise that half of the people there had precisely the opposite opinion but by then the die was cast.

Then I started to say that for the first six months at least I would have to concentrate on the job of working out what should be kept, using very pragmatic criteria. After the 1989 earthquake, buildings in the city had been classified into five categories, according to how badly they had been damaged. Buildings in category one had suffered only slight damage while those in category five were beyond repair and due for demolition. Most of the museum's buildings were in categories three, four or five.

One thing that was immediately obvious was that the plaza would have to stay. Named "the Piazza", it is the hub around which the museum's pavilions are deployed.

The Piazza is the heart of the entire concept, a space that has more significance than any of the volumes. This point of view, which I put forward at the first meeting, made a fairly big impression and nearly all the members approved.

That Sunday, we started to lay down a few ground rules.

It was all a bit like tackling a complicated mathematical equation with too many variables. The first thing to do was remove some of them and try to understand the core issues.

Something else I said from the first was that the roof of the new building would have to be roughly where the old one was, at the height of about ten metres.

There was also the problem of the Planetarium and the Biosphere. It doesn't take long to work out that you can't put a rain forest with thirty metre-tall trees inside a building with ten-metre ceilings. You're going to need somewhere at least three times as high.

The same went for the new Planetarium, which unlike the old optical one, would have a state-of-the-art digital system. Nor would it be used only to project the stars.

Questa riflessione, che feci già durante il primo incontro, li colpì abbastanza, più o meno tutti trovarono che fosse giusta. Quel giorno cominciammo a fissare alcune cose.

Era un po' come avere davanti un'equazione matematica troppo complicata, con troppe variabili: la prima cosa da fare è toglierne alcune in modo da riuscire a capirci un po' di più. Un'altra cosa che dissi subito è che il tetto del nuovo edificio avrebbe dovuto essere più o meno dov'era quello originario, ovvero più o meno a 10 metri.

C'era però il problema del Planetario e della Biosfera: ci vuole poco a capire che non si può riprodurre una foresta pluviale con alberi che raggiungono i 30 metri in un edificio alto 10, ci vuole un'altezza almeno tripla.

Lo stesso valeva per il nuovo Planetario, che a differenza di quello esistente non avrebbe avuto un sistema ottico ma un sistema digitale, che è più attuale. E non sarebbe servito soltanto a proiettare le stelle, ma anche a far vedere l'interno del corpo umano, o la profondità del mare. Fu subito chiaro che il Planetario, se volevamo che contenesse 300 o 400 persone, aveva bisogno di un'altezza di 20 metri.

Allora nacque il primissimo schizzo, che poi è diventato in qualche modo il simbolo di questo progetto: è una specie di diagramma in cui disegnai il tetto all'altezza, più o meno, di quello esistente, con curve a salire e a scendere.

Nel pomeriggio stesso andai a misurare l'altezza dell'edificio, e scoprii che eravamo a 35 piedi (che corrispondono a 10 metri abbondanti). E quindi capii subito che quell'altezza non sarebbe bastata, per cui fatalmente il tetto avrebbe dovuto salire e scendere, come d'altronde faceva già nell'edificio originale. Qualcuno del board alla fine della riunione andò sul tetto a controllare quello che avevo detto.

E scoprirono che era vero: la cupola del Planetario, che allora era coperta di bizzarre tegole rosse, spuntava fuori. Ed era un po' la prefigurazione di quella curva che io avevo appena disegnato.

Quindi quel giorno, più che un vero e proprio colloquio, feci un lungo ragionamento con loro, ed in questo ragionamento c'era di tutto: c'erano silenzi e titubanze, pentimenti e rivelazioni improvvise.

Tutto cominciò così, e poi fummo scelti per fare il progetto. In seguito venni a sapere che Norman Foster, (che è un architetto straordinario, beninteso) arrivò con una manciata di assistenti, ed un paio di giorni prima dell'incontro fece un sopralluogo in elicottero, per fotografare il sito.

Arrivarono all'appuntamento con il progetto praticamente finito. Non che questo sia sbagliato, per carità, però chi era alla riunione mi disse, che loro più che di una soluzione avevano bisogno di discutere, di capire.

Questo la dice lunga sul fatto che in architettura il dialogo con il cliente, il confronto, il desiderio di capire, l'arte dell'ascoltare e di dibattere (che non coincide con l'arte di trovarsi d'accordo, anzi...) sono molto importanti.

Insomma, vincemmo la selezione e cominciammo a lavorare. Non fu tutto facile.

Il progetto si fece nel nostro ufficio di Punta Nave, a Genova. Mark Carroll è stato il responsabile insieme a Shunji Ishida e Olaf de Nooyer. Per almeno due o tre anni abbiamo lavorato

The new Planetarium would also show the innards of the human body and the abysses of the oceans. It was obvious that if we wanted the Planetarium to hold three or four hundred people, it would have to be twenty metres high.

At that point, I did my very first sketch, which later became the project's symbol. It's diagrammatic and shows a sweepingly curved roof roughly as high as the previous one.

That afternoon, I measured the building's height, which turned out to be thirty-five feet, or just over ten metres. Clearly, that was not going to be high enough so the roof would have to rise and fall, as in fact it had in the original edifice. After the meeting, one or two board members went onto the roof to check.

It was true. The dome of the Planetarium, at that time clad in bizarre red tiles, protruded from the roof in what was a precursor of the curve I had just sketched. It wasn't so much an interview that Sunday morning as a leisurely exchange of ideas that had a bit of everything, including silences, hesitations, changes of mind and flashes of inspiration.

That's how it all started. We were selected for the project. Afterwards, I discovered that Norman Foster, who is of course an outstanding architect, had arrived with a gaggle of assistants and, a couple of days before the meeting, made a site inspection by helicopter to photograph the location.

Foster's group had turned up with a project that was almost complete. Obviously, there's nothing wrong with this. However, some of those present at the meeting told me that they did not so much need a "ready made" project as to talk things over and acquire insight.

This is highly significant. In architecture, dialogue with the client is very important. It is all about exchanging points of view, wanting to understand and the arts of listening and debating, which is not the same thing as saying "yes" to everything. So, we were selected and got down to work. But it wasn't all plain sailing. The project was drafted at our Punta Nave offices in Genoa. Mark Carroll was in charge, flanked by Shunji Ishida and Olaf de Nooyer. For at least two or three years, we worked just on the plans. There were difficult moments, when someone would come back to us with the old story of making the functions distinct and try to persuade us to build a research centre and a separate exhibition space. Tempers rose over this. Patrick Kociolek threatened to resign and I sided with him, saying I would walk out as well.

This is how it is with projects. Everything seems to be going smoothly but there are moments of high drama when catastrophe looms. Working on the California Academy of Sciences enabled me to meet a lot of interesting people, including city officials, who tended to defend the park. Remember that this is San Francisco, the city that was environmentalism's incubator and the place that in the late 19th century saw the foundation of the Sierra Club, America's oldest, most influential ecology organisation.

In fact, the museum might never have been built if it hadn't been in San Francisco, a city that has always been green-friendly and championed sustainability. There is a feeling for nature in San Francisco, where sea lions swim undisturbed in the bay and no one would dream of hunting them.

solo alla progettazione. E ci sono stati anche momenti molto difficili, in cui qualcuno tornò alla carica con la vecchia storia della separazione delle funzioni, proponendoci di fare da una parte un centro per la ricerca, e da un'altra un edificio per la mostra. E lì si scatenò un pandemonio: Patrick Kociolek minacciò di dare le dimissioni, e io lo seguii dichiarando che avrei lasciato il progetto. Perché nei progetti è così, apparentemente è tutto liscio, ma nella realtà ci sono momenti drammatici in cui rasenti la catastrofe.

Lavorare a questo progetto mi ha permesso anche di conoscere molte persone interessanti, compresi i rappresentanti della città, che erano in qualche modo i "difensori" del parco. Ricordiamoci che siamo a San Francisco, città che è stata l'incubatrice dell'ambientalismo, dove alla fine del 1800 nacque il Sierra Club, la più antica e importante organizzazione ecologista degli Stati Uniti.

Se non si fosse trattato di San Francisco, una città che da sempre insegue la sostenibilità e un profondo rapporto con il verde, forse questo edificio non si sarebbe fatto. C'è una vocazione per la natura, basta pensare che nella baia i leoni marini nuotano indisturbati senza che nessuno si sia mai sognato di cacciarli. Questo è il livello di legame con la natura, e questa è la città di San Francisco.

La prima fase di ogni progetto comprende un lavoro che definirei "politico", ed uso questo termine nella sua accezione più alta e nobile, come momento di apertura verso l'interlocutore. Iniziai a conoscere più approfonditamente i nostri partner, e con alcuni di loro nacque in qualche modo un'amicizia, come con John Mc Cosker.

Ricordo un'indimenticabile telefonata con John, che ad un certo punto mi avvisò che entro breve sarebbe caduta la linea; io credevo che stesse entrando in una galleria, ed invece mi disse che si stava immergendo in batiscafo, ed oltre una certa profondità il cellulare avrebbe perso campo.

Ci sono tante storie legate ai ricercatori, alcune drammatiche, finite male.

Mi ricordo di aver conosciuto uno di loro mentre era convalescente dal morso di un cobra. Era un cobra di una specie nota, e poiché i ricercatori viaggiano sempre portandosi dietro gli antidoti, poterono intervenire. Ma qualche mese dopo ripartì per una nuova spedizione nella foresta della Nuova Guinea, e scoprì un cobra fino ad allora sconosciuto. La bella notizia è che avevano aggiunto una specie in più ai 20 milioni della loro collezione, ma la pessima notizia era che, essendo un cobra sconosciuto, non esisteva ancora nessun antidoto. Il ricercatore fu morso dal cobra e morì.

È una storia terribile, ma aiuta a capire il lavoro dei ricercatori: sono persone che sacrificano la vita alla ricerca, hanno una sorta di ostinazione, di passione feroce per scoprire i segreti della Terra. È anche il senso dell'avventura che li spinge ad andare avanti...

Questa storia non la racconto per il gusto dell'aneddoto, ma perché ha rinforzato in me la convinzione che la conoscenza della natura e la consapevolezza della sua fragilità sono elementi importanti, in grado di sostanziare un progetto.

E tutti i progetti ne hanno bisogno: che si parli di una sala da concerto, che si sostanzia con la passione totale e onnivora dei

It shows how deep the relationship with nature is, and with the city of San Francisco. The first stage of any project is what I would call "political", in its noblest, most elevated sense of engagement with one's interlocutor. I also started to get to know our partners better, and struck up a friendship with some of them, like John McCosker.

There was one memorable phone call when at a certain point John told me that he was going to be cut off soon. I thought he might be going into a tunnel but he told me that he was actually in a bathyscaphe. Below a certain depth, the cell phone signal disappears.

There are so many other stories about research scientists, some of them dramatic and with unhappy endings.

Once, I met a researcher who was convalescing after a cobra bite. It was a cobra of a known species and since researchers always travel with antidotes, they'd been able to take appropriate measures. But a few months later, the same man left on another expedition to the forests of New Guinea, where he discovered a hitherto unknown species of cobra.

The good news is that the museum was able to add a new species to the twenty million in the collection but the bad, indeed tragic, news is that there was no known antidote for the cobra's poison. The snake bit the researcher, who died.

It's a dreadful story but it does help us to understand how researchers work. They sacrifice their lives for research, stubbornly and with a fierce passion, striving to unravel the Earth's mysteries.

They are also driven by a spirit of adventure. I'm not telling you this simply because it is a compelling story. It reinforced my conviction that the knowledge of nature, and an awareness of how fragile it is, are fundamental elements that can imbue a project with substance. And every project needs substance, whether it's a concert hall that draws on the all-consuming passion of musicians and music lovers, or a museum, where the passion focuses on art.

The architect's job is provide an activity with a shelter, somewhere it can feel at home. And the more powerful the activity – the more it is driven by sheer passion – the more substantial the project becomes.

There were two extremely important aspects to this project, aspects from which it derived growing momentum.

One was the presence of the researchers and their stubborn defence of the Earth, their desire to explore the planet and convey their knowledge to others while the second key aspect was the city's acknowledgement of the museum's and the Golden Gate Park's importance. It is impossible to build anything in San Francisco in less than two or three years because of the deep-rooted local custom of discussing everything. And a discussion duly took place but there was nothing pre-ordained about it. The aim wasn't to persuade one or other of the parties.

To the contrary, the aim of the discussion was to acquire understanding. It then became clear that the project had to embody the very nature of its content.

When you are planning a natural science museum in a city like San Francisco, it has to be very clear that the project is founded on the following ideas: the Earth is fragile and needs

musicisti, o di un museo, e allora la passione è quella
per l'arte. Il mestiere dell'architetto è proprio quello di dare
una casa, di provvedere un riparo ad una attività.
E più è forte quell'attività, più è spinta da una passione
smodata, più il progetto diventa sostanziale.
Ci furono due elementi di grandi importanza in questo
progetto, che gli diedero progressivamente sempre più forza.
Uno era proprio la presenza dei ricercatori con la loro
ostinazione nel difendere la Terra, nel conoscerla, nello
scoprirla e nel trasferire questa loro conoscenza agli
altri. E l'altro era la consapevolezza, da parte della città,
dell'importanza di quella istituzione e del Golden Gate Park.
Nella città di San Francisco è impossibile costruire qualcosa
in meno di due o tre anni, perché esiste una radicata
abitudine al dibattito. Ed infatti la discussione ci fu,
ma non era una discussione "furba", fatta per convincere
o per persuadere una delle parti.
Al contrario, era una discussione fatta per capire.
E allora cominciò ad essere evidente come il progetto si
dovesse sostanziare della natura stessa del contenuto.
Ed in una città di questo genere, nel progettare un museo
di scienze naturali, bisognava che venisse fuori molto
chiaramente che il progetto nasceva da questa idea:
che la Terra è fragile e va difesa, e che la natura è un mondo
ancora piuttosto sconosciuto sul quale fare luce.
Quasi immediatamente si impose anche la sfida del risparmio
energetico, tema che allora era più "europeo".
All'inizio del duemila è innegabile che fosse un argomento
più sentito in Europa; basta pensare alla nota vicenda del
protocollo di Kyoto non sottoscritto proprio dagli Stati Uniti.
Ma la California, l'ho già accennato, è sempre stata un po'
diversa dal resto degli U.S.A.
E allora presero immediatamente terreno tutti i ragionamenti
sull'energia, sul tetto "verde", dove c'erano due milioni di
piccole piante, sul sogno di non mettere l'aria condizionata,
ma di ventilare naturalmente, di usare e i pannelli solari di
nuova generazione a microcristalli.
Quindi il progetto da un lato prese forma sulla base delle
premesse che ho raccontato prima; ma subito fu chiaro che
l'edificio avrebbe dovuto diventare esso stesso "exhibit".
Anzi, doveva diventare l'exhibit numero uno, il portatore
del messaggio: dovevamo costruire un museo delle scienze
che fosse esso stesso oggetto di studio naturalistico,
un contenitore che fosse al tempo stesso contenuto.
I complici di questa fase furono gli scienziati stessi.
Ad esempio i botanici: furono loro i primi a parlarmi
di specie vegetali native che non hanno nulla a che fare
con le piante d'importazione che invadono la California.
Come ho già accennato anche il Golden Gate Park è così
lussureggiante perché l'intervento dell'uomo ha trasformato
il suolo arido della Baia in un giardino, pompando acqua
dalla falda freatica sotterranea. Ma un giorno bisognerà
pur smettere di prosciugare il sottosuolo. Dovevamo quindi
scoprire quali essenze californiane avrebbero potuto
sopravvivere sul tetto, con la semplice umidità del microclima
di San Francisco. Questa copertura "verde" e vivente era stata
pensata anche per creare una condizione climatica migliore

to be protected; and nature is still largely a mystery waiting
to be revealed. One of the first issues to come up was energy
saving, at that time still a relatively "European" concern.
In the early 2000s, energy was more pivotal to the debate in
Europe than in the United States. Look at the failure of the
US to sign the Kyoto protocol.
However as I have already said, California has always been
a little bit different from the rest of the United States.
We got straight down to the nuts and bolts of energy saving,
the living roof with more than two million small plants and
the dream of doing away with air-conditioning.
There would be natural ventilation instead, and state-of-the-
art microcrystalline solar cell-based panels. So while the
project started out with the rationale I have just outlined,
it was quickly obvious that the building itself would have to
be an "exhibit", or rather be the main exhibit. The museum
would be the message. We had to build a science museum that
would itself become a model of studio, a container that would
embody its own content.
At this stage, our collaborators were the scientists themselves.
Botanists, for instance, were the first to tell me about the
native plants, which are completely different from the
imported species that have invaded California. As I said,
the Golden Gate Park is particularly verdant because human
intervention has transformed the arid bay-area soil into a
garden by pumping water from underground.
One day, though, it will no longer be possible to drain the
subsoil. This means we had to find local Californian plants
that could survive on the roof, nourished only by the humidity
of San Francisco's climate. Our green, living roof was also
designed to create better climate-conditioning inside the
building. Obviously, a green roof retains dampness during
the night and releases it during the day. It's beautiful not
just because it is natural: there is special beauty in its high
thermal inertia. It means that a green roof does not influence
the climate of the building underneath, which can be cooled
by natural ventilation.
Initially, it really was a dream. Then we started to discuss
the idea and look at it from various perspectives, including
the criteria of the LEED system (Leadership in Energy and
Environmental Design). LEED is an American scheme widely
applied all over the world to assess a building's sustainability.
This complex system takes a wide range of parameters into
consideration, such as material recycling, energy consumption
and pollution levels.
During our discussions, it never crossed our minds we
might obtain LEED platinum certification, the very highest
level, partly because it had only been awarded for the odd
experimental project but never for a full-scale building.
As it turned out, our museum was given the award on the day
it opened. No one thought we would obtain it and I have to say
it was not our foremost thought. We shared the same concern
of the scientists, botanists and engineers who wanted to create
a significant building, emblematic of this attention to nature.
In fact, we were already working on this when we started
in 2000. For instance, our team, the researchers and the
agronomists set out to find a place with soil that had the same

all'interno dell'edificio. Perché è chiaro che un tetto verde, che si inumidisce di notte e che cede l'umidità di giorno, non solo è bello perché è naturale, ma soprattutto ha una grande inerzia termica, quindi consente di non condizionare l'edificio sottostante, che potrà essere rinfrescato dalla ventilazione naturale.

All'inizio era davvero un sogno, ma poi cominciammo a ragionare anche sulla base del sistema LEED (Leadership in Energy and Environmental Design). Si tratta di un criterio americano, oggi molto diffuso anche nel resto del mondo, per misurare la sostenibilità di un edificio. È un sistema complesso, che considera molti diversi parametri: il riciclo dei materiali, il consumo di energia, i livelli di inquinamento.

Allora non avremmo mai sperato di ottenere il "platinum", il livello più alto in assoluto. Anche perché nessuno ci era ancora riuscito con un edificio "importante", ma soltanto con qualche esperimento. Alla fine, il giorno dell'apertura, l'edifico ottenne il riconoscimento.

Nessuno ci sperava, ma devo dire che non era quella la nostra maggiore preoccupazione.

Piuttosto condividevamo con scienziati, botanici e ingegneri il desiderio di fare un edificio che fosse "significativo", che fosse esso stesso emblema di questa attenzione verso la natura. E quindi cominciammo, già nel 2000, a lavorare su questo. Ad esempio, insieme ai ricercatori e agli agronomi, cercammo un terreno che avesse lo stesso identico microclima del nostro sito. E in questo terreno, a una ventina di miglia dal Golden Gate Park, iniziammo a testare le essenze che sarebbero state utilizzate per piantumare il tetto.

Cominciammo con venti o trenta specie diverse, per poi arrivare a nove. Sono le essenze che possono sopravvivere sul tetto senza innaffiatura.

E questo è importante, perché la vegetazione della California è questa, e non ha bisogno di pompare acqua dal suolo per sopravvivere. Queste specie furono poi piantate sul tetto del museo, erano un milione e settecentomila, tutte messe in "vassoi" di un materiale perfettamente organico che dopo la radicazione spariscono e diventano terra.

Questa scelta assunse poi grande importanza, e tutta la lunga ricerca delle essenze giuste fu premiata il giorno dell'apertura, come vedremo. Forse posso spiegare il tetto con un'immagine: è un prato sospeso nel cuore del Golden Gate Park.

Come se un lembo del parco fosse stato tagliato con un cutter e sollevato a circa dieci metri di altezza, per farci scivolare sotto l'edificio. Alcune delle funzioni del museo sono troppo alte, per cui sollevano il tetto.

Altre devono essere più basse, pensiamo alla piazza, ed ecco allora che il tetto sprofonda e diventa una piazza aperta, ventilata naturalmente ed esposta alla pioggia. Quindi quest'idea del tetto vegetale ha a che fare con tanti ambiti: con la storia topografica e geografica di San Francisco e della California, con la memoria dei luoghi, con l'eredità di chi ha abitato quella terra da nativo, con la scienza, con l'energia.

Ma ha a che fare, soprattutto, con questa indomita voglia di scoprire che è quella tipica dei ricercatori.

characteristics as the terrain of our site. On this location, about twenty miles from Golden Gate Park, we started experimenting with species to plant on the roof. Gradually, we whittled the initial twenty or thirty down to just nine species, the ones that could survive on the roof without irrigation. It's a crucial point because California's vegetation is like that. It doesn't need to suck water from the ground to survive. One million seven hundred thousand examples of these species were then planted on the roof in biodegradable organic trays that would break down into soil when the plants took root.

The choice was pivotal. All our efforts to find the right plants were rewarded on the opening day, as we shall see. Perhaps I can explain the roof with an image: like a meadow suspended over the heart of the Golden Gate Park. It looks as if a piece of the park has been cut away and lifted about ten metres above the ground to slide the museum underneath. Some of the museum's spaces are higher than this so the roof rises. Others, like the Piazza, need to be lower so the roof descends to become an open, naturally ventilated square exposed to the rain. The green roof idea ties in with so many fields, from the topographical and geographical history of San Francisco and California, to the memory of places and the heritage left by the generations who born here, to science and to energy. Mainly, however, it has to do with the irrepressible urge of researchers to make discoveries, an urge that also brought forth the idea of the spider's web, the delicate steel structure that covers the Piazza. During the day, its reticular structure opens to allow the air in for ventilation and at night, when the temperature drops, the mesh closes.

This relatively complex covering system can be regulated for available light, rather like the eye's contracting and expanding iris. There are three separate fabric screens. The first keeps out the damp, the second provides shade from the sun and the third creates the right acoustics for music in the Piazza, turning the central square into another organic space.

A further development was the idea of setting a canopy of photovoltaic panels round the building. Cover provided by the panels is not total and light can filter through the spaces. What the canopy offers is a living, vibrant shade, much like cover provided by trees in summertime.

These panels, with a total of 60,000 photovoltaic cells, generate more than five percent of the building's energy needs. It was a project that constantly shifted focus from practical, concrete, science and energy-related requirements to the imperatives of expression. In the event, one of my greatest sources of pride was a series of articles in the American press that indicated the California Academy of Sciences as proof that an environmentally friendly building needn't be ugly. Yes, there's a conviction that sustainability in a building is a moral obligation to be put up with.

But in our case, we experienced the germinating awareness – although these things never come out of the blue – that we were on the threshold of exploring a new architectural language. We started to ask ourselves a number of questions. What language of architecture celebrates recent awareness of the Earth's fragility and the need for sustainability?

E tutto è nato da quella voglia, anche l'idea dello "spider web". Si tratta di una delicata ragnatela d'acciaio che copre la piazza: una struttura reticolare che di giorno si apre e consente la ventilazione, mentre di notte, quando la temperatura si abbassa, si chiude.

Un sistema di copertura piuttosto complesso le permette di regolarsi in funzione della luminosità: un po' come l'iride dell'occhio che si contrae.

La copertura si articola attraverso tre serie diverse di tende: la prima ripara dall'acqua, la seconda dal sole e la terza permette di creare delle condizioni acustiche corrette per poter fare musica nella piazza.

In questo modo anche la piazza diventa un luogo organico. Ed è così che è nata anche l'idea di mettere dei pannelli fotovoltaici tutti intorno all'edificio, che non sono completamente coprenti e quindi permettono che nello spazio fra l'uno e l'altro passi la luce.

In questo modo l'ombra che si crea a terra è un'ombra vivace e "vibrante", come l'ombra che si crea d'estate sotto le chiome degli alberi.

E questi pannelli, costituiti da 60.000 cellule fotovoltaiche, coprono più del 5% del fabbisogno energetico dell'edificio.

In questo progetto c'è un continuo rimbalzare fra le esigenze pratiche, concrete, scientifiche ed energetiche e quelle espressive. Tanto che uno degli elementi di maggiore orgoglio per me sono stati alcuni articoli apparsi sulla stampa americana che citavano la California Academy of Sciences come la prova che un edificio ecologico non deve essere per forza brutto. E sì, perché c'è un po' la convinzione che la sostenibilità di un edificio sia una necessità morale da subire, un obbligo. Invece in noi cominciò a prendere corpo – anche se queste cose non avvengono mai d'improvviso – la consapevolezza che si poteva esplorare un nuovo linguaggio dell'architettura. Iniziammo a porci una serie di domande. Qual'è il linguaggio dell'architettura che celebra questa recente scoperta, cioè la fragilità della Terra, la necessità di essere sostenibili?

È possibile trovare un linguaggio di bellezza, di poesia, per cui fare un edificio sostenibile non sia un'obbligazione morale da subire come una maledizione?

Prima ho accennato alla stampa: ricordo in partcolare sul Newsweek l'articolo della critica americana Cathleen McGuigan, che osservava come nella norma l'architettura sostenibile sia "brutta", abbia qualcosa che non funziona dal punto di vista estetico. E citava invece il caso della Californa Academy of Sciences come la scoperta che l'architettura sostenibile può anche essere bella, può anche essere un'architettura vivace, trasparente, gioiosa e allegra. Naturalmente aggiungeva che una brutta architettura sostenibile è sempre preferibile ad una brutta architettura non sostenibile, e questo è senz'altro vero.

Ma quello che sto cercando di dire, che non era delineato chiaramente agli inizi del progetto, ma è diventato via via più evidente, è che all'inizio del XXI secolo una delle fonti di ispirazione più forti è proprio la consapevolezza che la Terra è fragile, e che si debba lavorare su costruzioni sensibili, che rispettino la natura.

Can a language of beauty and poetry be found to express the sustainability of a building, that is not a curse-like moral obligation? I was talking about the press before. There was one article I particularly remember in Newsweek by the American critic Cathleen McGuigan, who pointed out that sustainable architecture was generally ugly and had something aesthetically wrong with it. To show the other side of the story, she mentioned the California Academy of Sciences as an example of how sustainable architecture could also be beautiful, vibrant, easy to understand, joyous and happy. Of course, McGuigan added that an ugly green building is better than an ugly non-green building, which is undeniable. What I am trying to say, and was not explicit from the start of the project, emerging gradually instead as it unfolded, is that one of the greatest sources of early 21st-century inspiration is the realisation that the Earth is fragile and that we should be working on environment-sensitive buildings that respect nature. Preserving natural resources and energy and protecting the environment are worldwide emergencies. In my view, it was right that a major institution for natural sciences should be emblematic of this challenge to architecture. We have to confront the issue and shoulder our responsibility to solve it. Architects cannot step aside. In some sense, every century has presented architects with new sources of inspiration.

As we know, the 20th century and the modern movement brought freedom from decoration, followed by the globalisation of building and everything else. Compare that with the steel construction culture of the entire 19th century, and the lightness made possible by steel-based technology. Each century has its physical sources of inspiration, just as it has its academic moments, for academe is always lurking in the wings, peddling its spurious inspirations. But to go back to the genuine version, it looks increasingly evident that one of the 21st century's greatest epiphanies will emerge from the debate over what architectural language should explore our engagement with nature. A need has to be translated into an aesthetic, and then we have to build buildings that exist in, and communicate with, nature: buildings that breathe.

All this sounds terribly theoretical until you actually go into the California Academy of Sciences but we'll come back to this in a short time. Underpinning the project was the awareness that we were working on a museum of natural sciences, and could not ignore the nature issue. There were ethical, moral and cultural reasons for confronting it.

All these factors gave substance to the project, albeit a multitude of crises. Just about every project has to go through a stage where it all seems to be coming apart, perhaps because it is costing too much. In our case, for example, the final project decision was to start almost from scratch. Parts of two structures did of course remain but in essence, the California Academy of Sciences was completely rebuilt. The budget topped 400 million dollars so we are talking about a pretty significant project. The construction site was operational for about three years. It was all fairly complicated and it took the best part of a year to move in all the plant and animal species

La salvaguardia delle risorse naturali e la tutela dell'ambiente sono emergenze mondiali, mi sembrava quindi doveroso che la sede di una grande istituzione di scienze naturali diventasse simbolo di questa sfida architettonica.

Dobbiamo cimentarci con il problema e assumerci la responsabilità di risolverlo, gli architetti non possono tirarsi indietro. Ogni secolo ha in qualche maniera fornito agli architetti nuove sorgenti di ispirazione.

Il XX secolo come è noto si è liberato dalla decorazione, con il movimento moderno. Poi la globalizzazione del mondo, e del costruire. Tutto il XIX secolo è stato invece ispirato al costruire in acciaio; ed alla leggerezza che è conseguita alla sua scoperta tecnologica. Ogni secolo insomma ha fonti "reali" di ispirazione, ed allo stesso modo ha fasi accademiche. Perché anche "l'Accademia" è sempre in agguato, pronta a fornire delle false ispirazioni.

Ma parlando di quelle "vere", appare sempre più evidente che una delle maggiori fonti di ispirazione del XXI sarà certamente questa: quale linguaggio l'architettura dovrebbe andare ad indagare nel confrontarsi con la natura? Si tratta di tradurre in poetica una necessità, e quindi fare degli edifici che vivono e dialogano con la natura, che respirano.

Tutto questo discorso appare abbastanza teorico finché non si va, fisicamente, in questo edificio.

Ma di questo parleremo tra poco. Il progetto fu cadenzato da questa consapevolezza: stavamo lavorando a un edificio che, essendo un museo di scienze naturali, non poteva essere indifferente a questo tema. Doveva esserlo per ragioni etiche, morali, culturali.

Questi furono gli elementi che sostanziarono il progetto, sebbene tra mille crisi, anche di carattere finanziario.

Quasi tutti i progetti passano attraverso fasi in cui sembra che tutto stia per crollare, magari perché costano troppo. In questo caso, ad esempio, scelta progettuale definitiva fu quella di ricostruire quasi tutto. Sì, restarono in piedi due edifici, alcuni frammenti, ma sostanzialmente la California Academy of Sciences è stata ricostruita.

Il budget di questo progetto è stato di oltre 400 milioni di dollari, parliamo quindi di un progetto piuttosto importante. Il cantiere è durato circa tre anni, ed è stato piuttosto complicato, e poi c'è voluto quasi un anno, dopo la fine del cantiere, per effettuare il trasferimento di tutte le specie vegetali ed animali che durante i lavori erano state portate altrove.

Si tratta di 20 milioni di campioni, non è uno scherzo…

Un cantiere lungo e complesso ma privo di grandi sorprese, perché il terreno non nascondeva reperti archeologici, ed essendo sabbioso era facile da scavare.

Durante i cantieri quasi sempre troviamo qualcosa: a Roma i resti di una villa patrizia, a Los Angeles gli scheletri di mammuth, a Berlino bombe inesplose, ma qui non abbiamo avuto sorprese. È stato però un cantiere cadenzato da molti tests, da innumerevoli prove, esperimenti e prototipi.

Forse la cosa più complicata è stata la messa a punto del tetto vegetale. Come ho già detto abbiamo cercato la combinazione giusta di vegetali per tre o quattro anni, fino ad arrivare a selezionare le nove specie che abbiamo piantato sul tetto.

that had been taken elsewhere while work was under way. We are talking about twenty million samples, which is no laughing matter.

Building work was challenging and took its time but nothing unexpected cropped up. There were no archaeological finds lurking beneath the sandy soil and it was easy to excavate. On almost all of our sites, we unearth something or other. In Rome, we found a patrician villa; in Los Angeles, it was a mammoth; and in Berlin, we came across unexploded bombs. But there were no surprises in Golden Gate Park.

Work was, however, interrupted by endless tests, trials, experiments and prototypes, of which perhaps the most complex was finding a solution for the living roof. I have already said that we spent three or four years looking for the right combination of vegetation until we whittled the species down to the nine we finally planted on the roof.

Planting wasn't easy. In the end, we made 50,000 trays from organic materials, which were filled off-site before being shipped in and put in place. Eventually, these coconut-fibre trays break down into soil, a process that takes a year and a half. This was a relatively complex phase of construction work. We now come to the final stage of the project, which was opening the museum to the public.

The complex was inaugurated just before Barack Obama's election, a not insignificant coincidence.

Every so often in life, you create a building that may not exactly change history but does celebrate it. This had happened to me before. I might just be lucky but thirty years ago, for example, while the Centre Pompidou in Paris may not have transformed the role of museums in cities, it did celebrate that change. The Centre Pompidou happened when it was destined to happen. Museums, no longer intimidating, dust-covered institution, were becoming cultural spaces. Spaces for social exchanges, knowledge and discovery.

In a sense, and certainly not from any merit of ours, the Centre Pompidou neatly represented, and indeed physically embodied, this transformation.

In the 1970s, there was a radical change in the perception of the museum space and the "Beaubourg", as I still call it, is its most flamboyant representation. The museum-as-refinery was undoubtedly over the top but it did bring down the wall of diffidence, eliminating distrust of museums and introducing something nobler and more beautiful, which was curiosity. That curiosity was consciousness-raising, the start of a cultural process, particularly for those who are not what we would call "cultivated". Up till then, museums had been places for the elite, for those who are cultured and are often rather snobbish with it. The Beaubourg immediately took on the role of ice-breaker, fending the floes that separate ordinary people from culture.

In a sense, the California Academy of Sciences in San Francisco is a similar phenomenon, but in this case what is at stake is our relationship with nature, not culture. Of course, it could just be a coincidence. Whether or not it was "serendipity", it happened at just the right moment. A month before Obama's election, at a time when it was clear that America would have to reconsider its stance vis-à-vis the

L'impianto non è stato facile: abbiamo dovuto costruire 50.000 "vassoi" di materiale organico, che sono stati assemblati altrove e poi trasferiti e piantati.

Questi vassoi di fibra di cocco con il tempo diventeranno terra, nell'arco di un anno e mezzo.

Questa è stata una fase abbastanza complessa del cantiere. Veniamo alla fase finale del progetto, l'apertura al pubblico. L'edificio è stato inaugurato poco prima dell'elezione di Barack Obama, che non è una cosa da niente.

Ogni tanto capita, nella vita: fai un edificio che non cambia la storia, questo no, ma celebra il cambiamento storico in atto. A me è già successo.

Forse sarò fortunato, ma ad esempio trent'anni fa il Centre Pompidou di Parigi se non ha cambiato il ruolo dei musei nelle città, certamente ne ha celebrato il cambiamento.

Il Centre Pompidou è successo quando doveva succedere: quando la nozione stessa di museo cessava di essere quella di un luogo istituzionale e intimidente, marmoreo e statico, noioso e pieno di polvere, e si preparava a diventare un luogo di civiltà. Un luogo di civiltà perché luogo di scambio, di conoscenza, di scoperta.

Ed in qualche maniera il Centre Pompidou, non certo per merito nostro, rappresentava bene questo passaggio, ne era il materializzarsi.

Gli anni Settanta portarono alla trasformazione nella percezione del luogo-museo, e "Beaubourg" (come io continuo a chiamarlo) ne era una specie di rappresentazione esagerata. Un museo come una raffineria era sicuramente un'esagerazione, però certamente faceva crollare il muro di diffidenza, di paura dei musei, per introdurre invece una cosa ben più nobile e più bella, che era la curiosità.

La curiosità come momento di consapevolezza, e quindi come inizio di un momento culturale, soprattutto per una persona cosidetta "non coltivata".

I musei erano sempre stati, fino ad allora, luoghi di élite, per le persone che già avevano questa coltivazione, questo atteggiamento che spesso era anche abbastanza snob.

Beaubourg si è presentato subito come un modo per rompere questo ghiaccio, questo gelo tra le persone comuni e la cultura.

E la California Academy of Sciences di San Francisco in qualche modo rappresenta un fenomeno simile, in cui però non è in gioco il rapporto con la cultura, ma il rapporto con la natura.

Può essere un caso, naturalmente. Ma, che si tratti di fatalità o no, è accaduto nel momento giusto. Proprio un mese prima dell'elezione di Obama, e in un momento in cui è evidente che l'America deve rivedere il proprio atteggiamento rispetto agli accordi di Kyoto, e proprio a San Francisco, che è la punta di diamante dell'ecologia in quel paese, si realizza il primo edificio che è "platinum" del sistema LEED.

Quindi un edificio che non ha aria condizionata, che consuma pochissima energia, e che diventa esso stesso emblema di un modo di fare architettura.

E come succede sempre questa cosa all'inizio non era chiara, lo si è capito solo alla fine.

Prendiamo il Centro Pompidou: all'inizio non sapevamo assolutamente che sarebbe diventato il vessillo di un

Kyoto protocol, and in San Francisco, the very first LEED platinum-certified building was opened. It had minimum air-conditioning, very low energy requirements and became emblematic of an approach to architecture.

As always, this was not clear at the outset, emerging only at the end of the project.

Take the Pompidou Centre. In the beginning, we had absolutely no idea that it would become a flagship for change. In the same way, it was not at all clear that the California Academy of Sciences would be the objective correlative for another step change. But it is.

It is interesting because we architects do tend to work with our heads in the clouds. In the first place, we do not choose what to do. Clients commission jobs, we simply take part in these rituals, which sometimes carry us a very long way, following their destiny and going where history takes them.

It was no coincidence that Al Gore, a politician who is very much keyed into these issues, should visit the site several times and recently came back to see the finished building. It is one of things that gives meaning to our work because the architect contributes to these processes, building spaces for activities that, satisfyingly, turn out to be at the cutting edge, activities that transform reality.

It is part of the architect's utopia. There's a writer's utopia, an artist's utopia, a politician's utopia, so why not an architect's utopia? In our case, it's changing the world.

A mad dream, I know. An absurd and totally irrational one, but it exists, and it's a good thing it does.

In some sense, then, the California Academy of Sciences is part of that utopia. I would even say it is the most political part, and I am still using the word "political" in its most noble sense of "polis". But there is another, obvious, aspect of the building that shrewder critics in America and Europe were quick to focus on.

The California Academy of Sciences also reveals the search for a language that belongs to us and to this new century. One British critic, the Guardian's Jonathan Glancey, pointed out that thirty years ago, I started building "soft machines" with the Menil Collection in Houston.

That museum was a machine created to softly filter the sunlight and illuminate the interior naturally. Similarly, according to Glancey, the California Academy of Sciences is a soft machine designed to explore the building's relationship with nature and the environment.

Not just with the splendid Golden Gate Park, itself one of the environmental icons of America, but also with history, at a time when the United States has to take a clear stance on ecology. We are talking about something important both politically and in terms of expression.

Because one of its most significant characteristics you notice if you visit the building personally is its simplicity of conception. In essence, it is a flying roof, or rather a piece of the park that has taken to the air.

All round the edge is a band of photovoltaic cells, which as I have already mentioned provide five percent of the museum's energy requirements while creating a peripheral area of shade and protection. Inside is the Piazza, which was there in the

cambiamento, così come non era assolutamente chiaro che la California Academy of Sciences sarebbe diventato il materializzarsi di una trasformazione.

Però è accaduto.

Questa cosa è interessante, perché noi architetti, in fondo, lavoriamo con la testa un po' tra le nuvole. Intanto perché non scegliamo noi cosa fare; sono i clienti che ci commissionano il lavoro. E noi partecipiamo semplicemente a questi riti che talvolta ci conducono lontano, seguono la loro strada e vanno dove li porta la storia.

Non è un caso che Al Gore, ad esempio, che è un personaggio politico molto attento a questi fenomeni, sia venuto tante volte in cantiere ed ancora recentemente abbia visitato l'edificio. Ecco, questa è una cosa che conferisce un senso al nostro lavoro, perché l'architetto partecipa a questi processi, costruisce ripari per attività che è bello scoprire essere quelle di punta, quelle che trasformano la realtà.

Fa parte dell'utopia dell'architetto.

C'è l'utopia dello scrittore, dell'artista, del politico, perché no, ma c'è anche l'utopia dell'architetto, che è quella di cambiare il mondo. È un sogno folle, lo capisco, assurdo e completamente irragionevole, però c'è, ed è un bene che ci sia. Quindi l'edificio in qualche maniera appartiene a questa utopia, e questa è una parte oserei dire più "politica", e continuo ad usare questa parola nella sua accezione più bella, nel senso di "polis". Però c'è anche un altro aspetto in questo edificio, che appare evidente, ed è stato ben colto dalla critica più sottile, americana ed europea.

Ed è come questo edificio rappresenti la ricerca di un linguaggio che ci appartenga, che appartenga a questo nuovo secolo. Un critico inglese, Jonathan Glancey del Guardian, ha scritto che io cominciai a costruire delle "soft machines" trent'anni fa con la Menil Collection di Houston.

Il museo della Menil Collection era una "macchina gentile" costruita per filtrare i raggi del sole ed illuminare naturalmente l'edificio.

Allo stesso modo, secondo Glancey, la California Academy of Sciences è una "macchina gentile" pensata per esplorare il rapporto tra l'edificio e la natura, l'ambiente.

Non solo nei confronti del Golden Gate Park, che è bellissimo ed è esso stesso uno dei vessilli ambientalistici dell'America, ma anche nei confronti della storia, in un momento in cui gli Stati Uniti devono prendere posizioni nette nei confronti dell'ecologia.

Stiamo quindi parlando di un dato importante sul piano politico ed anche sul piano espressivo. Perché una delle cose più importanti che si possono osservare andando a visitare l'edificio è la semplicità della sua impostazione.

È sostanzialmente un tetto che vola, anzi, è una porzione di parco che vola.

E tutto il bordo attorno è coperto da cellule fotovoltaiche, che come ho già detto provvedono più del 5% del fabbisogno energetico dell'edificio, ma creano anche uno spazio protetto e ombroso che circonda il museo.

Ed all'interno dell'edificio si trova questa piazza, che c'era già, ed è uno degli elementi di memoria degli edifici precedenti, che avevano già un secolo.

original museum. It is part of the memory of a complex that was more than a century old.

There is not one single point inside the museum from where it is not possible to see the outside world. You can always feel the presence of the Golden Gate Park.

You are talking about nature in the midst of nature. These are aesthetic considerations that have nothing to do with politics. Instead, they are related to the intangible we call "beauty". It is hard to describe this sense of place, of transparency and of lightness. The roof itself is a landscape.

One man told me that the curves of the roof reminded him of San Francisco's hills but that is just fantasy. The hills of San Francisco never crossed my mind. If anything, since I wanted to keep the roof at a height of ten metres, and also had to locate the thirty metre-high Planetarium and Biosphere underneath it, I was thinking that the roof obviously couldn't be flat. The fact remains that even now, only a year and a half after it was planted, the roof is already looking the way I hoped and wanted it to. It is highlighting diversity.

The south-facing side of the hill is constructed in such a way that some of the plants will be stronger than others whereas the northern side grows differently. Even the birds and butterflies exhibit a range of behaviours.

This is how the roof was constructed, not to mirror the San Franciscan hills but to create a native microcosm.

It will be another fifteen years before we know what will survive. Architecture takes a long-term view of things. Like forests, rivers and mountains, architecture needs time. It does not reveal itself in the short term. Fashion and trends are the short-term winners. We'll see.

The California Museum of Sciences is undoubtedly a much-loved building. A few days ago, I heard from Greg Farrington, who took over as director from Patrick Kociolek.

He told me the only problem was the very large number of visitors. Last Saturday, there 12,000 of them.

When you finish a building, you should always ask yourself what remains of the initial dream. When more than half is still there, you are doing well. We will see with the passage of time but I reckon a lot of the California Academy of Sciences' dream is still there.

It is been said that the California Academy of Sciences is already considered as a landmark project, a building that designers will, in some way, have to measure themselves against in the future.

From now on, it will be difficult to justify erecting a building that pays no attention to energy consumption saying "it can't be done". It is not true because we proved it can.

When the museum was inaugurated on 27 September 2008, I hid behind one of the pillars to watch people's reactions, the way I always do. It is an old trick I learned from Roberto Rossellini in 1977, when he was shooting his last film here at the Centre Pompidou. He told me: "Don't watch the building. You're young. You don't understand anything. Don't watch the building. Watch the faces of the people who are looking at the building. You can see from them what you've created".

That is what I have done ever since. On opening day, visitors' faces showed an irrational, instinctive sense of wonder,

E non c'è un solo punto, all'interno del museo, in cui non si veda
fuori, in cui non si percepisca la presenza del Golden Gate Park.
Parli di natura e sei immerso nella natura.
E queste sono voci poetiche, non hanno a che fare con la politica,
ma con una cosa imprendibile che si chiama "bellezza".
Una cosa difficilmente evocabile: questo senso di appartenenza
al luogo, questo senso di trasparenza, questo senso di leggerezza.
Il tetto stesso è un paesaggio.
Qualcuno mi ha detto che queste ondulazioni del tetto
rammentano le colline di san Francisco.
Ma sono storie, io non ho mai minimamente pensato alle colline
di San Francisco, casomai pensavo che, volendo mantenere
il tetto a dieci metri, e dovendo collocare sotto questa quota
il Planetario e la Biosfera alte trenta metri, evidentemente la
copertura non poteva essere piana.
Resta il fatto che queste colline già adesso, dopo un anno
e mezzo che le piantumazioni sono state fatte, cominciano a dare
l'effetto che mi aspettavo e speravo, cioé ad evidenziare delle
diversità. La faccia esposta a sud della collina è fatta in modo
tale che alcune delle essenze prendono più forza di altre, la
faccia a nord agisce diversamente. Persino le farfalle e gli uccelli
si comportano in maniera differenziata.
Questo tetto è nato così, non dall'echeggiare le colline di San
Francisco, ma dall'idea di creare un microcosmo "native",
nativo. Ci vorranno forse ancora quindici anni per capire cosa
resterà. L'architettura vive di tempi lunghi.
Ha bisogno di tempo: come le foreste, i fiumi, le montagne.
Non si manifesta e non si rivela nell'immediato.
Nell'immediato vincono la moda, la tendenza. Vedremo.
È certamente un edificio molto amato.
Ho sentito pochi giorni fa Greg Farrington, che è il direttore che
ha preso il posto di Patrick Kociolek. Mi ha raccontato che il loro
unico problema è l'affluenza di troppi visitatori; sabato scorso
c'erano dodicimila persone.
Quando si finisce un edificio bisogna sempre domandarsi quanto
è rimasto del sogno iniziale, e quando ne è rimasta più della
metà va già bene. Vedremo con il tempo, ma in questo edificio
mi sembra che di sogno ne sia rimasto parecchio.
Qualcuno ha scritto che il museo comincia ad essere riconosciuto
come un nuovo "landmark", un punto di riferimento,
un edificio che in qualche maniera obbligherà i progettisti a
misurarsi con il proprio esempio.
Sarà difficile d'ora in poi giustificare l'aver fatto un edificio
disattento ai consumi energetici con la scusa del "non si può",
perché non è vero: noi abbiamo provato che si può.
All'inaugurazione, il 27 settembre 2008, come sempre mi sono
nascosto dietro ai pilastri per spiare le reazioni dei visitatori.
È un vecchio trucco che mi insegnò Roberto Rossellini nel 1977,
quando girò il suo ultimo film qui al Centre Pompidou.
Mi disse: "non guardare l'edificio. Tu sei giovane, non capisci
niente. Non guardare l'edificio, ma la faccia della gente che
osserva l'edificio. Attraverso di loro capirai che cosa hai fatto".
Da allora io lo faccio, e il giorno dell'apertura nello sguardo
dei visitatori si coglieva un senso di meraviglia, irrazionale e
istintivo, ma anche un senso di appartenenza a quell'edificio
così aperto, trasparente, luminoso.

mingling with a sense of belonging to this transparently open,
light-filled building.
There was also an awareness that the scientists, who for
a century and a half have been making this miracle of
knowledge possible, were not somewhere else far away
but there in the building, carrying out their experiments.
The museum is much-loved, as is the idea that science is
a marvellous terrain for exploration, research, love and
affection. The California Academy of Sciences is loved
because it can be understood pretty much instinctively.
But perhaps the most prestigious acknowledgement was the
speech given on the day of the inauguration by a young Native
American, the descendent of the American Indians who
owned the site. At the start of the ceremony, he said something
touchingly beautiful. He said he could see we had made good
use of the piece of land that had belonged to his forefathers,
adding that he would gift it to us in perpetuity. Obviously, the
act had no legal value because the site already belonged to the
city of San Francisco but it had a huge moral significance.
He then performed a brief ceremony with fire and an eagle's
wing that he used to waft the smoke towards us, explaining
that he was giving us the site because it was the only piece of
native land left for miles around.
A little bit of California soaring over the city.

E c'era anche la sensazione che gli scienziati, che per
centocinquant'anni hanno dato luogo a quel miracolo di
conoscenza, non erano lontani, da un'altra parte, ma erano
lì a fare i loro esperimenti. Certamente l'edificio è amato,
ed è amata l'idea che la scienza sia terreno straordinario di
esplorazione, di ricerca, di amore, di affetto.
È amato ed è anche capito in maniera abbastanza istintiva.
Ma forse il riconoscimento più prestigioso è stato il discorso
tenuto proprio il giorno dell'inaugurazione da un giovane
nativo americano, discendente dall'indiano d'America
proprietario del terreno. All'inizio della cerimonia disse una
cosa molto bella e toccante: disse di aver capito che avevamo
fatto un buon uso di quel pezzo di terra che apparteneva
ai suoi avi, e aggiunse che ce ne avrebbe fatto dono
definitivamente. La cosa non aveva, ovviamente, un valore
legale, perché il terreno era già di proprietà della città
di San Francisco.
Però aveva un valore morale molto importante.
Questo giovane indiano, con il breve rito che fece con il fuoco
e l'ala di aquila che spingeva il fumo verso di noi, ci spiegò
che ci avrebbe fatto dono del terreno perché quello era l'unico
pezzo di "native California", di California nativa, che era
rimasto nel giro di miglia.
Come dicevo, è una piccola prateria che vola sulla città.

Renzo Piano, 2010

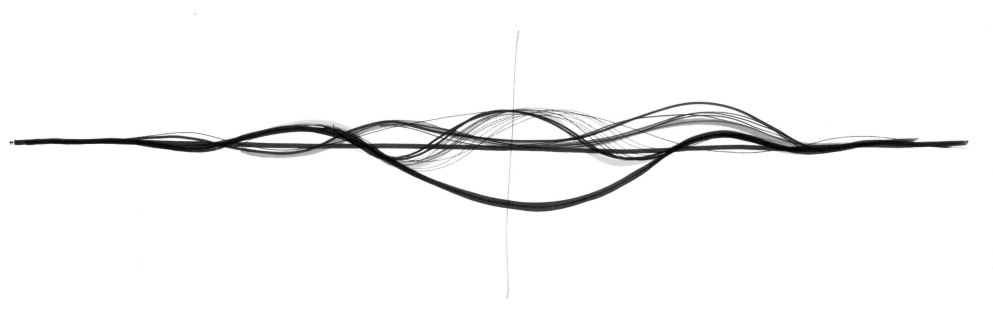

2000-2008
California Academy of Sciences
San Francisco, USA

Client
California Academy of Sciences

Renzo Piano Building Workshop, architects
in collaboration with Stantec Architecture
(San Francisco)

Design team
M. Carroll, O. de Nooyer
(partner and partner in charge)
with S. Ishida (partner),
B. Terpeluk, J. McNeal, A.De Flora,
F. Elmalipinar, A. Guernier, D. Hart, T. Kjaer,
J. Lee, A. Meine-Jansen, A. Ng, D. Piano,
W. Piotraschke, J.Sylvester;
and C. Bruce, L. Burow, C. Cooper, A. Knapp,
Y. Pages, Z. Rockett, V. Tolu, A. Walsh;
I. Corte, S. D'Atri, G. Langasco,
M. Ottonello (CAD Operators);
F. Cappellini, S. Rossi, A. Malgeri,
A. Marazzi (models)

Consultants
Ove Arup & Partners
(engineering and sustainability);
Rutherford & Chekene (civil engineering);
SWA Group (landscaping);
Rana Creek (living roof);
PBS&J (aquarium life support systems);
Thinc Design, Cinnabar, Visual-Acuity (exhibits)

General contractor: Webcor Builders

California Academy of Sciences

Concezione della collana editoriale
Conception of the book series
Lia Piano
Franco Origoni
Giorgio Bianchi
Milly Rossato Piano
Stefania Canta
Carlo Giordanetti

Volume a cura di / Book edited by
Lia Piano

Concezione e realizzazione del volume
Book conception and realization
Lia Piano e Franco Origoni
con / with
Shunji Ishida (partner RPBW)
Olaf de Nooyer (partner RPBW)

Con la partecipazione di
With the partecipation of
(Renzo Piano Building Workshop)
Stefania Canta
Chiara Casazza
Nicoletta Durante
Giovanna Giusto
Giovanna Langasco
Justin Lee
Marco Profumo
Con / with
(California Academy of Sciences)
Danielle Castronovo
Daniel S. Ransom

Progetto grafico e impaginazione
Layout
Franco Origoni e Anna Steiner
Con / with
Roberta Cesani

Fotolito e Stampa / Print
StampArte S.r.l. (Firenze)

© Fondazione Renzo Piano
Editore SOFP Società Operativa Fondazione Piano srl

Si ringraziano
Special thanks to
Alistair Guthrie
Paul Kephart
Patrick Kociolek
Bill Lacy

Crediti Fotografici
Photos Credits
John A. Benson
Alessandro Bertoglio
California Academy
of Sciences Archives
Paolo Colonna – RPBW
Michel Denancé
Tom Fox – SWA Group
Stefano Goldberg – Publifoto
Google
Tim Griffith
Shunji Ishida – RPBW
Caroline Kapp
Justin Lee – RPBW
Nic Lehoux
Jonathan Mc Neal – RPBW
National Geographic Channel
Brett Terpeluk – RPBW
Monica Terpeluk

Traduzione / Translation
Giles Watson
e / and
Catherine Chapelle
Grosz, Italy